855

# Folk and Fairy Tales

Fairy-Tale Mother. Illustration from a collection of German fairy tales. Carl and Theodor Colshorn, *Märchen und Sagen* (Hannover: Verlag von Carl Rümpler, 1854), frontispiece.

# Folk and Fairy Tales

## A Handbook

*D.L. Ashliman*

Greenwood Folklore Handbooks

**GREENWOOD PRESS**
*Westport, Connecticut • London*

**Library of Congress Cataloging-in-Publication Data**

Ashliman, D.L.
    Folk and fairy tales : a handbook / D.L. Ashliman.
        p. cm.—(Greenwood Folklore Handbooks, ISSN 1549–733X)
    Includes bibliographical references and index.
    ISBN 0-313-32810-2 (alk. paper)
    1. Fairy tales—History and criticism. 2. Fairy
tales—Classification. 3. Folklore—Classification. I. Title.
GR550.A77 2004
398.2—dc22        2004004321

British Library Cataloguing in Publication Data is available.

Library of Congress Catalog Card Number: 2004004321
ISBN: 0–313–32810–2
ISSN: 1549–733X

First published in 2004

Greenwood Press, 88 Post Road West, Westport, CT 06881
An imprint of Greenwood Publishing Group, Inc.
www.greenwood.com

Printed in the United States of America

The paper used in this book complies with the
Permanent Paper Standard issued by the National
Information Standards Organization (Z39.48–1984).

10  9  8  7  6  5  4  3  2  1

# Contents

# Preface

Among the most enduring memories of most adults are tales heard in childhood, both those that were read or told as bedtime stories by adult caregivers and those exchanged in the neighborhood by playmates. Many such stories evolved from oral traditions that have remained amazingly constant for centuries and across diverse cultures. This handbook examines the origins of these traditions and their development into the body of literature known today as folk and fairy tales.

Questions addressed in the following pages include these: Why do we tell stories? Where do our familiar fairy tales come from, and how old are they? If more than one version of a folktale exists, can one determine which form is "correct"? Do fairy tales have hidden meaning? How do scholars from various disciplines—including psychology, anthropology, and literary criticism—use folk and fairy tales in their work? What do the popular entertainment forms of today—television programs, films, fantasy novels, and such—have in common with traditional tales inherited from the distant past?

This handbook is designed both as a reference tool and as an introduction to the study of folk and fairy tales. It was written for storytellers, teachers, and all who love to read and hear traditional tales. No special expertise is assumed, except for curiosity about one of humankind's most enduring traits: the creation and dissemination, for the most part by ordinary people, of fantasy fiction.

The handbook is divided into five chapters and additional resources. The chapters contain an introduction to and an overview of folk and fairy-tale studies. Chapters 1 and 2 identify and describe the most important traditional collections of folktales in the Indo-European tradition, trace the emergence of folklore as an academic discipline, and define the various genres and types of folk and fairy tales. Chapter 3 offers full-text examples, with interpretive commentary, of each category. Chapter 4 outlines and evaluates the various scholarly approaches that have dominated folktale studies from classical antiquity to the present day. Chapter 5 shows how traditional folk and fairy tales have been used by artists in diverse fields, including literature (both for children and adults), music, opera, drama, and filmmaking.

Readers using this handbook as a reference tool are advised first to consult the index. Other helpful features of the book include a glossary, which defines specialized terms used in folk and fairy-tale scholarship, and a comprehensive bibliography, arranged thematically, that lists the most important folk and fairy-tale anthologies as well as books about the tales. The bibliography focuses on English-language publications, although selected titles in other languages are included. Finally, in recognition of the growing importance of the Internet in scholarly research, the book includes an overview of World Wide Web resources for folk and fairy-tale studies, including concrete tips on how to most efficiently use search engines, electronic libraries, and academic sites.

While recognizing that storytelling is a universal human activity, one practiced throughout history and in all cultures, this handbook focuses on the stories that have evolved from Indo-European folktales. The stories told from India to northwestern Europe (and carried by travelers and settlers to other continents as well) form a unified folkloric tradition. Other cultures have storytelling traditions equally rich, and also fully deserving of careful study.

# One

# Introduction

## ONCE UPON A TIME

"Tell me a story" are magic words in all cultures. Storytelling is a universal human activity. Every known society on earth, at every period of recorded history, has told stories: some as oral history, some as part of religious rituals, some for instruction, and some for pure entertainment. Folk and fairy tales, with few exceptions, fall into the last two categories. These are stories that admit to being fictitious; they are products of fantasy, make-believe stories that create new worlds, thus providing an outlet for our frustrations and fears and a platform for our hopes and dreams. They are also stories that instruct, but they do so entertainingly.

### "Once upon a time" in the languages of western Europe

| | |
|---|---|
| Danish | Der var engang... |
| Dutch | Er war eens... |
| English | Once upon a time... |
| French | Il était une fois... |
| German | Es war einmal... |
| Italian | C'era una volta... |
| Norwegian | Det var en gang... |
| Portuguese | Havia uma vez... |
| Spanish | Habia una vez... |
| Swedish | Det var en gång... |

## WHY DO WE TELL STORIES?

### Fantasy Wish Fulfillment

The types of stories usually referred to as folk and fairy tales (more about story types in chapter 2) are told first and foremost as entertainment. Originated by anonymous oral storytellers and passed on by word of mouth from generation to generation, such stories rely on their ability to satisfy for their survival. Stories that fail to entertain—like bad jokes even today—are soon forgotten and lost. The psychology of entertainment is complicated, and different listeners can be attracted to a particular story for quite different reasons. Fairy tales—stories with a strong make-believe component— satisfy a number of personal and social needs. Perhaps most important, they provide a mechanism for fantasy wish fulfillment. The problems of fairy-tale heroes and heroines are real: poverty, sibling rivalry, unjust persecution, finding an appropriate mate, and many more. The fairy-tale solutions to these real-life problems are literally and figuratively out of this world. A persecuted scullery maid marries a prince and thus escapes from the kitchen into the castle. A slow-witted swineherd marries a princess and inherits a kingdom. A woman is forced to take a beast as her husband, and he turns into a handsome prince.

### Expression of Fears and Taboos

Closely related to wish fulfillment is a fairy tale's ability to provide an acceptable outlet for the expression of fears and taboos. Helpless children are abandoned in a forest, then threatened by a cannibalistic witch, but they survive (Grimm 15). A wolf entices a naïve girl into bed, where he devours her; but she is miraculously rescued, and afterward inflicts fitting revenge upon the beast (Grimm 26). A 15-year-old girl falls asleep, and a hedge of thorns grows up to protect her from unworthy suitors. She awakens when the right man approaches, apparently one chosen by fate, and they marry on the same day (Grimm 50). A child's fear of abandonment, even if not founded in reality, can be terrifying. An appropriate fairy tale assures him or her that everything will be all right. Similarly, must a girl's flirtation with an unprincipled man result in her destruction? In real life the answer may be yes, but in a magic tale she gets a second chance. And finally, how can one best confront the conflicts and uncertainties so often associated with puberty and courtship? A fairy-tale solution is simply to fall asleep and let nature take its course; fate will make the right decisions.

ANTONIO · IS · NOT · AFRAID ·
OF · THE OGRE

Illustration by H.J. Ford. Andrew Lang, *The Grey Fairy Book* (London: Longmans, Green, and Company, 1900), p. 345.

## *Explanation*

Myths deal with the great issues of life: the creation of the world, the nature of good and evil, and the relationships between deities and mortals. Folktales too address the nature of things, but usually in a less profound and less authoritative manner than do myths. With varying degrees of seriousness, they offer explanations to life's questions, both trivial and fundamental. For example: Why are cats and dogs enemies? Why do bears have short tails? Why is the sea salty? Why are some people rich and others poor? How long should one mourn the death of a child? Why are some babies born deformed? How should a man and a woman divide household tasks? Why do some die young and others old? Why are we strong in our youth but feeble in old age? For many of us any answer to a perplexing question is better than no answer. Each of the preceding questions is answered by one or more traditional folktales, and even if the answers sometimes seem superficial or comical, the stories provide a vehicle for talking about issues of concern.

### Education

Another common function of folktales is to preserve and promote cultural and personal values, but they must do so entertainingly, or they will not endure. Like the sugar coating on a bitter pill, the fictitious plot of a moral story guarantees its delivery. All cultures tell didactic stories, and some of our most ancient tales have strong moralizing components—for example, *The Jataka* and *The Panchatantra* from India, Aesop's fables from Greece, and stories from the Old and New Testaments.

Charles Perrault concluded each of the fairy tales in his *Mother Goose* collection with an appended moral, but whether stated or not, "the moral of the story" usually is not difficult to ascertain. In traditional fairy tales morals typically center around the preservation of existing values and the maintenance of social stability. There is much to praise in the messages of ancient tales. Many of the values that then held families and communities together in a hostile world, enabling them not only to survive but sometimes to thrive and prosper, seem timeless in their merit: diligence, honesty, generosity, dependability, perseverance, courage, and a unique balance of self-reliance and selflessness.

But other values, equally well represented in traditional stories, are embarrassing to sensitive modern readers. Sexism, racism, anti-Semitism, persecution of people deemed to be witches, and an almost pathological drive toward retribution are among the ideals unapologetically advanced by traditional tales that modern readers find offensive. Furthermore, social structures that promote inequality, such as monarchies and rigid class systems, are often described but seldom challenged in fairy tales. A true moralist, it is said, loves the sinner but hates the sin. Thus students of ancient folklore can love the stories but criticize at least some of the standards that they reflect. Perhaps we can learn not only from the ethical successes of our forebears, but also from their shortcomings.

## MULTIPLE LEVELS OF MEANING

The so-called *Grimms' Fairy Tales,* first published in 1812, constitute the world's best-known collection of folktales. The actual title of the work is *Kinder- und Hausmärchen* (Children's and Household Tales). The two-part title is significant, showing as it does the duality of the collection's contents: stories for children and stories for the rest of the household. Indeed, "duality" is an understatement, because traditional preindustrial households often included extended families crossing several generations: a grandmother, an invalid cousin, a widowed aunt, a live-in farmhand, a foster child, and an itinerant tradesman seeking temporary shelter—all in addition to the nuclear family of parents and children. This is true not only of the households mentioned in the Grimms' title but of storytelling families everywhere. A storyteller wishing to address the needs and expectations of her entire audience would have to create tales, or—at the least—groups of tales, with multiple levels of meaning. This can be done in different ways. A simple plot, easily followed by a child, can be augmented with meaningful details. Events can be depicted with purposeful ambiguity, so that individuals with different backgrounds will interpret them differently. Images can be drawn with words that through free association suggest different ideas to all members of an audience, in much the same way that two people may see quite different things in the same Rorschach inkblot. Emotions can be evoked through musicality of language and vividness of imagery. And—related to all of the preceding strategies—the storyteller can build her tale around events and things that elicit symbolic interpretation.

The Grimms' fairy tales, and others of the genre, contain numerous episodes that children and adults will understand differently. Foremost in this category are discussions of pregnancy. For example, the opening scene in "Little Brier Rose" (Grimm 50) describes a husband and wife wishing for a child. One day, the story continues, while the woman was sitting in her bath a frog emerged from the water and told her that within a year she would give birth to a daughter. Children will surely interpret this unusual harbinger of pregnancy differently than will adults.

Similarly, "Thumbthick" (Grimm 37) begins with the description of a peasant who sat poking the fire every evening, all the while bemoaning the fact that he and his wife had no children. His wife responded that she would be satisfied if they had but one, even if it were no larger than a thumb. After that, the story continues, "the wife took ill, and seven months later she gave birth to a child. All of his parts were perfectly formed, but he was no larger than a thumb." Again, the various elements of this depiction will be understood differently by children than by adults, especially the seven-month pregnancy (which under primitive delivery conditions would probably not have produced a live birth).

The well-known story "Rapunzel" (Grimm 12) offers an example that was apparently too daring for the early-nineteenth-century public, and the Grimms removed the suggestive passage from the second and all following editions of their collection. Rapunzel, imprisoned in a tower, lets down her hair, thus allowing a prince to climb up and visit her. According to the first edition, her guardian learns of these forbidden trysts when one day Rapunzel says to her, "Frau Gothel, tell me why it is that my clothes are all too tight. They no longer fit me." Hearing this, the guardian punishes Rapunzel by cutting off her hair (a traditional punishment for sexual indiscretion) and banishing her to a wilderness. The naïve girl's complaint that her clothes no longer fit will mean nothing to a child hearing this story, but every adult will understand.

## SYMBOLS IN FAIRY TALES

### Natural and Traditional Symbols

Symbols are things or acts that communicate meaning beyond themselves. Countless objects from the natural world suggest extended meaning, and storytellers use such items repeatedly. For example, eggs and flowers suggest both fragility and fertility. Bread or grain make logical symbols for life. A forest, one of the most-used symbols in fairy tales, represents both freedom and danger. A pathway suggests order and security. The sun, with its life-giving rays, works well as a symbol for God. The uncountable stars symbolize eternity. Different animals have observable or purported qualities that lead to symbolic interpretation; thus lions represent courage, wolves viciousness, owls wisdom, ants and bees diligence, foxes cunning, bears laziness, and eagles nobility. Fantasy beasts and composite animals, such as dragons, unicorns, griffins, mermaids, and sphinxes, appear regularly in fairy tales and have special symbolic meaning. Bodies of water often symbolize a dividing line between two realms. In this regard wells and springs are often seen, symbolically or even literally, as passageways between this world and an underground world inhabited by fairies, elves, trolls, and a host of earth-spirits.

Institutions of all types—clans, guilds, fraternities, religions, armies, and nations—develop sets of symbols that provide identification and meaning for their members. These can be abstract designs (such as a Scottish plaid or the Star of David), designs drawn from nature (like the moon-inspired Islamic crescent), or special objects from a group's past (for example, a cross or a fish for Christianity). Crowns, orbs, chalices, rings, lamps, dragons, unicorns, and innumerable patterns from traditional heraldry all can and do appear in fairy tales, usually with symbolic meaning.

### Number Symbolism

In a sense the most common number used in fairy tales is two. Although the number itself is not always named, the feeling of a universal duality of things is never far beneath the main text. Typical fairy-tale settings are both of this world and of another world. Humans consist of body and soul, and they are constantly faced with good and evil. Fairy tales thrive on simplification, focusing on polar opposites rather than on the complex continuum that connects them. A decision is right or wrong. One turns to the left or to the right. A secondary character is either for or against the hero.

Beyond this elemental dualism, the most common number in fairy tales is three. Possibly based on structures of the natural world and the human mind, three is universally seen as a special number. A triangle is the most stable of all simple designs. We start a race with the three-part command "ready, set, go." The basic family consists of father, mother, and child. And, of course, the Christian Godhead is a trinity, further endorsing the number three's positive character. Fairy-tale episodes are typically repeated three times. If a set number of wishes is granted, the number is almost always three.

Four, the number of cardinal directions and sides in a rectangle, is also a special number, often representing rectitude or completeness. Seven also symbolizes completeness, as derived from the seven days of creation and the seven planets of Greek antiquity. Twelve gains its special meaning from the Judeo-Christian tradition: the 12 tribes of Israel and the 12 apostles of Jesus. Thirteen brings unbalance to the stability of 12, as, for example, in the 13 participants at the last supper of Jesus. Two, three, four, seven, 12, and 13 are thus the special numbers of traditional folktales. When they occur within a fairy-tale plot they likely represent more than just arithmetic counters.

Arabic calligraphy in the shape of a triangle. Cover design for Richard Burton's translation of the *1,001 Nights* (1885–1888). *The Book of the Thousand Nights and a Night: A Plain and Literal Translation of the Arabian Nights Entertainments,* trans. Richard F. Burton, 10 vols. plus 6 supplemental vols. (Privately printed by the Burton Club, 1885–1888). Cover design on each volume.

### Color Symbolism

Color symbolism is often suggested by nature. Blood and fire are red, so red might represent danger or courage. Red is also the color of menstrual blood, and can thus suggest sexual maturity and fertility. A large number of fairy tales—two examples are "The Juniper Tree" (Grimm 47) and "Little Snow-White" (Grimm 53)—depict a young wife who pricks her finger and then sees drops of blood in the snow, which she correctly interprets as a sign that she soon will become pregnant. This interpretation is given added credibility when one considers that arranged marriages in preindustrial Europe often involved girls who had not yet come of age.

New plant growth is green, making that color a natural symbol for hope. The heaven is blue, leading to connotations of purity and piety (Saint Mary is traditionally clothed in blue). Old people's hair (and sometimes their skin) is gray, associating that color with both the problems (failing health) and the benefits (wisdom) that come with age. White, the color of new snow and bleached cloth, often symbolizes purity, as does colorless transparency, as in Cinderella's glass slippers.

Gold, both the metal and the color, appears in countless fairy tales, often symbolizing any positive quality, not merely its obvious representation of wealth. A good example of the word *gold* depicting something other than the shiny metal is found in "The Gold-Children" (Grimm 85), a tale that features twin boys "who were entirely golden" but (unlike King Midas's daughter) still able to function like ordinary people.

The symbolic meaning of some colors varies substantially from one culture to another. In English green suggests jealousy, and blue sadness, but these connotations do not carry over into other languages. The preference of pink for girls and blue for boys is by no means universal. In Western cultures black represents mourning, a role played by white in the Orient. In Norse mythology blue symbolizes death and mourning. Unfortunately, colors can also reflect prejudicial and racist attitudes inherited from the past, with expressions such as dark or black designating undesirable qualities and light or white suggesting positive attributes. An embarrassing example is provided by "The White Bride and the Black Bride" (Grimm 135).

### Symbolic Images

In addition to natural and traditional symbols, fairy tales also contain innumerable images that beg for personal interpretation: a frog demanding to sleep with a princess (Grimm 1); a boy learning to shudder when his new bride throws a bucketful of minnows over him in bed (Grimm 4); a girl letting down her hair to allow a man access to the tower where she is imprisoned, then later discovering that she is pregnant (Grimm 12); two abandoned children killing a witch, then discovering that their abusive stepmother has died (Grimm 15); a confused suitor determining which woman is the right bride by how her shoe fits (Grimm 21); a wolf enticing a naïve girl to get into bed with him, then devouring her (Grimm 26); a girl refusing to carry an egg with her at all times, as demanded by her captor, and thus gaining control over him (Grimm 46); a creature, half boy and half hedgehog, riding on a rooster while playing bagpipes (Grimm 108); a boy seeking the key to a wild man's cage under his mother's pillow (Grimm 136). The list has no end.

The half-hedgehog, half-boy creature claims his bride (Grimm 108). Illustration by H.J. Ford (1892). Andrew Lang, *The Green Fairy Book* (London: Longmans, Green, and Company, 1892), p. 309.

The symbols described in the previous paragraph have significance beyond their literal meanings. Apologists for a specific philosophy—be it solar mythology, Freudianism, Marxism, or a particular religious creed—may advance a single, exclusive interpretation of a given symbol, but in many instances unbiased reflection will suggest other possibilities as well. Indeed, one of the reasons for the longevity and wide distribution of folktales is that they, by their very nature, say different things to different people. Storytellers and

Cinderella's stepsister cuts off her own toe (Grimm 21). Illustration by John D. Batten (1916). Joseph Jacobs, *European Folk and Fairy Tales* (New York: G.P. Putnam's Sons, 1916), p. 9.

their audiences have always recognized that an important part of a fairy tale's appeal lies in its extended meaning. It is not necessary, nor even desirable, for the storyteller to provide an interpretation of each symbol within a tale. Ambiguity is part of the charm. A child and an adult, a servant and a master, a believer and an agnostic can all hear the same story and feel satisfied, each listener for a different reason. But one conclusion is inescapable: The depiction of a half-human, half-hedgehog boy riding on a rooster while playing bagpipes represents something more than a half-human, half-hedgehog boy riding on a rooster while playing bagpipes.

## WHICH VERSION IS CORRECT?

Even a casual observer of the folklore scene will notice that oral stories, poems, and songs are remembered differently by different people. How does "Little Red Riding Hood" end? Does the wolf kill her, as claimed by Perrault, or does she miraculously escape, as depicted by the Grimms? Do Cinderella's sisters really cut off their heels and toes trying to make the glass slipper fit? Again Perrault and the Grimms tell the story differently. What turns the frog into a prince? A kiss? Sleeping for three nights with a princess? Being thrown against the wall by an impetuous heroine? The "correct" answer in each of these cases is "All of the above." Simply stated, the same story can be told (and remembered) differently by different people. And, does it not go without saying that the version of a story remembered and retold by a particular individual or group reflects on their psychological make-up and on their values?

Not all storytellers are equally gifted, and they sometimes relate episodes in an illogical order or add elements of one tale to another, a process called contamination. The end result can be satisfying, like a new recipe created by accident, but normally the addition is out of place. Nonetheless, the mistake, like a mutant gene, can be passed on, assuming a life of its own. A probable example is the final episode in the Grimms' first tale, "The Frog King; or, Iron Heinrich" (the full text is reproduced in chapter 3). Here the recently disenchanted young king and his new bride are joined by Heinrich, the king's faithful servant, who had had to bind his heart with iron bands to keep it from breaking when his master was transformed into a frog. Most versions of this popular tale (A-T 440) do not include this last episode, which was apparently added to the story as an afterthought decades, or maybe centuries, before the Grimms found the tale. In my judgment the details about Iron Heinrich do not contribute to the tale as a whole and can be considered a contamination, although it is clear from the Grimms' own comments that they valued the episode.

## AGE OF FOLK AND FAIRY TALES

### The Written Record

Most of the stories that we today know as folk and fairy tales were first recorded during the nineteenth century in the flurry of collecting and editing that followed the Grimms' pioneering work *Kinder- und Hausmärchen*. However, there is ample evidence that nearly all of these stories are substantially older. Curious audiences everywhere and at all times will have asked, "Where did this story come from? Has it always existed?"

By its nature storytelling is an oral art and does not normally leave a paper trail. However, a few ancient documents have survived that record or mention folktales, some that are still in circulation, hundreds and even thousands of years later. A folklorist must use this very sparse written record in much the same way that a paleontologist uses the fossil record of prehistoric animals; both specialists know that the preserved physical evidence represents only a tiny fraction of what formerly existed. The following survey of ancient folktale documentation extends to the Middle Ages, when the written record becomes much more abundant:

- About 1250 B.C. "Anpu and Bata," or "The Tale of Two Brothers" (A-T 318), was recorded on papyrus in Egypt.

- In the ninth or eighth century B.C. Homer built into his *Odyssey* the tale of "Odysseus and the Cyclops," a story that would live on for centuries as the independent folktale "Blinding an Ogre with a Stake" (A-T 1137).

- About 550 B.C. the story of "Jephthah and His Daughter" is recorded in the *Book of Judges,* based on events that happened 500 hundred years or more earlier. This tale of a father sacrificing his daughter because of a reckless oath would find extended life as a central motif in numerous fairy tales—for example, "The Girl without Hands" (Grimm 31) and "Hans-My-Hedgehog" (Grimm 108).

- About 425 B.C. Herodotus records the tale of "The Treasure Chamber of Rhampsinitus" (A-T 950) in his *History* of the Greco-Persian Wars.

- About 425 B.C. the same writer refers to Aesop, the fable writer, adding details that place him in the sixth century B.C.

- About 422 B.C. Elycleon, a character in Aristophanes's drama *The Wasps,* claims that one can make peace at a drinking party by telling "some comic story, perhaps one of those you have yourself heard at table, either in Aesop's style or in that of Sybaris [an ancient Greek city]. Everyone laughs and the trouble is ended."

- About 360 B.C. Plato criticizes storytellers for telling casual tales to children, tales that might instill beliefs that would prove untrue when the children become adults.

- About 200 B.C. the story of "The Grateful Dead" (A-T 505) is recorded in the *Book of Tobit.*

- About A.D. 10 Ovid records in his *Metamorphoses* two stories about King Midas, "The Golden Touch" (A-T 775) and "Ass's Ears" (A-T 782).

The Lamp

Psyche discovers that her husband is the handsome god Cupid, not a beast as she had feared. Illustration by John D. Batten. Joseph Jacobs, *European Folk and Fairy Tales* (New York: G.P. Putnam's Sons, 1916), p. 133.

- About A.D. 150 the Latin writer Lucius Apuleius records the story of "Cupid and Psyche" (A-T 425A) in his novel *The Golden Ass.*
- In the eleventh century A.D. the "Cantus de uno bove" (Song of One-Ox, A-T 1535) is recorded in the so-called Brussels Manuscript.

*Ancient Beliefs and Practices*

There is a consensus among scholars that individual motifs are often much older than the tales where they currently are found. Motifs, like used bricks, can be recycled into new tales of different types. Fairy tales are veritable catalogs of ancient beliefs and practices, some—like the acceptance of fairies or the belief in magic healing wells—that were active well into the twentieth century. Other motifs—like gaining control over a supernatural being by discovering and pronouncing his name (as in "Rumpelstiltskin," A-T 500) or foreseeing the future through the magic gift of understanding the language of birds—died out long ago as generally accepted beliefs but live on in fairy tales. The number of such beliefs inherited from the distant past and used by storytellers is very large.

Belonging to the list are mythical animals of every sort (including dragons, unicorns, and werewolves), magic weapons, charms, shape-shifters, seven-league boots and other magic items, giants, sorcerers, witches, magic invincibility, invisibility, hidden people and spirits of every description, enchanted springs and trees, talking animals, century-long sleeps, and much more. These items reflect the view prevalent in many primitive cultures that magic is omnipresent, but not omnipotent, and that its effects can be harmful or beneficial. The many types of supernatural beings represented in fairy tales are likely derived from ancient polytheistic religions where individual deities were neither inherently good nor evil, and often capricious in their dealings with humans. Fairy tales further reflect ancient beliefs in other realms (for example, a fairyland or spirit world) parallel to our own, with some individuals having the ability to cross back and forth between them.

*Nonsupernatural Ancient Practices*

Although supernatural powers form the soul of fairy tales, these stories also reflect their distant ancestry through ancient practices not involving magic. Ritualistic cannibalism apparently has both supernatural and this-worldly motivation, and both types find frequent mention in fairy tales. Thus Snow-White's stepmother desires to eat the girl's liver and lungs, apparently believing that they will renew her beauty and vitality, in other words, that the victim's qualities magically will be transferred to the person who eats her internal organs (Grimm 53). The stepmother in "The Juniper Tree" (Grimm 47) kills her stepson and feeds him to his unwitting father, apparently only as an expression of her self-centered wickedness. Another repugnant but well-documented ancient practice reflected in fairy tales is the right of parents to abandon unwanted children, leaving them to die of exposure. Never condoned, this practice is nonetheless depicted in numerous fairy tales, "Hansel and Gretel" (Grimm 15) being the most familiar example. These episodes suggest that at the time the tales were invented infanticide was still commonly practiced, or—at the least—that the fear of being killed by one's own parents was very real, even if not justified. The rigid rules of patriarchy are evident in many tales, including a man's right to execute his wife for suspected adultery. The absolute authority of kings over their subjects is seldom questioned in traditional fairy tales. Arranged marriages, including marriage by purchase, are depicted repeatedly, and for the most part without criticism. Marriage by capture happens frequently. Folktales collected in Hindu or Islamic cultures often depict polygamous marriages, as do a few European folktales—for example, "Gold-Tree and Silver-Tree" (Jacobs, *Celtic Fairy Tales,* no. 11). Human slavery is not unusual, although it may be called by some other name. However, calling a slave a servant or even an apprentice does not change the nature of the relationship between him and his master.

The preceding discussion presents evidence for the great antiquity of *some* fairy tales and fairy-tale components. However, one should not conclude that *all* traditional tales are prehistoric. There is good evidence that most of our popular tales—say those represented in the collections of Perrault and the Grimms—assumed their current forms in the late Middle Ages or the Renaissance, making them some 500 years old, give or take a century or two.

## MIGRATORY TALES

Since at least the beginning of the nineteenth century, scholars have known that variants of most of the stories circulating orally in a given region are found in other places as well. One explanation is that the sameness of the human psyche everywhere led to the independent invention of stories with similar plots (a process called polygenesis) in two or more regions. This view is defensible when such stories deal straightforwardly with commonly experienced human problems—for example, sibling rivalry or antagonism between social classes. However, when the plots are complex or are constructed from unusual motifs (for example, a lost slipper that later reveals the true bride, whose rightful position is threatened by her unworthy stepsisters), then reason dictates that the stories were not created independently of one another, but rather that they traveled, more or less intact, from one place to another (a process called diffusion).

Because many bilingual people inhabit both sides of language boundaries, such borders do not substantially hinder the exchange of stories. Even neighbors with languages that bear little resemblance to one another (for example,

Finnish and Swedish or Hungarian and German) typically share a large body of closely related folklore. Furthermore, even our distant forebears often made long journeys (consider the peopling of the Polynesian islands, the conquests of Alexander the Great, or the voyages of the Vikings, to name but three examples from different parts of the globe). When people travel they take with them their stories—together with other pieces of linguistic, cultural, and psychological baggage. Very often the transplanted stories, perhaps with a few alterations, flourish and multiply in their new environments.

It can sometimes be demonstrated with reasonable certainty where a given folktale type was born. For example, the migration of European tales to the New World and other corners of the earth followed the routes established by European explorers and colonizers. One can also show, with reasonable surety, how the rich storytelling heritage of the Arabic world and of India has made a permanent mark on European folklore and literature. However, much of the dissemination of folklore happened (and to an extent is still happening) outside of a recorded literary tradition, making it difficult—sometimes impossible—to determine when and where a given story was first told and how it traveled from its place of origin to its current home. Still, there is no doubt that folktales migrate. Thus Felix Karlinger's claim that "there are no German folktales, only folktales in the German language" (*Grundzüge,* p. x) can be applied to other nations as well. An Italian proverb expresses the same sentiment: "The fairy tale has no landlord" (quoted by Jones, *The Fairy Tale,* p. 29).

## National Differences

In spite of the similarities of folktales found in different places, a very large number of collections claim national or regional identity, using such titles as *Norwegian Folktales* or *Sicilian Folktales,* and this is appropriate, for even naturalized tales soon assume some characteristics of their new homelands. For example, in a Swiss version of "Little Snow-White," the seven dwarfs become angry at Snow-White for disobeying them, so—following longstanding Swiss democratic tradition—they put it to a vote whether or not to kill her. The majority votes to protect her, and thus she is allowed to continue living with them (as cited by Lüthi, *Es war einmal,* p. 42).

Many additional examples of such national, regional, and ethnic characteristics could be cited. However, just as immigrants seldom entirely overcome their foreign accents, migratory tales do not often lose all the traits of their countries of origin. The so-called *Jack Tales* of America's Appalachia offer a case in point. They talk freely of castles, kings, and princesses: motifs brought to the New World from Europe by storytelling immigrants. Similarly, fairy-tale characters in Icelandic stories go "into the woods" just as their continental European counterparts do, even though unlike Norway—the ancestral home of most Icelanders—Iceland has essentially no forests.

Castles, kings, princesses, and woods are admittedly superficial details. Migratory stories resemble one another also in terms of structure, theme, and function. As illustrated by the Aarne-Thompson index (more about this tool in chapter 2), a range of folktale types is at home in a broad swath of geography stretching from southern India to northwestern Europe. Thus animal fables, magic tales, trickster tales, and chain tales—all with similar plots—are told in Sri Lanka, Morocco, Russia, and Scotland. Furthermore, colonization and other more recent travels have carried Indo-European folklore to the Americas, East Asia, and beyond.

The often striking similarities between folktales found around the world should not lead to the conclusion that all cultures tell the same types of stories. All known societies tell stories for entertainment, education, and religious purposes, but the stories are often quite different from group to group, especially when one leaves the Indo-European linguistic and cultural area. For example, tales native to the indigenous peoples of the Americas, Africa, and the Pacific islands often bear little resemblance to each other or to the tales told in the Indo-European area. Drawing on a related observation, if Americans do not find British humor funny, should it surprise one that a Spaniard might struggle to find meaning in a traditional Maori tale?

## CLASSICAL COLLECTIONS

### Aesop

Aesop (also spelled Æsop) has been known since the fifth century B.C. as the Greek author of the world's best-known fables. However, most modern scholars doubt that he existed as a real person, maintaining instead that already in antiquity the name Aesop was invented to provide authorship for diverse fables from various anonymous sources. Supporting this theory, many of the earliest references to the stories of Aesop refer to *Aesopic* (or *Aesopian*) fables rather than *Aesop's* fables. Thus, the adjective *Aesopic* describes a kind of tale and a storytelling tradition but does not identify a specific author.

The most frequently cited ancient reference to the man Aesop is found in the *History* of the Greco-Persian Wars by the Greek historian Herodotus (ca. 425 B.C.). Here we learn little more than that Aesop lived during the sixth century B.C., was the slave of a Samian, and was murdered.

There are also a number of medieval manuscripts that depict the life of Aesop, but they often contradict each other, and many of the events they describe are so fantastic as to be unbelievable by modern standards. According to these accounts, Aesop was born a dark-skinned slave or possibly captured into slavery at a young age. He is reputed to have been ugly and deformed. Furthermore, in his early years he suffered from a speech impediment, but he was miraculously cured and became an eloquent orator. His quick tongue and sharp wit often got him into trouble, for he had a sarcastic response for every occasion, and he was an unrepentant trickster. With time Aesop's cunning, wisdom, and oratory skills brought him freedom from slavery, but in the end they cost him his life. The citizens of Delphi were so offended by his lack of respect for their aristocracy and for their principal deity, Apollo, that they planted a golden cup in his baggage, accused him of temple theft, and executed him by throwing him over a cliff.

The lack of surviving written records makes it impossible to establish an authoritative canon of stories attributable to Aesop. The oldest extant collection of Aesopic fables, containing some 94 tales, was recorded in Latin verse by Phaedrus during the first century A.D. It was based on earlier manuscripts, now lost. The oldest surviving collection of Aesopic fables in Greek was authored in the second century A.D. by Babrius, a hellenized Roman. This collection included more than 200 fables, 143 of which are still extant in their original verse form, with an additional 57 having survived in prose paraphrases. Many collections of "Aesop's fables" compiled in the Middle Ages were based on the versions of Phaedrus and Babrius.

Aesopic fables were highly valued as teaching tools in medieval and Renaissance Europe. The development of movable-type printing, beginning about 1455, greatly facilitated the publication of fable collections. In fact, various compilations of "Aesop's fables" were among the first books published in a number of European vernacular languages, including an English edition published in 1484 by William Caxton.

## The Jataka

Part of the canon of sacred Buddhist literature, *The Jataka,* a collection of some 550 anecdotes and fables, depicts earlier incarnations—sometimes as an animal, sometimes as a human—of the being who would become Siddhartha Gautama, the future Buddha. Traditional birth and death dates of Siddhartha Gautama are 563–483 B.C. The *Jataka* tales are dated between 300 B.C. and A.D. 400. In spite of the collection's sacred and didactic nature, it nonetheless includes elements—obviously derived from ancient folktales—whose primary function is entertainment. A number of the *Jataka* tales are also found in collections attributed to Aesop.

### The Panchatantra

Possibly India's most influential contribution to world literature, *The Panchatantra* (also spelled *Pañcatantra* or *Pañca-tantra*) consists of five books of animal fables and magic tales (some 87 stories in all) that were compiled, in their current form, between the third and fifth centuries A.D. It is believed that even then the stories were ancient. The tales' self-proclaimed purpose is to educate the sons of royalty. Although the original author's or compiler's name is unknown, an Arabic translation from about 750 attributes *The Panchatantra* to a wise man called Bidpai, a name probably derived from a Sanskrit word meaning "court scholar." Through oral folklore channels and by way of Persian and Arabic translations the tales of *The Panchatantra* found their way to Europe, where they substantially influenced medieval writers of fables.

### The Thousand and One Nights

Since its first translation into a European language between 1704 and 1717, the *1,001 Nights,* also known as *The Arabian Nights,* has been recognized as a universal classic of fantasy narrative. It is a much older work and one with a complicated genealogy. Based on Indian, Persian, and Arabic folklore, this work dates back at least 1,000 years as a unified collection, and many of its individual stories are undoubtedly even older. One of the collection's forebears is a book of Persian tales, likely of Indian origin, titled *A Thousand Legends.* These stories were translated into Arabic about 850, and at least one reference from about the year 950 calls them *The Thousand and One Nights.* Arabic stories, primarily from Baghdad and Cairo, were added to the ever-evolving collection, which by the early 1500s had assumed its more-or-less final form.

The framework of the *1,001 Nights* is well known: A sultan, convinced that all women are inherently disloyal, takes a new bride each night, then has her executed the following morning to ensure that he will never be deceived by an unfaithful wife. This gruesome pattern is broken when he marries Scheherazade, who entertains her husband each night with a story. However, she cleverly postpones each story's conclusion, so he always has to let her live one more day in order to find out how last night's tale ends. The pattern continues for 1,001 nights, by which time the king is sufficiently in love with Scheherazade that he abandons his plan to continue killing his wives.

This long and complicated work includes animal fables, love stories, adventures (everyone knows about Sinbad the Sailor), jests (including the universally known anecdote about the woman who hid five suitors in a closet), and some of the world's best-known magic tales, such as "Aladdin and His Magic Lamp" and "Ali-Baba and the Forty Thieves." Although they are today best known in heavily revised juvenile versions, most tales of the *1,001 Nights* are not for children. The stories lead their audience into a fantasyland, but the new realm includes many aspects of this world. Earthy humor, sensuality, passion, intolerance, and violence mark most of these unforgettable accounts. The *1,001 Nights* is by far the best known Arabic literary work in the non-Arabic world.

The *1,001 Nights* came to the Western world by way of France. Between 1704 and 1717 Antoine Galland translated the collection as *Les mille et une nuits* in 12 volumes, and for several generations this work was the basis for other European translations and editions. The most complete English version is the translation by the great adventurer-linguist Richard Burton, first published in London between 1885 and 1888 in 16 volumes, and "privately printed" to avoid conflict with Victorian antiobscenity laws. Burton's translation, although often praised for its accuracy, is not easy to read. His attempt to create an exotic and medieval style resulted in a florid, hybrid language that is neither ancient nor modern and neither Arabic nor English.

## Katha-saritsagara

Somadeva, a poet in the court of King Ananta of Kashmir, in the mid-eleventh century, assembled, from sources now lost, a monumental collection of Indian folklore into a work called *Katha-saritsagara* (Ocean of Streams of Story). A frame story extends across 124 sections called *taranga* (waves) and incorporates numerous interwoven retold stories into a continuous narrative. Many of the tales are built around motifs also found in the *1,001 Nights* and in medieval European jests and magic tales. These motifs include sexual adventures, ogres with external souls, vampires, and magicians.

### Medieval and Renaissance Jest Books

The birth of humanism in fourteenth-century Italy and its subsequent spread into northern Europe gave rise to numerous collections of short tales, often relying on anticlerical sentiment and scatological or sexual humor for their impact. Known generically as *facetiae* or *jests,* these tales were sometimes in Latin and sometimes in the vernacular, sometimes in verse and sometimes in prose, and a number of the writers, notably Hans Sachs, often turned them into short dramas. Their authors drew on oral sources as well as borrowing from competing collections for their raw material. Published tales often recirculated back into folklore channels through oral storytelling. Many tales—for example, "Unibos" (Song of One–Ox, A-T 1535) and "The Man from Paradise" (A-T 1540)—are found in different published jest books as well as in the oral folklore of numerous countries.

Among the best-known jest-book creators of this era are the Italians Franco Sacchetti, Giovanni Sercambi, and Gian Francesco Poggio Bracciolini (usually referred to simply as Poggio), and the Germans Johannes Pauli, Hans Sachs, and Jörg Wickram.

### Chapbooks and Broadsides

The Bible was the first book printed on Gutenberg's movable-print press, but the new technology soon yielded to lesser instincts. Cheaply printed (and usually anonymous) pamphlets and leaflets became an important part of European popular culture during the sixteenth, seventeenth, and eighteenth centuries. Typically carelessly written and poorly printed, these works mark the beginning of entertainment for the masses. In many instances their stories (often in the form of ballads) were taken from oral traditions. Many of the characters of these popular publications are household words even today: Tom Thumb, Jack the Giant Killer, Robin Hood, William Tell, Till Eulenspiegel, and Faust.

### Giovanni Francesco Straparola

Straparola's two-volume work *Le piacevoli notti* (1550–1553), called in English *The Nights of Straparola* or *The Facetious Nights,* contains some 75 novellas and fairy tales, some of oriental origin. Obviously patterning his collection after Boccaccio's *The Decameron,* Straparola depicts 13 nights of revelry in a luxurious villa on the island of Murano. The participants add to the entertainment by telling one another stories. Included are stories of magic and the supernatural as well as bawdy jokes and anecdotes. Although undistinguished as literature, Straparola's work is one of the earliest European collections of stories based largely on folklore, and as such is an important cultural document.

### Giambattista Basile

Following the tradition of the *1,001 Nights,* Boccaccio, Chaucer, and Straparola, Basile's *The Pentamerone* (1634–1636) is a collection of stories within

Storytelling in Renaissance Italy. Giovanni Francesco Straparola, *The Facetious Nights of Straparola,* vol. 1 (London: privately printed for members of the Society of Bibliophiles, 1898), frontispiece.

a frame story. The external story in this case is rather unlikely: A pregnant woman threatens to crush her unborn baby unless her husband, the king, meets her every whim, one of which is to hear fairy tales. He—at least for the present—gives in to her wishes and invites 10 gifted storytellers to the palace. Each woman tells five stories, and thus are born the 50 tales of *The Pentamerone*. These 50 stories draw heavily on oral traditions, as the frame story itself suggests. In fact, none of the stories in the collection is without analogues in Indo-European folklore. Many of our best-known fairy tales—for example, "Hansel and Gretel," "Rapunzel," "Sleeping Beauty," "Cinderella," "All-Kinds-of-Fur," "The Kind and the Unkind Girls," and "The Brothers Who Were Turned into Birds"—were recorded here, in some instances for the first time in a European language. Basile deserves recognition, both as a preserver of oral folklore and as a masterful and witty wordsmith. One reason he is not better known is that he wrote in an obscure Neapolitan dialect, making his book inaccessible to most of Europe for several generations.

### Charles Perrault

Like his contemporary Jean de La Fontaine, the famous author of rhymed fables, Perrault was a member of the Académie Française and a leading intellectual of his time. Ironically, his dialogue *Parallèles des anciens et des modernes* (Parallels between the Ancients and the Moderns, 1688–1697), which compared the authors of antiquity unfavorably with modern writers, served as a forerunner for the Age of Enlightenment in Europe, an era that was not always receptive to tales of magic and fantasy. Perrault could not have predicted that his reputation for future generations would rest almost entirely on a slender book published in 1697 and containing eight simple stories. Its unassuming title was *Histoires, ou contes du temps passé, avec des moralitez* (Stories, or Tales of Times Past, with Morals), with an added frontispiece containing the subtitle *Contes de ma mère l'Oye* (Tales of Mother Goose). Indeed, in a symbolically significant gesture, he did not publish the book in question under his own name but rather under the name of his 17-year-old son Pierre. The eight stories—"The Sleeping Beauty in the Wood," "Little Red Riding Hood," "Bluebeard," "Puss in Boots," "The Fairies," "Cinderella: or, The Little Glass Slipper," "Ricky with the Tuft," and "Little Thumb"—are almost universally known and loved. Perrault's fairy-tale legacy includes three additional titles—verse narratives published separately: "Griselda" (1691), "The Foolish Wishes" (1693), and "Donkey Skin" (1694).

Perrault chose his stories well, and he recorded them with wit and style. These 11 tales belong to an inheritance that has been shared by countless generations. He did not invent these tales—even in his day their plots were well known—but he gave them legitimacy.

## Le Cabinet des Fées *(1786–1789)*

France, influenced by Perrault's *Tales of Mother Goose* and to an even greater degree by Antoine Galland's pioneering translation of the *1,001 Nights,* took widespread advantage of the literary potential in the magic stories of folklore sooner than any other European country. The influential 41-volume anthology *Le cabinet des fées* (The Fairies' Cabinet, 1786–1789) is a good example of this interest. Edited by Charles-Joseph de Mayer, this collection included translations from the *1,001 Nights* plus fairy tales by such authors as Charles Perrault, Marie-Cathérine d'Aulnoy, and Jeanne-Marie Le Prince de Beaumont, who wrote one of the most memorable versions of "The Beauty and the Beast." The French Revolution brought this endeavor to an end. Interest in fairy tales moved across the Rhine to Germany, the homeland of the brothers Grimm.

### *Jacob Grimm and Wilhelm Grimm*

Influenced by the recently published folk poetry collection of Clemens Brentano and Achim von Arnim, *Des Knaben Wunderhorn* (The Boy's Magic Horn), Jacob and Wilhelm Grimm began to collect folktales in 1806. Their sources were varied, including chapbooks, broadsides, and other printed sources; but most of all they wrote down stories that were told to them by friends, neighbors, and associates. Most of their informants were women. In 1810 the brothers sent a manuscript containing 53 stories to von Arnim and Brentano, who had solicited folktales for a supplement to *Des Knaben Wunderhorn.* This folktale project never materialized, and the manuscript was not returned to its authors. However, the Grimms' interest in collecting and editing folklore did not falter. In 1812 they published their own collection of 86 tales, titled *Kinder- und Hausmärchen* (Children's and Household Tales). A second volume appeared in 1814 (dated 1815), adding 70 stories. A new edition, now numbering 161 tales plus an appendix of nine "Children's Legends," appeared in 1819. For this edition Wilhelm substantially revised most of the stories, creating a style that would become an international standard for printed fairy tales. A third volume, consisting of scholarly notes and titled *Anmerkungen* (Commentary) first appeared in 1822.

In 1825 the Grimms published a selection of 50 tales from their larger collection. This so-called "small edition" was very successful, going through a

# Kinder-
## und
# Haus - Märchen.

---

Gesammelt

durch

## die Brüder Grimm.

---

Berlin,

in der Realschulbuchhandlung.

1812.

Title page of the first edition of the Grimm brothers' *Children's and Household Tales. Kinder- und Hausmärchen, gesammelt durch die Brüder Grimm,* photographic reprint of 1812 edition, vol. 1 (Göttingen: Vandenhoeck and Ruprecht, 1996), title page.

total of 10 editions between that year and 1858. The "large edition" ran parallel to the smaller book, with new editions appearing in 1837, 1840, 1843, 1850, and 1857, growing to finally encompass 200 numbered stories plus an appendix of 10 "Children's Legends." Most modern editions and translations are based on the 1857 edition (number seven), the final version published during the Grimms' lifetimes. Although the Grimms used only 200 numbers in labeling their tales, their final collection actually comprises 206 stories (some numbers contain more than one entry), plus the 10 children's legends added as an appendix.

The Grimm brothers are best remembered for the magic stories in their *Children's and Household Tales,* but they also made a substantial contribution to another important folktale genre: the legend. Their collection *Deutsche Sagen* (German Legends) first appeared in two volumes in 1816 and 1818.

The Grimms' *Kinder- und Hausmärchen* with time has become the most widely read, the most frequently imitated, and the most influential book ever created in the German language. Its style, based on the idiom of ordinary people, maintains a careful balance between elegance and simplicity. In scope, it is one of the most complete folktale collections ever assembled in any language. Subsequent collectors, working in every corner of Europe and beyond, have independently discovered variants of nearly all of the Grimms' tales, which confirms that their stories were, indeed, of the people.

### After the Grimm Brothers

As the nineteenth century progressed, interest in folktale collection and publication spread throughout Europe. Influenced by the Grimms' technique and style, collectors—usually natives but sometimes foreigners—compiled and published folktale books from virtually every country and region. To name only the most important figures, Denmark had Svendt Grundtvig; England James Halliwell-Phillips; France Emmanuel Cosquin; Greece J.G. Hahn; Ireland Thomas Crofton Croker; Italy Giuseppe Pitré; Norway Peter Christian Asbjørnsen and Jørgen Moe; Russia Aleksandr Afanasyev; and Sweden Gabriel Djurklou. Geographically the list extends to many more countries, and chronologically it reaches even into the twenty-first century.

### WORKS CITED

Aarne, Antti, and Stith Thompson. *The Types of the Folktale: A Classification and Bibliography.* Helsinki: Suomalainen Tiedeakatemia, 1961. Abbreviated A-T. In-text citations refer to type numbers.

Grimm, Jacob, and Wilhelm Grimm. *Kinder- und Hausmärchen* (Children's and Household Tales, often named Grimms' Fairy Tales). Ed. Heinz Rölleke. 3 vols. Stuttgart: Reclam, 1980. Based on the 7th edition of 1857. In-text citations refer to the tale numbers, which are the same in all standard editions. Throughout this handbook I cite many examples from this collection, using my own translations. In most instances other tales would serve equally well, but I have given preference to the Grimms' collection because of its universal availability.

Jacobs, Joseph. *Celtic Fairy Tales.* New York: Putnam's, [1899].

Jones, Steven Swann. *The Fairy Tale: The Magic Mirror of Imagination.* New York: Twayne, 1995.

Karlinger, Felix. *Grundzüge einer Geschichte des Märchens im deutschen Sprachraum.* Darmstadt: Wissenschaftliche Buchgesellschaft, 1983.

Lüthi, Max. *Es war einmal: Vom Wesen des Volksmärchens.* Göttingen: Vandenhoeck und Ruprecht, 1973.

# Two
# Definitions and Classifications

**FOLKLORE**

Folklore can be defined as information communicated from person to person and from generation to generation by word of mouth and through personal demonstration. Excluded are items published or broadcast through the mass media as well as material standardized and transmitted by formal groups such as organized religions, governments, and schools. Folklore thus includes bedtime prayers learned at home and then later taught from memory to a new generation of children, but it excludes prayers preserved in a printed catechism. Folklore includes jump-rope rhymes learned at a playground from one's schoolmates, but it excludes crossword puzzles from newspapers. Folklore can be utilitarian (how to sharpen a knife), esthetic (decorating a quilt top), or spiritual (a saying to bring good luck). Most, but not all, folklore is verbal: proverbs and narratives recited from memory, or possibly made up extemporaneously to satisfy a particular need, then recalled and related by succeeding narrators, sometimes for many generations.

**FOLK**

The term *folk*—in compounds such as *folklore, folksong,* and *folktale*—came into English by a circular route. This pathway started in 1760 with the publication of *Fragments of Ancient Poetry, Collected in the Highlands of Scotland.* The ostensible collector and translator of these songs, attributed to a third-century blind Gaelic bard named Ossian, was the Scottish poet James Macpherson. Although time would reveal that Macpherson himself was the creator of this collection, not its discoverer and translator as claimed, the work had tremendous influence throughout northern Europe, especially in Germany, sparking interest in the ancient lore of the region, largely orally transmitted and until then underappreciated.

A second publication of traditional material from Britain appeared five years later (1765), the three-volume collection of 180 ballads titled *Reliques of Ancient English Poetry,* collected and edited by Thomas Percy. Unlike his predecessor Macpherson, Percy did indeed base his ancient poetry on long-forgotten documents, in this case a manuscript collection from the sixteenth century. However, in amending the fragments Percy gave them a decidedly eighteenth-century cast. Nonetheless, his ballads were accepted as authentic and were translated and imitated throughout northern Europe.

Among Percy's many disciples was the German poet Johann Gottfried Herder, who called himself "ein deutscher Percy." Through his anthologies and theoretical writings Herder did more than any German of his generation to promote interest in folk literature. In fact, he coined the terms *Volksdichtung* (folk literature), *Volkspoesie* (folk poetry), and *Volkslied* (folksong), consciously patterning them after then current English phrases containing the word *popular.*

Influenced by Herder and others, Jacob and Wilhelm Grimm collected and published their pioneering two-volume collection of *Kinder- und Hausmärchen* (Children's and Household Tales, 1812–1815), and soon afterward the internationally recognized center of preliterate culture studies established itself in Germany, where it would remain for at least the remainder of the century. Neighboring countries borrowed both concepts and vocabulary from Germany, and for England this included—as a substitute for *popular*—the term *folk,* a cognate with the German *Volk* (people). Thus, for example, the English expression *popular song* was translated by Herder into German as *Volkslied,* then found its way back into English as *folksong.*

The English word *folklore* has a similar and well-documented genealogy. In the periodical *The Athenaeum* dated August 22, 1846, William Thoms, writing under the pseudonym Ambrose Merton, proposed that the then current phrases *popular antiquities* and *popular literature* be replaced with "a good Saxon [Germanic] compound, *Folk-Lore*—the lore of the people." His recommendation found fertile ground, and within a year the term *folklore* had become a household word in England.

Other countries adopted both the concept and the word. Even in France, a country not usually friendly to foreign linguistic influence, the designation *folklore* found a place beside its Gallic counterpart *traditions populaires.* German scholars adopted a literal translation of *folklore: Volkskunde.* Curiously, in the late twentieth century the English-spelled *Folklore* (with an uppercase *F*, in keeping with German orthography) found its way back to Germany, now with a narrow field of meaning encompassing traditional costumes, dances, and folk music—for example, lederhosen, dirndl dresses, and oompah bands.

## FAIRY TALES

The term *fairy tale* came to England from France through an author whose name and works now are largely forgotten. Commencing in 1697, Marie-Cathérine le Jumel de Barneville de la Motte, Comtesse d'Aulnoy (usually referred to simply as Madame d'Aulnoy) began publishing volumes of fantasy stories under the collective title *Les contes des fées* (Tales of Fairies). These are contrived literary creations, based only marginally on folklore. Her stories, called fairy tales, were popular in England into the nineteenth century.

### Mother Goose

In France the year 1697 brought the publication of another collection of stories that in England would come to be known as fairy tales: *Histoires, ou contes du temps passé, avec des moralitez* (Stories, or Tales of Times Passed, with Morals) by Charles Perrault. An added frontispiece calls them *Contes de ma mère l'Oye* (Tales of Mother Goose). The earliest English translation kept the original French title essentially intact: *Histories; or, Tales of Past Times, with Morals* (Robert Samber, 1729). However, later translations added the phrase *fairy tales* to the title, as in, for example, the anonymously translated American edition *Fairy Tales, or Histories of Past Times, with Morals* (1794).

### The Brothers Grimm

Similarly, the most famous "fairy-tale" collection of all time, the Grimm brothers' *Kinder- und Hausmärchen* (Children's and Household Tales) did not come to be known as a book of *fairy tales* until several decades after the work was translated into English. Edgar Taylor, the Grimms' first English translator, named the collection *German Popular Stories* (2 vols., 1823–1826). An anonymous translation from 1853, identified only by its illustrator Edward H. Wehnert, is titled *Household Tales,* remaining true to half of the Grimms' original title. Apparently the first major translator to use the technically inaccurate and grammatically flawed but now familiar title *Grimm's Fairy Tales* was Mrs. H.B. Paull in 1868. She also translated the *Eventyr fortalte for børn* (literally, Adventures, Told for Children) of Hans Christian Andersen under the title *Hans Andersen's Fairy Tales* (1872). Subsequent translators of the Grimms have vacillated between the expression *fairy tales* and terms that more accurately describe the original German title. Some examples: *Household Tales* (Margaret Hunt, 1884); *Household Stories* (Lucy Crane, 1886); *Household Fairy Tales* (Ella Boldey, 1890); *Tales* (Wanda Gág, 1936); *German Folk Tales* (Francis P. Magoun Jr. and Alexander H. Krappe, 1960); *Fairy Tales* (James Stern, 1972); *Tales for Young and Old* (Ralph Manheim, 1977); and *Fairy Tales* (Jack Zipes, 1987).

The pattern in France is different. Following are some of the titles used by French translators of the Grimms over the years: *Les contes des frères Grimm* (Tales of the Brothers Grimm); *Contes de la famille* (Family Tales); *Les contes merveilleux* (Magic Tales); and *Contes pour les enfants et les parents* (Tales for Children and Their Parents). The phrase *contes des fées* is conspicuously absent in the titles of French translations of the Grimms' tales.

The designation *fairy tale* is problematic for students of folk narrative. In English that term is at the same time a synonym for the adjectives *fantasy, magical, ideal, fictitious,* or *untrue;* and in common usage a designation for essentially any kind of make-believe story, especially one with a marvelously happy ending. But strictly speaking, *fairy tale,* applied to such traditional tales as "Hansel and Gretel" or "Little Snow-White," is a misnomer. These are tales of magic, but no fairies are involved.

In conclusion, the expression *fairy tale* is a relative latecomer in English and does not accurately translate the original French, German, and Danish titles of some of our most popular "fairy-tale" collections. Furthermore, most stories known today as fairy tales are not about fairies at all, even though they do typically rely on magic powers for their resolution. A more accurate and historically more consistent designation would be *magic tale,* a term with close parallels in German *(Zaubermärchen),* French *(contes merveilleux),* and other languages. The label *magic tale* is preferred by specialists, but *fairy tale* is by now thoroughly established in English, and I will not attempt to dislodge it. Fairy tales, or magic tales—I shall use the terms synonymously—are an important part of a larger genre called collectively *folk narratives,* and it is to that broader category that we now turn.

## FOLK NARRATIVES

A basic activity of scholars in all disciplines is to separate their objects of study into related categories. Scholars of folk narratives divide their subject into three main groups or genres: myths, legends, and folktales. Numerous subcategories are possible within each larger group. These divisions are made according to various criteria: style, form, content, function, author's intent, and so on. Closely related to folk narratives are two separate categories of verbal folklore: proverbs and riddles. The boundaries between the major groups and the subdivisions are fluid, and many recognized kinds of narratives and sayings can best be defined as mixed genres.

## Myths

Myths constitute possibly the most elemental kind of folk narrative. These accounts, often rich with symbolic imagery, establish a context for humans within the cosmos; define our relationships with supernatural powers; and depict the deeds of deities, prophets, and superhuman heroes from the distant past. The issues of mythology—origins and purposes, good and evil, life and death—are also those of religion. The sacred beliefs and traditions of one culture are myths and legends to another.

## Legends

Legends and myths are often mentioned in the same phrase, and rightly so, for the two genres are closely related. Like myths, legends are presented as true accounts, but unlike the former, they are human centered; and they are more specific, more individual, and more local than myths. A legend, whether depicting the experience of an ordinary miller or of a famous hero such as Alexander the Great, relates a personal event. The stuff of legends may be mundane and trivial (George Washington slept here) or supernatural and dramatic (King Arthur and his knights will arise from their death-like sleep when Britain needs them most), but legends do not meet the elemental grandeur and cosmic authority of myths. Furthermore, they are typically reported in unadorned, everyday language.

The essential characteristic of a legend is that it claims to be true. Standards of credibility, of course, vary greatly from audience to audience and from generation to generation. Thus, accounts of dragons, fairies, trolls, and witches that would have been widely believed a few generations ago in today's skeptical age would be viewed by most as fictions and fantasies.

## Folktales

The word *fiction* leads to the next main category of folk narrative: folktales (also spelled as two words, or as a hyphenated word). Myths and legends were considered to be true by their originators and traditional tellers, however fantastic their contents are by later belief standards; but stories in the third category—folktales—are, for the most part, self-consciously fictitious. I say "for the most part" because there is evidence that at least some traditional audiences and storytellers have accepted many types of folktales as truth.

## TYPES OF THE FOLKTALE

Although scholars from the brothers Grimm onward have recognized that Indo-European folktales fall into fairly well definable groups, it was nearly a century before these observations were developed into a formal classification system. In 1910 the Finnish scholar Antti Aarne published his *Verzeichnis der Märchentypen* (Index of Folktale Types). In 1928 American folklorist Stith Thompson issued an expanded version of this pioneering work, now in English instead of German, titled *The Types of the Folktale*. A second revision, further enlarged, appeared in 1961. This final product has proven itself an indispensable tool for folktale researchers.

Using numbers 1 through 2,499, sometimes amended with letters or asterisks, the Aarne-Thompson index defines traditional folktale plots (primarily those found from India to northwestern Europe), assigning to each a type number. Usually referred to as A-T types, these classifications greatly aid scholars in the investigation of folktales and their distribution.

Folktales, fluid by their very nature, are not easy to define and to categorize. Even the word *folktale* resists easy definition. The following table, extracted from the contents of Aarne's and Thompson's *The Types of the Folktale*, while giving an overview of their system, also illustrates the lack of precision in the term *folktale*. In common usage, even among professional folklorists, all of the tale types represented in their book are folktales—after all, the word *folktale* is part of its title. Note, however, that one of the main subcategories under *folktales* is *ordinary folktales*. To confuse the issue even more, *fairy tales* are nowhere listed in this scheme (for reasons explained previously), although the designation *tales of magic* can serve as a synonym. Thus, although in everyday English usage folktales and fairy tales often are treated as two different kinds of stories (as witnessed, for example, by the title *Folk and Fairy Tales*), folklore specialists generally prefer the term *magic tales* over *fairy tales*. By either name, they form a subcategory of *folktales*, not a separate genre.

**Aarne-Thompson Folktale Types**

| Category | Type Numbers |
|---|---|
| Animal tales | 1-299 |
| Ordinary folktales | 300-1199 |

| Tales of magic | 300-749 |
| Religious tales | 750-849 |
| Novellas (romantic tales) | 850-999 |
| Tales of the stupid ogre | 1000-1199 |
| Jokes and anecdotes | 1200-1999 |
| Formula tales | 2000-2399 |
| Unclassified tales | 2400-2499 |

## ANIMAL TALES (TYPES 1–299)

Most of the items designated as animal tales in the Aarne-Thompson index qualify as fables. The fable's defining quality is its didactic function. Centuries ago in the Mediterranean area, India, and other parts of the world, our forebears observed that brief stories, often featuring animals and even inanimate things as actors, were highly effective tools in teaching moral concepts. In the popular mind fables are so closely connected with moralizing that we expect each one to conclude, "And the moral of the story is…" Indeed, a traditional fable, especially one attributed to Aesop, typically ends with an aphoristic restatement of the tale's ethical content. However, many of the best fables lack such a moral, and it can be argued that a well-written story does not require a summary any more than a well-told joke needs an explanation of its punch line.

Apart from its didactic nature, another attribute of the fable is its brevity. Many of the most memorable fables can be told in a half dozen or fewer sentences. For example, Aesop's "The Oak and the Reeds" (A-T 298C*) in the translation of V.S. Vernon Jones has but four sentences. The first sentence describes the situation: "An oak that grew on the bank of a river was uprooted by a severe gale of wind, and thrown across the stream." The second sentence, through the eyes of the fallen tree, reveals the paradox that the storm injured the strong while sparing the weak: "It fell among some reeds growing by the water, and said to them, 'How is it that you, who are so frail and slender, have managed to weather the storm, whereas I, with all my strength, have been torn up by the roots and hurled into the river?'" The final two sentences (which easily could be written as one) explain the paradox: " 'You were stubborn,' came the reply, 'and fought against the storm, which proved stronger than you. But we bow and yield to every breeze, and thus the gale passed harmlessly over our heads.'"

Nowhere in these few sparse sentences is there any dramatic buildup. Nothing is said about the relationship between the oak and the reeds prior to the fateful storm. Essentially nothing is said about the participants' emotional response to the tragedy. We learn nothing about other survivors or victims of

The oak and the reeds. Illustration by Richard Heighway (1894). *The Fables of Aesop* (London and New York: Macmillan, 1894), p. 89.

the storm, and nothing about how these events might influence their lives afterward. Nor is there any deliberation as to when and under what circumstances an individual should follow the reeds' example, and when it might be better to emulate the oak. A well-crafted fable does not say everything, leaving instead much to the imagination and interpretive powers of the reader.

In addition to brevity, this exemplary fable also illustrates that genre's propensity to function as an allegory. The oak is not simply an individual tree that falls because of its inability to bend with the wind; nor are the reeds just one family of fortunate plants who survive a particular storm. Instead, most readers of this fable will see in the oak and the reeds classes of people found everywhere and in every generation. The oak represents those who stubbornly resist change and refuse to compromise, whereas the reeds symbolize those who are willing to give and take in order to survive. The moral of this story, which in this version is not repeated in an appended aphorism, is controversial, for it teaches pragmatism and flexibility, rather than strict conformity to a particular code, precisely the opposite of messages taught by many religious and political systems.

The preceding tale's active participants are plants, but more often fables feature animals. In either case, the nonhuman actors play very humanlike roles. Three main advantages derive from the use of plants or animals as stand-ins for humans in these tales:

1. By casting negative players as nonhumans fabulists distance themselves from the targets of their criticism—who may be ruthless despots—thus gaining a greater degree of freedom to expose human foibles without fear of interference or retribution.

2. By repeatedly assigning specific traits to particular creatures, fabulists have developed a kind of shorthand, allowing their tales to be all the more concise. Thus when a fox is introduced, we—without further explanation—know that he is resourceful, crafty, and amoral. Similarly, the wolf is self-centered and greedy, but probably too slow-witted to bring his ill-conceived plans to fruition.

3. Talking and acting plants and animals have a universal audience appeal, especially for children. By engaging the listeners' imaginations and asking them to conceptualize situations that cannot be observed in real life, the fabulists elevate story-time to an otherworldly experience.

Although animals and things speak human language and exhibit human behavior only in a world of make-believe, in fables their words and deeds are still very much of this world. We may be told that the lion is the king of beasts, but in fables he represents a king of men, ruthless and powerful as long as his strength holds out, but highly vulnerable once his strength begins to fail. In short, Aesop's world is our world.

## MAGIC TALES (TYPES 300–749)

### A World of Magic

Fables, in spite of their plant and animal protagonists, are very much of this world, but this is not so with magic tales, also known as fairy tales. "In ancient times, when wishing still did some good" begins one of the best-known such tales, "The Frog King" (Grimm 1). The frog in this tale, like his counterparts in Aesopic fables, speaks and acts like a human, but his fairy-tale experiences are quite unlike those in fables. The Grimms' frog cavorts with a princess and turns into a prince. Aesop's frogs refuse to move from puddles in the road and are crushed by wagon wheels; or they request a powerful king and are given a stork, who forthwith begins to devour them. Aesop's frogs inhabit a world that appears to differ from ours: creatures talk and use logic (however flawed) to play out their lives. But in the end, theirs is a stork-eat-frog, all-too-human world.

On the other hand, the Grimms' frog king inhabits a world that only superficially resembles ours. Precious things get lost; promises are made and broken; fathers scold. But behind this real-world façade is a background of magic. It can be sinister and inexplicable: Before the story opens, as we later learn, a prince is turned into a frog for no given reason. But the magic is also wish fulfilling and emancipating: A princess frees herself from a demanding and repulsive companion and gains a desirable marriage partner merely by asserting herself. This is a world of fantasy, an enchanted world where wishing still does some good: a fairy-tale world.

Fairy-tale characters accept magic as a natural and expected part of their everyday world. The princess in "The Frog King" demonstrates no surprise when confronted by a talking frog. Lewis Carroll, in *Alice's Adventures in Wonderland,* one of the nineteenth century's most successful literary fairy tales, makes the same observation. His book opens when Alice sees a rabbit running along while saying to itself, "Oh dear! Oh dear! I shall be too late!" to which the narrator adds parenthetically, "when she thought it over afterwards it occurred to her that she ought to have wondered at this, but at the time it all seemed quite natural."

In many respects the world of fairy tales resembles the fairyland of ancient legends. Numerous accounts mention a realm inhabited by fairies or other such hidden people and imbued with supernatural powers. Variously described, this place can be in the sky, underground, underwater, or mysteriously integrated into our own world in a manner intangible and invisible to most humans. Fairy tales give their characters, and vicariously the readers, access to this alternate parallel world, a place where magic abounds. These powers are supernatural only by this-worldly standards. By fairy-tale standards they are natural and subject to their own laws. Magic may be inexplicable using ordinary human logic, but it is not arbitrary. If Ali Baba, his undeserving brother, or anyone else pronounces the magic phrase *Open Sesame* correctly, the magic mountain will open; otherwise it will not.

The heroine of "The Twelve Brothers" (Grimm 9) plucks 12 lilies, thus unleashing a curse that turns her brothers into ravens, a curse that she can undo only by remaining silent for 12 years. She satisfies the requirement, and her brothers regain their human forms. Illustrating the exactness of magic rules, in a Norwegian counterpart to this tale, "The Twelve Wild Ducks," the heroine, in addition to remaining silent for 12 years, must also make 12 shirts from thistledown. At the end of 12 years the last shirt is still lacking a sleeve, and when her brothers appear, the youngest has a feathered wing in the place of one of his arms. The laws of magic are inviolable.

Taking the Indo-European fairy-tale tradition as a whole, it is difficult to isolate a single source of magic, although in individual tales specific sources can be identified. There are magic lamps, rings, tables, sacks, cudgels, carpets, boots, and much more. Anyone who possesses them can control their power, if they only know the rules. Many tales, even some circulating quite recently, draw their magic from ancient religion. The underground goddess in "Frau Holle" (Grimm 24) magically rewards the virtuous heroine and punishes her selfish stepsister (as expected in a fairy tale), but she also causes it to snow on earth, a task normally associated with a major deity.

Frequently folktales, even far-traveled stories with a very ancient heritage, take on religious aspects from the cultures where they currently reside. Thus the tales of the *1,001 Nights* have a pronounced Islamic cast, while their European counterparts assume a Christian character, although neither group necessarily follows official theology. For example, the hero of "Bearskin" (Grimm 101) receives magic help from the devil under the following agreement: "For the next seven years you are neither to wash yourself, nor comb your beard and hair, nor cut your nails, nor say the Lord's prayer." He keeps the agreement and wins everything: wealth, power, and a beautiful bride, all because he abstained from washing and praying for seven years. At the tale's end we are even assured that the devil will not get his soul.

In some of our oldest tales the magic powers are directly associated with a deceased relative, usually a mother. For example, in many variants of "Cinderella" the heroine's magic help comes from a being connected to her dead mother. In the Grimms' version (21) Cinderella gets her beautiful dresses from a tree growing out of her mother's grave.

In other tales the magic power comes from within the protagonist's own self, suggesting that we all have untapped and undiscovered abilities. Perhaps the best example of this extraordinary inner power comes from "Fitcher's Bird" (Grimm 46). A Bluebeard-like sorcerer abducts two sisters in succession, killing and dismembering each one when she enters a forbidden room. Afterward he captures the third sister, and gives her the same restrictions. She too disobeys, but her very defiance seems to give her power over her despotic captor. Discovering the mutilated bodies of her sisters, she simply puts the pieces back together, and they magically come to life. She then tricks the ogre into carrying her now-living sisters back home, after which she makes her own escape. This tale offers no explanation as to the source of the heroine's power; it simply comes from within.

Another widespread group of tales that demonstrates inner power is known generically as "The Girl Helps the Hero Flee" (A-T 313). These stories depict a young couple's flight from an ogre. The woman is very much the leader, her magic powers enabling the pair to escape from a demonic force and start a new life together. But their flight is not simple. Typically the heroine throws down ordinary objects—such as a comb or a mirror—which turn into hindrances—a forest or a lake—for the pursuer. Alternatively the heroine hides herself and her companion by transforming herself and him into other beings. Nowhere is her magic power explained. It is simply something she draws from within at a time of need.

In many tales dreams are a source of supernatural help, especially as a means of foretelling the future and gaining instructions. The Grimms' "The Nixie in the Pond" (181) offers an excellent example. Here a young husband is abducted by a water sprite. His faithful wife, through a series of dreams, learns how he can be freed. She then literally follows her dreams and rescues her husband from the arms of another woman.

### Misuse of Magic

Magic, like fire, is a good servant but a bad master. Most of the examples in the preceding discussion show the benefits of magic, properly used. However, magic also can be misused, much to the detriment of the practitioner. A direct warning against such abuses is made in the "Sorcerer's Apprentice" (A-T 325), famously depicted in Walt Disney's film *Fantasia* (1941). Here an apprentice uses a charm from his master's magic book to help him carry water, but, knowing only half the formula, he cannot stop the ensuing flood, with nearly catastrophic results. Similarly, in "Why the Sea Is Salty" (A-T 565), a tale told around the world, a hand mill that magically grinds out salt on demand comes into the possession of someone who knows only part of the command and cannot bring it to a stop. In the end he saves himself from the relentless stream of salt by throwing the mill into the sea, where to this day it sits at the bottom churning forth salt.

A final example of misused magic comes from "The Hunchbacks and the Elves" (A-T 503). As the story is typically told, the first of two protagonists (both hunchbacks) happens upon a band of elves and joins in their song. Pleased with his singing, they take the hump from his back and send him home straight and strong. His misshapen companion, desiring the same cure, seeks out the elves and sings along with them. However, his singing offends the little people, and they punish him by adding the first singer's hump to his already deformed back.

*Fairy-Tale Structure*

Apart from the omnipresence of magic, traditional fairy tales are also marked by a fairly consistent structure, as numerous scholars have noted, most prominently Vladimir Propp in *The Morphology of the Folktale* (1928) and Joseph Campbell in *The Hero with a Thousand Faces* (1949). Although fairy-tale formulas are not as reliable and universal as some structuralists might posit, the following outline does apply to a very large number of tales:

1. Separation

2. Initiation

3. Return

Stephen Sondheim chose well when he selected the title *Into the Woods* for his 1987 fairy-tale musical. A departure from home into the woods is the starting point for countless tales. The forest is an obvious symbol for freedom from social conventions and restrictions, but also for risk and danger. The fairy-tale separation from familiar surroundings can be either voluntary or forced. Hansel and Gretel (Grimm 15) are taken into the woods and abandoned by parents who cannot or will not care for them. The boy who went forth to learn fear (Grimm 4) is disowned by his father and sent into the world to find his own way. The mutilated heroine of "The Girl without Hands" (Grimm 31), although apparently safe from further abuse, walks away from her father's house and into the woods. The youthful hero of "Iron Hans" (Grimm 136), fearing a beating from his father, runs away into the woods. The heroine of "All-Kinds-of-Fur" (Grimm 65) flees into the woods to escape her father's incestuous advances. The brave little tailor (Grimm 20), finding his workplace too restraining, abandons his trade and sets forth to seek a better life. Furthermore, with few exceptions, the leading characters of fairy tales must find their new way by themselves, independent of traditional social structures. Neither family, government, nor church offers aid. But the heroes and heroines are not alone. Magic pervades the woods, and through its help they prevail.

The initiation phase of a typical fairy tale is rife with conflict and often resembles the coming-of-age rituals of primitive cultures. These are quite different for males and for females. The leading ladies of fairy tales are typically faced with daunting domestic tasks: to spin straw into gold ("Rumpelstiltskin," Grimm 55); to separate peas and lentils from ashes ("Cinderella," Grimm 21); or to strip a large quantity of feathers from their quills ("The True Bride," Grimm 186). Alternatively, a fairy-tale heroine, now an emerging woman, may spend her time of initiation passively isolated: locked in a tower ("Rapunzel," Grimm 12); maintaining a vow of silence ("The Twelve Brothers," Grimm 9); comatose in a glass tomb ("Little Snow-White," Grimm 53); or asleep barricaded behind an impenetrable hedge of thorns ("Little Brier-Rose," Grimm 50). For males the initiation usually requires strength, valor, and fortitude. Familiar challenges include spending three nights in a haunted castle ("The Story of a Boy Who Went Forth to Learn Fear," Grimm 4); killing a dragon ("The Two Brothers," Grimm 60); or rescuing a princess from an ogre ("Strong Hans," Grimm 166).

Three is the most prominent number in European fairy tales. As already noted, fairy tales are typically constructed around a three-part frame: separation, initiation, and return. The central part of this formula, the initiation, is frequently further subdivided into episodes, often three in number. They are usually repetitive, with the second and third episodes being variations of the first. For example, in the center part of "Little Snow-White" (Grimm 53) the jealous stepmother three times attempts to poison the heroine, always using similar tricks. Twice she fails, but her third try is successful, at least until a prince revives the heroine from her deathlike trance.

Typically the leading characters are only children when they leave home. Snow-White is but 7; Hans-My-Hedgehog is 8; Rapunzel is 12; Strong Hans is 13; Brier-Rose is 15. Even if the age is not given, tradition implies that fairy-tale heroes and heroines are not far removed from childhood as their adventures begin. The initiation episodes obviously mark their coming of age. Immediately upon resolving the story's central conflict the protagonists marry. Both Snow-White and Brier-Rose, for example, fall into a magic sleep as girls and wake up as women, each immediately marrying the first man she sees upon awakening.

A fairy tale's third stage is the return of the hero or heroine to society. However, the path is not circular. The norm for fairy tales is not a return to one's original home, but rather the integration into a new community, and nearly always in a much more powerful and prestigious role. Upward mobility knows no limits in fairy tales. Heroines move from kitchen to castle. Swineherds and tailors are promoted to kings.

Although innumerable fairy tales fit the outline just described, it is not universal, nor should it be considered prescriptive. Many traditional tales are outliers. Not all fairy tales end happily. Some tales have a "cautionary" design, showing the negative results of bad behavior instead of letting good behavior lead to the proverbial "fairy-tale" ending. For example, in "The Fisherman and His Wife" (Grimm 19) the husband and wife fail their tests and go full circle, ending exactly where they began, living in a miserable hovel. An even more dramatic example of a cautionary magic tale is "Frau Trude" (Grimm 43), in which a strong-willed little girl, in violation of her parents' orders,

The fisherman returns to the magic fish to request a still larger mansion. Illustration from *Kindermärchen* (Children's Tales) by Albert Ludewig Grimm (no relation to the famous Grimm brothers). Albert Ludewig Grimm, *Kindermärchen* (Heidelberg: Mohr und Zimmer, 1809), facing p. 82.

pays a visit to the mysterious Frau Trude. The tale ends when Frau Trude turns her young visitor into a block of wood, which she throws onto the fire. The story's final sentence: "When it was thoroughly aglow Frau Trude sat down next to it, and warmed herself by it, saying, 'It gives such a bright light!'" This tale thus reverses the expected formula, with the little girl being burned to death and the wicked witch enjoying the happy ending.

There are other endings that depart from normal expectations. "The Little Lamb and the Little Fish" (Grimm 141) ends when a brother and sister, tormented by their evil stepmother, escape into the woods, "where they lived by themselves, contented and happy." Here there is no accustomed marriage and no return to society, although the storyteller does assure us that they were happy.

### Style

With the second edition (1819) of their *Children's and Household Tales* the Grimm brothers, especially Wilhelm, established a literary style for such stories that remains exemplary to this day. (Their first edition was written in a simpler, less formal mode. For an example of the style differences see the two versions of "The Frog King" presented side by side in chapter 3 of this handbook.) The literary style of Wilhelm Grimm, the principal caretaker and editor of their collection, departed substantially from the flowery, elaborate, and often artificially archaic language of other fairy-tale writers of the nineteenth and preceding centuries, and it is his style that quickly established itself as a pattern for later folktale collectors and editors of many nations.

Wilhelm's language is simple, but not primitive; literate, but not pretentious; child friendly, but not childish. Unlike the rambling, unfocused narratives often found in folklorists' field books and tape recordings, Wilhelm's plots are tightly constructed, avoiding parenthetical comments and unintended redundancies. Above all else, remaining true to the oral genre, the Grimms' fairy tales are action oriented. These narratives contain few descriptive passages, very sparse dialogue, and virtually no deliberation or reflection. The adventure itself is the message. Adventure is an almost stereotypical feature of fairy tales. Reflecting this observation, the Danish/Norwegian word for *fairy tale* is *eventyr* (root meaning: *adventure*).

### Fairy-Tale Themes

Although in theory almost any kind of human experience could be turned into a fairy tale, most storytellers within this genre have chosen their themes from a relatively narrow field.

Who are the leading characters in fairy tales? The stereotypical hero is a fellow named Hans, Jack, Jean, Juan, or Ivan; or even more likely, he is identified only as *the boy* or *the lad*. His female counterpart is called simply *the girl* or *the maiden*, possibly named Gretel, Mary, Marie, or Maria. Their occupations come from the extreme ends of the social structure. At the bottom are woodcutters, tailors, cobblers, peasants, swineherds, goose-girls, kitchen maids, cottagers, crofters, and discharged soldiers. At the top are princes, princesses, kings, and queens. However, fairy-tale heroes and heroines depicted as princes and princesses are such in name only and are typically quite powerless at the tale's beginning, as witnessed in the Grimms' tales "The Frog King" (1), "The Twelve Brothers" (9), "Little Snow-White" (53), and "Iron Hans" (136).

Fairy-tale protagonists typically have the least-favored position in a family: youngest son, youngest daughter, or stepchild. Often they are openly unwanted by their parents. Many are chided for being too small, and *Little* can even be a part of their names—for example, Little Thumb, Little Red Riding Hood, Little Brier-Rose, and Little Snow-White. Demeaning names such as Cinderella, Ash Lad, Donkey-Skin, or Hans-My-Hedgehog are common. Frequently the male protagonist is a simpleton, although curiously his reputed stupidity mentioned early in the tale rarely shows itself as the story advances.

By casting the heroes and heroines as ordinary, even disadvantaged folk, the storytellers make it easier for their listeners to identify with them and to vicariously share in their trials and ultimate victories. In keeping with this psychological strategy, the protagonists rarely depend on special skills, training, or resources in achieving their goals. They are aided by magic, but this they acquire more through luck than any other means.

An example is offered by "The Shoes That Were Danced to Pieces" (Grimm 133). A king with 12 daughters offers the hand of one of them in marriage to the man who can discover how they escape from their locked room every night and dance their shoes to pieces. Many princes attempt to learn their secret, but all fail, forfeiting their lives. A recently dismissed soldier, too severely wounded to continue his military service, is confronted by an old woman who, for no apparent reason, gives him a cloak that will render him invisible, then tells him how to use it to discover the princesses' secret. He follows the old woman's counsel and succeeds where many before him have failed. His wounds mentioned earlier play no role as the story progresses, but then neither does he rely on any special abilities. He succeeds because he has the magic cloak, a cloak that anyone could have acquired, had he been in the right place at the right time.

Although "The Shoes That Were Danced to Pieces" is told from the man's point of view, the female characters' problems are also addressed, if only at the margin. As the story opens they—against their father's will—are playing a courtship game by dancing each night with forbidden partners in an underground realm. The soldier with his magic cloak puts a halt to this, but in the end none of them are punished, although we are told that the enchanted princes with whom they were dancing have as much time added to their enchantments as they had spent with the princesses. Here the men, and not the women, are punished for conducting a forbidden relationship, a reversal of normal expectations.

Relationships between the sexes fill a large portion of fairy-tale plots. Indeed, "and they got married and lived happily ever after" is a stereotypical fairy-tale ending. But before they get married there are conflicts to resolve, and these—like the princesses dancing with forbidden partners—are symbolic of real-life anxieties and fantasies.

Extremely common are marriage arrangements (usually brokered through the heroine's father) between a princess and a seemingly undesirable partner. Animal-bridegroom tales fall into this category, in addition to many others where a beautiful woman is promised to an obnoxious suitor: simpleton, swineherd, beggar, or a man who refuses to wash. These tales reflect a marriageable woman's anxieties about a process that gives her but little control. Social realities notwithstanding, in fairy tales these problematic couplings always turn out to the bride's benefit. The beasts become handsome princes (with the transformation typically taking place in the bridal bedroom); simpletons turn out to not be so stupid after all; and even a man who has not washed for seven years cleans up very handsomely. In short, such tales of fantasy wish fulfillment help to calm fears that one might have about marriage.

Courtship can be worrisome for males as well, and a number of fairy tales depict a man's anxiety about the whole process. One such story ("The Boy Who Went Forth to Learn Fear," Grimm 4) hides the hero's marital concerns behind his ostensible concern that he is unable to "shudder." At the end of the tale, after the boy has miraculously overcome many ordeals and has married a princess, he bemoans the fact that he still cannot shudder. His young bride takes her cue, and that night in bed pours a bucketful of cold water and minnows over him. Awakening, he says, "Now I know how to shudder," and thus the tale has a happy ending.

Another tale, "The Three Feathers" (Grimm 63), resembles animal-bridegroom stories, but with gender roles reversed. Here a boy (the youngest of three brothers, and a simpleton) takes a toad for a wife; it is the best he can do. But before the story's end the toad-wife has turned into a beautiful lady, who outshines the brides brought home by his brothers and also makes possible the simpleton-hero's inheritance of his father's kingdom.

Fears concerning fertility are also common, and the tales that give them an outlet virtually always have a good outcome. Countless fairy tales begin with a husband and wife wishing for a child. A child is then born under miraculous but stressful circumstances (he or she is only thumb-sized, has the form of an animal, or is threatened by a demonic curse); but these problems are overcome, and in the end the parents have a son or daughter worthy of a royal marriage and the kingdom that goes with it.

Other fertility fears are often imbedded within longer tales. The so-called calumniated-wife motif appears in many tales. Here a villain steals a young wife's newborn child, sometimes replacing it with a baby animal, sometimes claiming that the mother cannibalized her own offspring. Either way the heroine stands accused of the most horrible breach of motherhood thinkable, but after a period of conflict and suffering, justice prevails. Her children are restored to her, the accuser is punished, and harmony returns to her marriage.

Sibling rivalry expresses itself in numerous fairy tales, and nearly always between same-sexed siblings. A brother and a sister usually cooperate with one another (think of Hansel and Gretel). Sisters (or even worse, stepsisters) compete with one another for a wealthy suitor. Brothers compete for an inheritance or for a beautiful bride.

Parent-child conflicts take a number of forms, the most common being the proverbial cruel stepmother's mistreatment of her husband's children. There are many cultural and psychological reasons why fairy-tale villains are so often cast as stepmothers. Family stories were primarily transmitted by women, and at first view it may seem odd that their standard evildoers were also female. One explanation is socialization, for in a strongly patriarchal society no one, not even in a fantasy tale, would be comfortable laying too much blame on male characters. Further, by placing other mother figures in exceptionally bad light, the female storytellers made themselves look good by comparison. Finally, these tales of female cruelty also serve as a warning to the man of the house, who—given the realities of human mortality—soon might be looking for a new wife. "Choose carefully, and keep your eye on her" is a message that emerges from between the lines of many tales.

A few tales suggest that mothers too should be careful about entering into new domestic relationships. In "The Blue Belt" from Norway a woman with a young boy takes up residence with a troll, who early on says to his guest, "We two might live here quite happily together could we only be rid of this son of yours." The following episodes depict the couple's attempts to kill the unwanted boy, but he—with magic help—always prevails, and in the end it is he who gets rid of them.

Perhaps the greatest overall theme treated in fairy tales is the restoration of justice. Many other topics, including those previously discussed, fit within this framework: A child is denied his or her rightful position in a family; a young adult is denied personal choice in the selection of a mate; a mother is wrongly accused of killing her child or of giving birth to a monster. Additional tales add to this list of grievances.

Several types of stories—for example, the Grimms' "Little Brother, Little Sister" (11) and "The Goose-Girl" (89)—regularly include a "false bride" episode, where an interloper kidnaps (or even kills) the true bride, then assumes her place. The unwitting husband (hard to believe, but true) does not discover the substitution until magical powers bring it to light, punish the intruder, and restore the deposed bride to her rightful place. A similar breech of justice is corrected in many animal-bridegroom tales, and other types as well—for example, the Norwegian tales "East of the Sun and West of the Moon" and "Mastermaid." Here the heroine's husband or fiancé is spirited away from her and given to another woman to marry. But with magical help the true bride intervenes, is recognized by her beloved, and is taken back as his legitimate and deserving wife.

One final example of justice restored: In the Grimms' "The Blue Light" (116) an unfairly dismissed soldier gains possession of a magic lantern, through which he has the services of a powerful dwarf. Wanting revenge for his mistreatment, he commands the dwarf to bring the king's daughter to his house every night to do maid service. After a few evenings the soldier is caught and sentenced to die, but for a last wish he is allowed to smoke a pipeful of tobacco. Taking up his magic lantern to light his pipe, he unleashes the dwarf, who strikes down the king's men on every side. Fearing for his own life, the king surrenders his kingdom to the soldier, and gives him the princess in marriage.

This tale shares a number of details with other stories about the restitution of justice. Most important, fairy tales typically represent the viewpoint of only one leading character—here the dismissed soldier. He has been hurt and deserves compensation, so he forces the king's daughter to serve him, a woman who had nothing to do with his grievance. Furthermore, the soldier's reward, by any real-life standard, is excessive: marriage to a princess and the immediate inheritance of an entire kingdom, all for having been unfairly discharged. But this is a fairy tale, set in a time when wishing still did some good.

Fairy tales evolved in cultures where injustice—by modern standards—prevailed for most. Kings, patriarchs, and priests enjoyed indisputable authority within their respective realms. Fairy tales expose and correct individual cases of the misuse of power, but the institutions are never challenged. An individual king, priest, parent, or overseer may be deposed, but monarchy, priesthood, patriarchy, and class structure are never faulted. Furthermore, the injustices exposed and corrected in fairy tales are virtually always personal, with only a single victim—the hero or heroine. Thus "The Blue Light" says nothing about the grievances of other soldiers under the king's charge, nor is any assurance given that the former soldier will rule any more justly than did the now overthrown king.

### Time

Fairy tales are timeless, both in their enduring appeal and in their depiction of days and years. Designations such as 7, 12, or 100 years are symbolic expressions, not literal measurements of time. A character such as Rip Van Winkle thinks he has slept a few hours, but in the world external to his own perception some 20 years have lapsed. Conversely, Little Brier-Rose (Grimm 50) is cursed with a 100-year sleep, but when she awakens none of her surroundings have changed. The change is wholly internal. She fell asleep a child and awoke a woman ready for marriage. Similarly, Little Snow-White (Grimm 53) was driven from home at the age of seven. Following a seemingly short apprenticeship in housekeeping with seven dwarfs, then a sleep of unspecified length, she, too, is ready for marriage. Hansel and Gretel (Grimm 15), subsequent to an adventure in the woods of what appears to be only a few days, cross a body of water (that was not mentioned on the first leg of their journey) to get back home, where they assume the responsibility of supporting their surviving parent, a role normally taken by middle-aged relatives, not young children. Hans-My-Hedgehog (Grimm 108) leaves home at the age of eight, herds animals in the woods for an unspecified time, then marries and assumes the support of his now aged father. Fairy tales are timeless.

### Functions of Fairy Tales

A narrative's utility for its tellers and listeners helps to define its genre. Stories with similar contents can be told for quite different reasons and could thus be assigned to different genres. An example is Charles Perrault's "Little Red Riding Hood." The tale's beginning is too well known to require summarizing, but its ending is less familiar. The final sentence tells all: "The wicked wolf fell upon Little Red Riding Hood, and ate her all up." Perrault's tale offers no second chance, no miraculous rescue from the wolf's belly. The heroine pays for her misunderstanding of the wolf's true intentions with her life. This is a cautionary tale with an obvious didactic function: to teach young girls the dangers of getting involved with strange men. Although normally classified as a fairy tale (A-T 333), the story, as told by Perrault, has all the qualities of a fable: didactic function, brevity, and animal actors.

Much the same tale is also told by the Grimm brothers, and with a similar title, "Little Red-Cap" (26). Curiously, in the English-speaking world this story is usually known with Perrault's title, but with the Grimms' content. The two versions are essentially the same until the wolf eats the heroine. There Perrault ends the tale, but the Grimms continue: A huntsman happens upon the scene, cuts open the sleeping wolf, rescuing both the grandmother and the girl. Then they fill the wolf's belly with stones and sew him shut. Upon awakening, the wolf tries to run away, but the stones are too heavy, and he falls down dead.

Of these two versions, only the Grimms' follows the typical fairy-tale formula with its initiation process and happy ending. Their story does not function as a cautionary tale, but rather as story of fantasy escape and wish fulfillment. This version offers listeners hope for a second chance, a rebirth. Furthermore, again unlike Perrault's tale, it warns any would-be tempter of little girls that he, like the wolf, may not escape the wrath of an intended victim and her protectors. By offering make-believe solutions to real-life problems it functions in a time-honored fairy-tale tradition.

Another common function of fairy tales is to offer storytellers and their audiences a socially acceptable platform for the expression of otherwise unspeakable fears and taboos. There is no better example of this than the Grimms' "All-Kinds-of-Fur" (65), the tale of a girl whose father attempts to marry her. The story starts innocently enough. A dying queen extracts from her husband the promise that if he remarries it will be only to a woman who has the same golden hair as the queen, and who is as beautiful as she. When the time comes for the king to take a new wife, the only woman he can find who meets these requirements is his own daughter, and he presses his suit with her. Horrified at his advances, she flees into the woods, where she is discovered by another king and put into service in his kitchen. In Cinderella fashion she appears at three succeeding balls dressed in beautiful gowns. He falls in love with her and they marry. This story is about incest, possibly humankind's most universal taboo. Anyone who has ever been sexually threatened by a member of his or her own family (or even anyone who has perceived such a threat) will find relief in this story, identifying with the heroine through her trials and ultimate fulfillment. Even if such happiness is denied a victim of real-life sexual abuse, he or she will surely find at least some cathartic relief through the account of another's successful escape.

However important the functions of fantasy wish fulfillment and catharsis may be in fairy tales, it will all come to nothing if the story is not entertaining. Entertainment is the most important function of fairy tales (probably of all folktales), because if a story does not please its listeners it will die. Folktales do not have the organized support of governments, religions, and commerce. They live because they please. Millions of stories have been made up and told throughout the ages, but only those relatively few that resonate with their listeners will be remembered and retold.

## RELIGIOUS TALES (TYPES 750–849)

As already mentioned, folktales of many types and with diverse genealogies often take on the religious character of their homeland, be it native or adopted. If the religious character of a folktale moves from the backdrop to center stage, the tale will fall into the "religious tales" category of the Aarne-Thompson index. These tales resemble magic tales in their structure and function, but they draw from a more limited bank of themes than do their secular counterparts. Supernatural intervention is common, even expected, in both genres, but in religious tales it comes from a relatively well-defined deity (or devil) rather than from an amorphous magical universe. The themes of religious tales are the topics of catechisms and theological treatises: faith, miracles, repentance, conversion, forgiveness, and redemption. However, many of these tales take decidedly unorthodox turns.

The famous story of the knight Tannhäuser offers an example. As recorded in the Grimms' *German Legends* (171, A-T 756), this story tells how Tannhäuser reveled with beautiful women in the Mountain of Venus (an enigmatic statement with both erotic and pagan overtones). Afterward he sought forgiveness from the pope, who bluntly told him that leaves would grow from the papal staff before he would be forgiven. Heavyhearted, the knight returned to the Mountain of Venus. Shortly thereafter the pope was astounded to see green leaves growing from his staff. He sent for Tannhäuser, but it was too late. He had already chosen a lover inside the mountain. The storyteller leaves unanswered the question as to how Tannhäuser will fare at God's final judgment day, but it is made clear that the pope was wrong in rejecting his penance.

"The Woman Who Had No Shadow" is a very similar story from Scandinavia with a Protestant backdrop. Here a pastor's wife magically prevents the birth of future children. Her husband discovers her secret and disowns her, sending her away with a curse. He swears that flowers will blossom from his slate roof before she will receive divine forgiveness. At the story's end the rejected woman returns to the parsonage and dies. The next morning the pastor sees that his slate roof is covered with blossoming flowers.

Another version, "The Flourishing Staff," features Jewish actors. Here a man "who had left the faith of the fathers" asks forgiveness of a rabbi, who rejects him with the now familiar curse "As little as this staff in my hand will blossom and produce green leaves, can you hope to obtain pardon and forgiveness for your sins." True to the formula of type 756 tales, a short time afterward the rabbi's staff bursts forth with green leaves. Upon further enquiry the rabbi learns that the man, in spite of his lack of faith, previously had testified in a court of law that Jews do not practice ritual murder, and that his testimony had helped to stop the persecution of Jews in that region. Thus the rabbi learned that this man's honesty and courage weighed more in God's balance than did his lack of faith.

Not all religious tales have happy endings, at least not from a this-worldly perspective. "The Singing Bone" (Grimm 28, A-T 780) represents a large group of tales in which a guiltless hero is killed. Many years later the murderer is brought to justice through the miraculous singing of a horn mouthpiece made from one of the dead man's bones. Such tales admit that this world is flawed. Undeserved pain, suffering, and death do occur, and the victim's loss may be irreversible. In this world at least, the best we can hope for is the punishment of the perpetrators.

Religious folktales often feature Bible characters in apocryphal or even unBiblical roles. Within the Jewish tradition, tales about Adam and Eve, Cain and Abel, and the prophet Elijah are common. A semi-Biblical hero, El Khudr, plays an important role in Islamic folklore. Saint Peter and Jesus appear in numerous Christian-based folktales, often in comic routines with Jesus playing the straight man to his slow-witted sidekick Peter. An example is the tale "How Saint Peter Lost His Hair" (A-T 774J). As the story goes, Jesus and Saint Peter stopped at a farmhouse, and Saint Peter went inside to beg for some food. The housewife gave Peter three pancakes, still sizzling from the pan. Not wanting to share them equally, Peter hid one pancake under his hat before returning to his waiting master. The hot pancake burned the hair off Peter's head, and he remained bald for the rest of his life.

## ROMANTIC TALES OR NOVELLAS (TYPES 850–999)

Katherine M. Briggs has called novellas "naturalistic fairy tales," adding that in such tales, "The loutish simpleton of a hero gains the hand of the princess, but without the help of a golden goose; the constancy and truth of the ill-used heroine wins her happiness in the end, but there is no fairy godmother or magical hazel-nut to help her" (*Dictionary of British Folk-Tales,* pt. A, vol. 2, p. 367).

There is no better example of a loutish simpleton gaining the hand of a princess than the tale known generically as "The Princess's Birthmarks" (A-T

850). This tale is told with varying degrees of raciness throughout Europe as well as North and South America. Hans Christian Andersen, a very cautious writer, stated that he had heard a version of this tale as a child that was "quite unprintable." The following summary attempts to suggest the tale's inherent coarseness without crossing over Andersen's line of unprintableness: A king promised his daughter in marriage to any suitor who could describe her hidden birthmarks. A swineherd knew how to make his pigs dance by playing a flute. He caused his pigs to dance in view of the princess, who asked to have one. The swineherd promised to give her one, but only if she would lift up her skirt for him. This she did, and thus he learned that she had three golden hairs on her belly. With this information he won her hand in marriage (Ranke, "The Swineherd Who Married a Princess," *Folktales of Germany*, no. 46).

This tale has essentially the same structure as a traditional magic tale, but instead of killing a dragon or rescuing a princess from a giant, the hero here wins the princess's hand by making a pig dance. This tale's lack of magic plus its burlesque details almost make it a parody of a fairy tale. Aarne and Thompson classified it as a type 850 folktale, their first number under the category *novella*.

*Novella* is a literary as well as a folkloric term, and as such it immediately brings the name Giovanni Boccaccio to mind. The 100 tales that make up his *Decameron* are exemplary novellas, many of which have oral folktales as analogues. A famous example is the parable of "The Three Rings" (A-T 912) and its accompanying frame story. Boccaccio's version takes place during the rule of the great Muslim sultan Saladin. In this tale, Saladin, in order to cover a temporary monetary shortfall, devised a plan to extort money from a wealthy Jewish subject named Melchizedek by asking him the question Which of the three major religions is most authentic—Judaism, Christianity, or Islam? Knowing that any direct answer would cause him or his ruler embarrassment, and thus set him up for extortion, Melchizedek responded with a parable: A man possessed a ring of extraordinary beauty and value that for many generations had been passed on to the most favored son. This man had three sons, all equally loved, so he had a jeweler make two exact copies of the ring and then gave one ring to each son. Each of the three brothers thought that he alone possessed the authentic ring, but upon closer examination no differences could be ascertained, so the question of final authenticity could not be settled. Saladin, seeing that Melchizedek cleverly had evaded his question, decided to ask him directly for a loan. Melchizedek gladly complied, and the two parted as friends.

"The Three Rings" and "The Princess's Birthmarks" each relates in a compact plot a series of unexpected events leading to an almost miraculous conclusion, all achieved without recourse to magic. These are the defining qualities of the novella. There are other themes and plots in folktales of this category, but these features remain constant.

## TALES OF THE STUPID OGRE (TYPES 1000–1199)

The ogres featured in the next group of folktales have two things in common with one another. The first is revealed in the category's title: They are stupid. Their second quality is related to the first: They can be defeated easily by ordinary humans. The names and descriptions of the featured ogres vary from tale to tale, depending upon where and when each was told. Trolls, boggarts, hobgoblins, giants, monsters, satyrs, and devils all take their turns being humiliated by their human adversaries in these tales.

Mortals play these roles also, with overseers and masters being cast as ogres, only to be put down by their nominal subordinates. Such tales frequently feature a labor contract involving the so-called anger bargain (A-T 1000). These tales open when a master and his new servant agree that whichever of the two first loses his temper will pay by forfeiting a strip of skin from his back (or other similarly cruel punishment—these are not genteel stories). As the tale progresses the servant makes one mistake after the other, all apparently mindless, but in truth slyly designed to anger the master. For example, when told to "light the way" for the master, who is returning home after dark, the servant sets his master's barn afire; or when charged with harvesting apples, the servant cuts down the entire orchard to make the job easier. A-T numbers 1001–1029 define the trickster's various pranks. A storyteller typically chains together a number of such episodes, finally letting the master lose his temper, who then must submit to whatever humiliating punishment was agreed upon at the tale's beginning. Many tales featuring Till Eulenspiegel, Germany's most famous trickster, fit into this category. His feigned foolishness hides his carefully contrived capers, all of which harm his various masters.

The appeal of these tales in a class-structured society is obvious. Exploited and often abused, apprentices and servants had little recourse in real life but to bite their lips and bide their time. These stories reverse social injustice and give the upper hand to the underdog, if not in the real workplace, then at least in the world of make-believe. Such tales almost never involve magic, only cleverness. Furthermore, the master is typically his own worst enemy. He is the one who sets up the conditions and gives the orders that lead to his own defeat.

Closely related to the work-contract tales are tales of types 1030–1114, which describe partnerships and contests between humans and ogres. Here too the weaker person always wins. A well-known tale from this group depicts an agreement between a peasant and the devil to share a harvest (A-T 1030). The devil accepts the peasant's proposal that he, the devil, will take everything that grows above the ground, with the peasant receiving everything that grows below the ground. The peasant plants turnips, and the devil's share is only the greens. The devil now insists that next year he receive everything growing beneath the ground. The peasant agrees and plants cabbages. This time the devil must be satisfied with the worthless roots.

Many of these tales appear to have their origins in the pre-Christian era, with the dupes being identified as satyrs, trolls, giants, and other such mythical demigods. After converting to Christianity, European storytellers did not abandon their heathen tales but often changed a few details to give them at least the appearance of having a Christian background. One of the most common such changes was to replace heathen ogres with the devil, at least in name. However, the devil in these tales bears but little resemblance to the Satan of Christian theology. The folktale devil is easily tricked, and human protagonists seem to risk nothing (certainly not their souls) by accepting him as a partner.

As with the master-servant stories discussed earlier, the appeal of these tales is self-evident. In real life, ordinary people are often victims of natural and social forces, ranging from crop failures to excessive taxation, over which they have little influence. In these tales they take control of their lives and fortunes. Partnership with a devil or ogre brings an added source of power unavailable in real life, and—as evidenced by countless tales—there are essentially no risks. This make-believe devil is so stupid that he always loses.

## JOKES AND ANECDOTES (TYPES 1200–1999)

A joke is defined as a short narrative that concludes with a humorous twist: a punch line. Jokes, also called facetiae or jests, are some of the oldest of all recorded folktales. Renaissance jest collections were among the earliest printed books in a number of European countries. And in much of the world jokes are among the last surviving examples of living oral folk narratives. Few people in our literate and mass-culture dominated society tell other kinds of stories for entertainment, but—the Internet notwithstanding—jokes are still transmitted primarily by word of mouth.

A short time ago an acquaintance told me "the latest joke" about a fellow who borrowed $500 from a friend, promising to pay it back within a few days. He then approached the friend's wife and offered her $500 if she would sleep with him. She accepted, and the exchange was made forthwith. A short time later the fellow told his friend that he had repaid the loan to his wife. When the husband asked his wife, she, of course, could not admit to the circumstances surrounding the transaction and had to give the money to her husband as repayment of the loan.

My acquaintance did not tell the joke very well, but I laughed politely, pretending not to have heard it before. I did not have the heart to tell him that his "latest joke" has been in circulation for more than 600 years. The same story (A-T 1420C) was used by Boccaccio in his *Decameron* (written between 1348 and 1353) as well as by Chaucer in his *Canterbury Tales* (written between 1387 and 1400). It is not recorded how many times the joke has since been retold at work sites and in taverns.

Tales of adultery and seduction fill a large part of the "jokes and anecdotes" section of the Aarne-Thompson index, just as they feature very prominently in the collections of Boccaccio and Chaucer. Two other subjects are also very well represented among folktale jokes: fools and tricksters.

Everyone knows the story attributed to Aesop about the man, the boy, and the donkey (A-T 1215): A man and a boy were walking along a road beside their donkey when a passerby chided them, saying that at least one of them should ride, so the boy mounted the beast. The next passerby criticized him for not letting his father ride, so they exchanged places. Then someone said that the boy should not have to walk, so the man pulled him up beside him. The next person shamed them both for overloading the poor animal, so, having tried every other alternative, they tied the donkey's feet together and carried it between them on a pole. Struggling to get free, the donkey fell over a bridge and drowned.

Why do we delight in such tales? Apart from the moral lesson that we draw from this tale (do not try to please everyone), it also gives every person who hears it a reason to feel superior. Who among us would try to carry a donkey suspended from a pole? Or exchange—in a sequence of trades—a clump of gold for an ordinary cobblestone (A-T 1415)? Or plan for a harvest of salt by sprinkling salt in a field (A-T 1200)? Our forebears took great delight in tales of foolishness, as evidenced by the very large store of such tales still extant.

There is often a fine line between tales of fools and tales of tricksters, and for two quite different reasons. Many traditional tricksters (Nasreddin Hoca from Turkey, Till Eulenspiegel from Germany, and Brer Rabbit from the American South come to mind) feign foolishness to achieve their tricks. Furthermore, every trickster needs a foolish dupe, so trickster tales almost inevitably feature fools as well.

One of the most widespread of all trickster tales is the story of the visitor from paradise (A-T 1540). Found throughout Europe, the story typically begins when a beggar introduces himself to a woman as a student from Paris. The woman, a remarried widow, understands "paradise" and gives the man a bundle of clothes for her deceased husband. When her new husband arrives home and hears what has happened, he senses fraud and mounts his horse to overtake the trickster. The thief sees him coming and hides the bundle. When asked if he has seen a man carrying a package, the trickster says that the guilty man just ran into the woods. The husband asks him to hold his horse so he can pursue the villain through the thicket. The trickster retrieves his package, mounts the horse, and quickly rides away. The husband returns home on foot and, unwilling to admit that he too has been duped, he tells his wife that he gave the student the horse to aid him on his journey back to paradise.

This tale is refreshingly evenhanded in its treatment of men and women. Reflecting male-dominated societies, most traditional trickster tales depict women as easy dupes, while treating men much more kindly. But here the husband is no less stupid than his wife, and furthermore, he is too proud to admit his mistakes.

There are many reasons for the lasting popularity of trickster tales. Like tales of fools, they too let us feel superior to the dupes, although in some instances the tricks are genuinely clever, with even intelligent people falling victim to them. In such cases their popularity derives from our pleasure in seeing a well-executed maneuver (as in watching a skilled athlete perform), as well as in vicariously sharing the gains of an ordinary person beating the system. Most often the trickster is an outsider or an underling, while his victim is a person of wealth and power.

Virtually all the genres defined and discussed in this chapter can be mixed, resulting in hybrid tales of unusual parentage. Jests are especially amenable to such mixtures, traditional storytellers having been willing to compose jokes about everything, even nominally sacred topics. Creation stories, for example, usually belong to religious myths or legends, but when told in a playful manner, perhaps tongue-in-cheek, such tales assume the function of jests. For example, a German legend tells how an early Christian missionary thanked a generous woman with the promise that her first task of the next day would be blessed. Her first task was to measure a little piece of linen that she had woven, and miraculously she continued to measure it until the linen filled her whole house. An envious and selfish neighbor asked for the same blessing, and the missionary granted it to her. The selfish woman planned to start her next day by counting the money she had saved in a jar, hoping thus to multiply it as her neighbor had multiplied the flax. However, before she could begin counting she had to answer a call of nature, and she could not stop until she had flooded the peninsula where she lived, thus creating the island of Hiddensee in the Baltic (Haas, *Rügensche Sagen und Märchen*, pp. 178–79).

This grotesquely humorous tale combines elements of three genres. Its burlesque conclusion, complete with punch line, makes it a jest. Its religious elements and the specific setting are typical of legends. Its subject matter, creation, gives it affinity with myth, although the creation stories of true myths are serious and grand, unlike this whimsical little piece.

## FORMULA TALES (TYPES 2000–2399)

Most of the tales in the preceding sections have followed a formula, to at least some extent, but in this last section, the formula itself becomes the tale. The most beloved of formula tales are chain tales, often describing long and involved sequences, but with only the sparsest of plots. The performance is more important than the story, with every listener wondering if the storyteller will finish the tongue-twisting, ever-growing progression correctly.

A favorite is the English tale "The Old Woman and Her Pig" (A-T 2030), which begins when a woman buys a pig at the market, but on their way home the pig refuses to jump over a stile. She asks a dog to bite the pig, but the dog refuses. So she asks a stick to beat the dog, but the stick refuses. She continues with her requests, all received negatively, until finally a cow does give her some milk, setting loose the following chain, as described in the tale's final sentence: "As soon as the cat had lapped up the milk, the cat began to kill the rat; the rat began to gnaw the rope; the rope began to hang the butcher; the butcher began to kill the ox; the ox began to drink the water; the water began to quench the fire; the fire began to burn the stick; the stick began to beat the dog; the dog began to bite the pig; the little pig in a fright jumped over the stile; and so the old woman got home that night" (Jacobs, *English Fairy Tales*, no. 4).

Other popular formulas include rounds that loop back into their own text; nonsense tales that consist of nothing but self-contradictory sentences; and any number of mock stories—tales that at their beginning appear to be traditional stories but that end abruptly and without a resolution. The most famous of these in the English tradition is the nonstory of Jack-a-Nory, used by storytellers to mark the end of story-time: "I'll tell you a story about Jack-a-Nory, and now my story's begun. I'll tell you another about Jack and his brother, and now my story is done!" Many generations of British and American children know that after this pronouncement any further pleading for another story is fruitless.

A formula tale with somewhat more substance, but still no resolution, is the last story in the Grimms' *Children's and Household Tales* (200). It is titled "The Golden Key":

> Once in the wintertime when the snow was very deep, a poor boy had to go out and fetch wood on a sled. After he had gathered it together and loaded it, he did not want to go straight home, because he was so frozen, but instead to make a fire and warm himself a little first. So he scraped the snow away, and while he was thus clearing the ground he found a small golden key. Now he believed that where there was a key, there must also be a lock, so he dug in the ground and found a little iron chest. "If only the key fits!" he thought. "Certainly there are valuable things in the chest." He looked, but there was no keyhole. Finally he found one, but so small that it could scarcely be seen. He tried the key, and fortunately it fitted. Then he turned it once, and now we must wait until he has finished unlocking it and has opened the lid. Then we shall find out what kind of wonderful things there were in the little chest.

This story was added to the Grimms' collection as the final tale of their second edition (1819), and from that edition onward it has occupied the last position in the collection (excluding the appendix of 10 *Children's Legends*). By closing their collection with this enigmatic tale without an end, the Grimms seem to be saying that folktales, too, are endless. There is no final word.

## WORKS CITED

Aarne, Antti, and Stith Thompson. *The Types of the Folktale: A Classification and Bibliography.* Helsinki: Suomalainen Tiedeakatemia, 1961.

Briggs, Katherine M. *A Dictionary of British Folk-Tales in the English Language.* Pt. A, 2 vols. Pt. B, 2 vols. London: Routledge, 1970–1971.

Campbell, Joseph. *The Hero with a Thousand Faces.* 2nd ed. Princeton: Princeton UP, 1968. First published 1949.

Haas, A. *Rügensche Sagen und Märchen.* Stettin: Burmeister's, 1903.

Jacobs, Joseph. *English Fairy Tales.* 3rd ed. New York: Putnam's, [1898].

Propp, Vladimir. *The Morphology of the Folktale.* Trans. Laurence Scott. 2nd ed. Austin: U of Texas P, 1968. First published 1928 in Russian.

Ranke, Kurt. *Folktales of Germany.* Trans. Lotte Baumann. Chicago: U of Chicago P, 1966.

# Three
## Examples and Texts

## ALLEGORY

*"Dharmabuddhi and Pâpabuddhi"* (The Panchatantra)

In a certain place there lived two friends, Dharmabuddhi, which means "having a just heart," and Pâpabuddhi, which means "having an unjust heart." One day Pâpabuddhi thought to himself, "I am a simpleton, plagued with poverty. I am going to travel abroad with Dharmabuddhi, and earn money with his help. Then I will cheat him out of it and thus gain a good situation for myself." One day he said to Dharmabuddhi, "Listen, friend! When you are old, which of your deeds will you be able to remember? You have never seen a foreign country, so what will you be able to tell the young people? After all, don't they say: *His birth has borne no fruit, who knows not foreign lands, many languages, customs, and the like.* And also: *One never properly grasps knowledge, wealth, and art, until joyfully one has wandered from one land to another.*"

Dharmabuddhi, as soon as he had heard these words, took leave from his parents with a joyful heart, and one happy day set forth for foreign lands. Through their diligence and skill, Dharmabuddhi and Pâpabuddhi acquired great wealth on their travels. Happy, but also filled with longing, they turned homeward with their great treasure. For it is also said: *For those who gain wisdom, art, and wealth in foreign lands, the absence of one hour has the length of hundreds.*

As they approached their city, Pâpabuddhi said to Dharmabuddhi, "Friend, it is not prudent for us to return home with our entire treasure, for

Unless otherwise noted, all translations and revisions were done by D.L. Ashliman.

our families and relatives will want part of it. Therefore let us bury it some-where here in the thick of the forest and take only a small part home with us. When the need arises, we can come back and get as much as we need from here. For they also say: *A smart man does not show off his money, not even in small amounts, for the sight of gold will agitate even a good heart.* And also: *Like meat is devoured in the water by fish, on land by wild animals, and in the air by birds, he who owns money is everywhere at risk.*"

Upon hearing this, Dharmabuddhi said, "Yes, my friend, that is what we will do!" After having thus buried their treasure, they both returned home and lived happily together.

However, one day at midnight Pâpabuddhi went back into the forest, took the entire treasure, refilled the hole, and returned home. Then he went to Dharmabuddhi and said to him, "Friend, each of us has a large family, and we are suffering because we have no money. Therefore, let us go to that place and get some money."

Dharmabuddhi answered, "Yes, my friend, let us do it!" They went there and dug up the container, but it was empty. Then Pâpabuddhi struck himself on the head and cried out, "Aha! Dharmabuddhi! You and only you have taken the money, for the hole has been filled in again. Give me my half of what you have hidden, or I will bring action against you at the king's court."

Dharmabuddhi said, "Do not speak like that, you evildoer. I am in truth Dharmabuddhi, the one with a just heart! I would not commit such an act of thievery. After all, it is said: *The person with a just heart treats another man's wife like his own mother, another man's property like a clod of earth, and all be-ings like himself.*"

Quarreling thus, they proceeded to the court where they told their stories and brought action against one another. The top judges decreed that they submit to an Ordeal of God, but Pâpabuddhi said, "No! Such an ordeal is not just. After all, it is written: *In a legal action one should seek documents. If there are no documents, then one should seek witnesses. If there are no witnesses, then wise men should prescribe an Ordeal of God.* In this matter the goddess of the tree will serve as my witness. She will declare which one of us is a thief and which one an honest man."

To this they all replied, "What you say is right, for it is also written: *An Or-deal of God is inappropriate where there is a witness, be he even a man of the low-est caste, to say nothing of the case where he is a god.* We too are very curious about this case. Tomorrow morning we shall go with you to that place in the forest."

In the meanwhile, Pâpabuddhi returned home and said to his father, "Fa-ther! I have stolen this money from Dharmabuddhi, and one word from you will secure it for us. Without your word, we shall lose it, and I shall lose my life as well."

The father said, "Child, just tell what I have to say in order to secure it!"

Pâpabuddhi said, "Father, in thus and such a place there is a large mimosa tree. It has a hollow trunk. Go hide yourself in it. When I swear an oath there tomorrow morning, then you must reply that Dharmabuddhi is the thief."

Having made these arrangements, the next morning Pâpabuddhi bathed himself, put on a clean shirt, and went to the mimosa tree with Dharmabuddhi and the judges. Once there, he spoke with a piercing voice, "Sun and moon, wind and fire, heaven and earth, heart and mind, day and night, sunrise and sunset, all of these, like dharma, know a man's deeds. Sublime goddess of the forest, reveal which of us is the thief!"

Then Pâpabuddhi's father, who was standing in the hollow trunk of the mimosa tree, said, "Listen! Listen! The money was taken away by Dharmabuddhi!"

Having heard this, the king's servants, their eyes opened wide with amazement, searched in their law books for an appropriate punishment for Dharmabuddhi's theft of the money. While they were thus engaged, Dharmabuddhi himself surrounded the tree's opening with flammable material, and set it on fire. When it was well ablaze, Pâpabuddhi's father emerged from the hollow tree. His eyes streaming, he cried out bitterly.

"What is this?" they asked him.

He confessed everything, and then died. The king's servants forthwith hanged Pâpabuddhi from a branch of the mimosa tree, but they had only words of praise for Dharmabuddhi.

*Source: Pantschatantra: Fünf Bücher indischer Fabeln, Märchen und Erzählungen, trans. from the Sanskrit into German by Theodor Benfey, vol. 2, bk. 1 (Leipzig: F.A. Brockhaus, 1859), story 19.*

## Commentary

Known generically as "The Two Travelers" (A-T 613), this is one of the oldest and most widespread of all folktales. Typically, as is the case in the preceding story, the two adversaries' names, as well as their actions, reveal the basic principles that they represent: True and Untrue, Right and Wrong, Justice and Injustice. This is not merely an account of a specific battle between two individuals, but rather a morality play about the universal conflict between good and evil. Furthermore, each party uses traditional wisdom in the form of proverbs to promote his cause. Philosophically, the story claims that both good and evil are inherent in the world but that victims of injustice need not meekly accept their lot. Virtue too can fight fire with fire.

Most type 613 tales include a magic element missing in the tale reproduced here. Typically the evil traveler puts out the eyes of his virtuous companion, but later the innocent victim's sight is miraculously restored, symbolizing the ultimate triumph of good over evil.

## ANECDOTE

### "Avarice" (England)

The following extraordinary instance of avarice lately occurred in Cumberland. A person, who had amassed considerable wealth by every act of meanness, and oppression of the poor, and who had for some years excused himself from the payment of taxes by pleading extreme poverty, being apprehensive that his money might be discovered, resolved to conceal it in a hole under part of his house, which he made large and deep enough for the purpose, with a door and spring lock, which, on closing, would securely fasten. Some days afterwards, he was missing, and after near a week's search after him, he was found in this hole, dead. It was supposed, he had locked himself in, and could not release himself, as the place was with great difficulty opened. Near his body was a candlestick; the candle, it is conjectured, he had, from extreme hunger devoured; and thus he died for want, in the midst of his treasure.

February 12, 1796.

*Source: Anecdotes for Children: Collected from the Best Authors, and Recent Occurrences* (London: Darton and Harvey, 1796), pp. 41–42.

### Commentary

This brief anecdote has some of the qualities of a legend, without the specific details usually associated with that genre. The locale is identified in broad terms (Cumberland was formerly a county in northwest England), although no specific place is mentioned. Similarly, the piece ends with a date, but the readers are not told whether this represents the time of the dead man's discovery or the issue of a newspaper reporting the incident. Like a fable, the story has an obvious moral, although to the writer's credit it is not explicitly stated. Even the youthful readers for whom this tale is intended will readily conclude that the man depicted here brought about his own destruction through his selfishness and greed.

# BALLAD

*"Sweet William's Ghost" (Scotland)*

There came a ghost to Margaret's door,
With many a grievous grone,
And ay he tirled at the pin;
But answer made she none.

Is this my father Philip?
Or is't my brother John?
Or is't my true love Willie,
From Scotland new come home?

Tis not thy father Philip;
Nor yet thy brother John:
But tis thy true love Willie
From Scotland new come home,

O sweet Margret! O dear Margret!
I pray thee speak to mee:
Give me my faith and troth, Margret,
As I gave it to thee.

Thy faith and troth thou'se nevir get,
Of me shalt nevir win,
Till that thou come within my bower,
And kiss my cheek and chin.

If I should come within thy bower,
I am no earthly man:
And should I kiss thy rosy lipp,
Thy days will not be lang.

O sweet Margret, O dear Margret,
I pray thee speak to mee:
Give me my faith and troth, Margret,
As I gave it to thee.

Thy faith and troth thou'se nevir get,
Of me shalt nevir win,
Till thou take me to yon kirk yard,
And wed me with a ring.

My bones are buried in a kirk yard
Afar beyond the sea,
And it is but my sprite, Margret,
That's speaking now to thee.

She stretched out her lilly-white hand,
As for to do her best:
Hae there your faith and troth, Willie,
God send your soul good rest.

Now she has kilted her robes of green,
A piece below her knee:
And a' the live-lang winter night
The dead corps followed shee.

Is there any room at your head, Willie?
Or any room at your feet?
Or any room at your side, Willie,
Wherein that I may creep?

There's nae room at my head, Margret,
There's nae room at my feet,
There's no room at my side, Margret,
My coffin is made so meet.

Then up and crew the red red cock,
And up then crew the gray:
Tis time, tis time, my dear Margret,
That I were gane away.

No more the ghost to Margret said,
But, with a grievous grone,
Evanish'd in a cloud of mist,
And left her all alone.

O stay, my only true love, stay,
The constant Margret cried:
Wan grew her cheeks, she clos'd her een,
Stretch'd her saft limbs, and died.

*Source:* Thomas Percy, *Reliques of Ancient English Poetry,* vol. 3, bk. 2 (London: Swan Sonneschein, Lebas, and Lowrey, 1886), no. 6, pp. 130–33. First published in 1765.

*Commentary*

This famous poem demonstrates the close relationship between ballads and folktales. The narrative is a type 365 folktale, often titled "The Specter Bridegroom." The story is sometimes presented as a true occurrence, with characters, places, and historical events specifically identified. In most versions the heroine, unlike Margaret in the preceding narrative, does not immediately know that the man taking her away is a ghost. All forms of the tale rely on a belief in spirits and in their ability to communicate with the living. In most versions the heroine suffers a violent death, suggesting that the living should allow the dead to rest in peace.

Note on the text: "And ay he tirled at the pin" refers to a notched iron noisemaker attached to a door, a precursor to knockers or doorbells.

## CALENDAR STORY

### *"The Clever Pilgrim" (Switzerland/Germany)*

A number of years ago a tramp was making his way through the country. He claimed to be a pious pilgrim on his way from Paderborn to the Holy Sepulcher in Jerusalem.

In Müllheim he asked at the Post Tavern, "How far is it to Jerusalem?"

He was told, "Seven hundred hours, but if you go by way of Mauchen, taking the footpath, then you will save a quarter of an hour."

So in order to save the quarter of an hour he went by way of Mauchen. And that was not a bad thing. If you don't take advantage of little benefits you will never get any large ones. We more often have the opportunity to save or to earn a batzen [a small German coin] than a florin, but fifteen batzen make one florin. And if someone on a journey of seven hundred hours could save a quarter of an hour every five hours, how much would he save during the whole trip? Who wants to figure it out?

In any event, none of this was very interesting to our disguised pilgrim. He was pursuing only leisure and good food, so he really did not care at all where he was. As the old proverb says, a beggar can never take a wrong turn. It would be a bad village indeed if he couldn't recover more there than what he used up on his soles getting there, even if he were going barefoot.

But still, our pilgrim did want to get back on the high road as soon as possible, where there were wealthy houses and good cooking. This rascal, unlike a genuine pilgrim, was not interested in common nourishment extended to him by a pious and sympathetic hand, but wanted to eat nothing but nourishing pebble soup.

Whenever he came to a good tavern by the side of the road, for example, the Posthaus in Krozingen, or the Baselstab in Schliengen, he would go inside and ask—hungrily, humbly, and in God's name—for some water soup with pebbles, adding that he had no money.

When the sympathetic waitress said to him, "Pious pilgrim, the pebbles are going to lie hard in your belly," he said, "Right! That's why I choose them. Pebbles last longer than bread, and it is a long way to Jerusalem. But if you could give me a little glass of wine with them, in God's name, then of course I could digest them more easily."

Then when the waitress said, "But, pious pilgrim, such a soup can surely give you no strength," he answered, "Indeed, if you would use meat broth instead of water it would of course be more nourishing."

When the waitress brought him such a soup, saying, "The sops haven't softened up yet," he said, "You are right, and the soup does seem to be quite thin. Wouldn't you have a few forkfuls of vegetables, or a little piece of meat, or both?"

Then when the sympathetic waitress put some vegetables and meat into the dish, he said, "God bless you. Now just give me some bread, and I'll eat the soup."

With that he pulled back the sleeves of his pilgrim's robe and attacked the work with pleasure. And when he had consumed the last crumb, strand, and drop, of the bread, wine, meat, vegetables, and meat broth, he said, "Waitress, your soup has filled me up so much that I can't eat the wonderful pebbles. That is too bad, but do save them. When I return I shall bring you a holy mussel from Askalon or a rose from Jericho."

*Source:* Johann Peter Hebel, "Der schlaue Pilgrim," *Der Rheinländische Hausfreund; oder, Neuer Calender auf das Jahr 1808.* Hebel's source: "Die Jesuiten in Wien," *Schweizerbote,* vol. 1, no. 38 (September 21, 1804).


*Commentary*

Johann Peter Hebel, a Swiss and Swabian schoolmaster, is even today famous for his dialect poetry and calendar stories. These tales, often based on folklore, were published in farmers' almanacs and were marked by rustic simplicity, good-natured humor, and gentle didacticism. The preceding story is a literary elaboration on the famous folktale "Stone Soup" (A-T 1548). Hebel could have communicated the gist of the story in half the space, as folk storytellers normally do, but his digressions, descriptions, and conversations create an easygoing mood and add to the story's unpretentious charm.

## CANTE FABLE

*"Old Hildebrand" (Jacob and Wilhelm Grimm)*

Once upon a time there was a peasant whose wife appealed to the village priest. The priest wanted ever so much to spend an entire day alone with her, and the peasant's wife was quite willing.

One day he said to her, "Listen, dear woman, I've thought it through, and I know how the two of us can spend an entire day together. On Wednesday tell your husband that you are sick and lie down in bed moaning and groaning. Carry on like that until Sunday, when in my sermon I will preach that if anyone has a sick child at home, a sick husband, a sick wife, a sick father, a sick mother, a sick sister, brother, or anyone else, then that person should make a pilgrimage to Mount Cuckoo in Italy. There, for a kreuzer, one can get a peck of laurel leaves, and this person's sick child, sick husband, sick wife, sick father, sick mother, sick sister, brother, or anyone else, will be healed on the spot."

"I'll do it," said the peasant's wife. So on Wednesday she went to bed, moaning and groaning. Her husband did everything for her that he could think of, but nothing helped. Sunday arrived, and the peasant's wife said, "I'm so miserable that I must be near death, but before I die, I would like to hear the sermon that the priest is going to give today."

The peasant answered, "Oh, my child, you can't go out. If you get up it might make you worse. Look, I'll go to church and pay close attention and tell you everything that the priest says."

"Good," said the peasant's wife. "Go and pay close attention, and then tell me everything that you have heard."

So the peasant went to church, and the priest began to preach, saying that if anyone had a sick child at home, a sick husband, a sick wife, a sick father, a sick mother, a sick sister, brother, or anyone else, then that person should make a pilgrimage to Mount Cuckoo in Italy, where a peck of laurel leaves costs one kreuzer, and this person's sick child, sick husband, sick wife, sick father, sick mother, sick sister, brother, or anyone else, will be healed on the spot, and that anyone who might want to undertake this trip should come to him after the mass, and he would give him a sack for the laurel leaves and a kreuzer.

No one was happier than the peasant, and immediately following the mass he went to the priest and asked for the laurel sack and the kreuzer. Then he went home, and even before going inside called out, "Hurrah! My dear wife, you are just as good as cured. The priest preached today that whoever has a sick child at home, a sick husband, a sick wife, a sick father, a sick mother, a sick sister, brother, or anyone else, then that person should make a pilgrimage to Mount Cuckoo in Italy, where a peck of laurel leaves costs one kreuzer, and this person's sick child, sick husband, sick wife, sick father, sick mother, sick sister, brother, or anyone else, will be healed on the spot, and I got the laurel sack and the kreuzer from the priest, and am going to take off immediately, so you can get better as soon as possible." And with that he set forth.

He had scarcely left before his wife got out of bed, and the priest arrived. But let's leave them for awhile and see what happened to the peasant. He was hurrying along in order to arrive at Mount Cuckoo as soon as possible, when he met a kinsman. Now this kinsman was an egg man, who was just returning from market, where he had sold his eggs.

"Bless you!" said the kinsman. "Where are you off to in such a hurry?"

"In all eternity!" said the peasant. "My wife has become sick, and today in the priest's sermon I heard that if anyone has a sick child at home, a sick husband, a sick wife, a sick father, a sick mother, a sick sister, brother, or anyone else, then that person should make a pilgrimage to Mount Cuckoo in Italy, where a peck of laurel leaves costs one kreuzer, and this person's sick child, sick husband, sick wife, sick father, sick mother, sick sister, brother, or anyone else, will be healed on the spot, and I got the laurel sack and the kreuzer from the priest, and now I am on my way."

"Listen, kinsman," said the peasant's kinsman. "Don't be so simple as to believe that. Do you know what? The priest wants to spend an entire day alone with your wife. He has given you this task just to get you out from under his feet."

"My!" the peasant said. "How I would like to know if that is true!"

"Do you know what?" said his kinsman. "Just climb into my egg basket, and I will carry you home, and you can see for yourself."

And that is just what happened. The peasant got into the egg basket, and his kinsman carried him home. When they arrived there, the good times had already started. The peasant's wife had slaughtered almost everything in the farmyard and had made pancakes, and the priest was there with his fiddle. The kinsman knocked at the door, and the peasant's wife asked who was there.

"It's me, kinswoman," said the kinsman. "Can you give me shelter for the night? I did not sell my eggs at the market, so now I have to carry them back home, but they are too heavy, and I can't make it. It is already dark."

"Well," said the peasant's wife, "you have come at a very inconvenient time, but it can't be helped. Just sit down over there on the bench by the stove." So the kinsman took a seat on the bench and set his pack basket down beside him. And the priest and the peasant's wife proceeded to carry on.

After a while the priest said, "Listen, my dear woman, you are such a good singer. Sing something for me."

"No," said the peasant's wife, "I can't sing anymore. I could sing well when I was younger, but that's all behind me now."

"Oh," said the priest, "do sing just a little."

So the peasant's wife started to sing:

> I sent my husband out, you see,
> To Mount Cuckoo in Italy!

And the priest sang back:

> I wish he'd stay away a year
> The laurel leaves don't interest me
> Hallelujah!

Then the kinsman chimed in (oh, I have to tell you that the peasant's name was Hildebrand), and sang out:

> Hey, you my kinsman Hildebrand,
> What are you doing on that bench?
> Hallelujah!

The peasant, from inside the basket, sang forth:

> This singing I can bear no more,
> Here I come!
> Trala tralore!

With that he jumped from the basket, and with blows he drove the priest out of the house.

*Source:* Jacob Grimm and Wilhelm Grimm, "Der alte Hildebrand," *Kinder- und Hausmärchen* (Children's and Household Tales), no. 95. The Grimms' source: An unnamed informant from Austria. This tale was added to the Grimms' collection with the second edition (1819).

*Commentary*

A cante fable or tale is a narrative that includes a song or rhyme, sung or chanted by traditional storytellers. These imbedded songs and rhymes are remarkably consistent from one variant to the next, even when the tale travels across linguistic boundaries. Such is the case with this widespread jest, a folktale of type 1360C. Versions of it in many different countries retain the sung responses by the various characters as the tale reaches its climax.

Stories of wayward wives and philandering churchmen were common in medieval and Renaissance jest books, and the tale of "Old Hildebrand" has been traced to a Flemish story from the fifteenth century. It may come as a surprise to find such a story in the Grimms' family-oriented collection. But families consist of adults as well as children, and this particular tale represents adult humor, although it does so in a way that few would find offensive.

This tale was presented by the Grimms in a pronounced Austrian dialect, lost in translation, which identifies the priest as a Roman Catholic, who should be practicing celibacy. The story thus corroborates a longstanding joke in Catholic Germany and Austria: "There is no reason for priests to marry as long as peasants have wives."

## CAUTIONARY TALE

### "Friday" (Russia)

There was once a certain woman who did not pay due reverence to Mother Friday, but set to work on a distaff full of flax, combing and whirling it. She span away till dinnertime, then suddenly sleep fell upon her—such a deep sleep! And when she had gone to sleep, suddenly the door opened and in came Mother Friday, before the eyes of all who were there, clad in a white dress, and in such a rage! And she went straight up to the woman who had been spinning, scooped up from the floor a handful of the dust that had fallen out of the flax, and began stuffing and stuffing that woman's eyes full of it! And when she had stuffed them full, she went off in a rage—disappeared without saying a word.

When the woman awoke, she began squalling at the top of her voice about her eyes, but couldn't tell what was the matter with them. The other women, who had been terribly frightened, began to cry out, "Oh, you wretch, you! You've brought a terrible punishment on yourself from Mother Friday."

Then they told her all that had taken place. She listened to it all, and then began imploring, "Mother Friday, forgive me! Pardon me, the guilty one! I'll offer you a taper, and I'll never let friend or foe dishonor you, Mother!"

Well, what do you think? During the night, back came Mother Friday and took the dust out of that woman's eyes, so that she was able to get about again. It's a great sin to dishonor Mother Friday—combing and spinning flax, forsooth!

*Source:* W.R.S. Ralston, *Russian Folk-Tales* (London: Smith, Elder, and Company, 1873), p. 200. Ralston's source: Aleksandr Afanasyev.

### Commentary

Cautionary tales depict the bad consequences of unacceptable behavior, thus preaching caution to their listeners. By today's standards the behavior deemed unacceptable in this tale—spinning on a Friday—is scarcely worthy of condemnation. W.R.S. Ralston, writing shortly after the tale was first published, offers a logical explanation: "The Russian name for that day, *Pyatnitsa* (from *pyat* = five, Friday being the fifth working day), has no such mythological significance as have our own *Friday* and the French *vendredi*. But the day was undoubtedly consecrated by the old Slavonians to some goddess akin to Venus or Freyja, and her worship in ancient times accounts for the superstitions now connected with the name of Friday" (p. 198). Thus this tale illustrates the survival in folklore of ancient beliefs and practices, long after they ceased to be active in the culture at large.

## CHAIN TALE

### "The Cock and the Mouse" (Italy)

Once upon a time there was a cock and a mouse.

One day the mouse said to the cock, "Friend cock, shall we go and eat some nuts on yonder tree?"

"As you like."

So they both went under the tree, and the mouse climbed up at once and began to eat. The poor cock began to fly, and flew and flew, but could not come where the mouse was. When it saw that there was no hope of getting there, it said, "Friend mouse, do you know what I want you to do? Throw me a nut."

The mouse went and threw one and hit the cock on the head. The poor cock, with its head broken and all covered with blood, went away to an old woman. "Old aunt, give me some rags to cure my head."

"If you will give me two hairs, I will give you the rags."

The cock went away to a dog. "Dog, give me some hairs. The hairs I will give the old woman. The old woman will give me rags to cure my head."

"If you will give me a little bread," said the dog, "I will give you the hairs."

The cock went away to a baker. "Baker, give me bread. I will give the bread to the dog. The dog will give hairs. The hairs I will carry to the old woman. The old woman will give me rags to cure my head."

The baker answered, "I will not give you bread unless you give me some wood!"

The cock went away to the forest. "Forest, give me some wood. The wood I will carry to the baker. The baker will give me some bread. The bread I will give to the dog. The dog will give me hairs. The hairs I will carry to the old woman. The old woman will give me rags to cure my head."

The forest answered, "If you will bring me a little water, I will give you some wood."

The cock went away to a fountain. "Fountain, give me water. Water I will carry to the forest. Forest will give wood. Wood I will carry to the baker. Baker will give bread. Bread I will give dog. Dog will give hairs. Hairs I will give old woman. Old woman will give rags to cure my head."

The fountain gave him water. The water he carried to the forest. The forest gave him wood. The wood he carried to the baker. The baker gave him bread. The bread he gave to the dog. The dog gave him the hairs. The hairs he carried to the old woman. The old woman gave him the rags. And the cock cured his head.

*Source:* Thomas Frederick Crane, *Italian Popular Tales* (Boston: Houghton, Mifflin, and Company, 1885), no. 80, pp. 252–53.


*Commentary*

Popular among children from India to northern Europe, and beyond, chain tales rely less on their actual plots than on a storyteller's ability to successfully manipulate the ever-expanding sequence of phrases. Such tales are as much games as they are narratives. *What* happens is less important than *how* the storyteller enacts it.

Similarly, another popular English chain tale, "The House That Jack Built," has essentially no plot, deriving its appeal instead from the playful musicality of its language. Its final sentence tells all: "This is the farmer that sowed the corn, that fed the cock that crowed in the morn, that waked the priest all shaven and shorn, that married the man all tattered and torn, that kissed the maiden all forlorn, that milked the cow with the crumpled horn, that tossed the dog, that worried the cat, that caught the rat, that ate the malt that lay in the house that Jack built."

Strictly speaking, chain tales belong to a broader category called cumulative tales, and it is to that group that we now turn.


## CUMULATIVE TALE

### "The Thick, Fat Pancake" (Germany)

Once upon a time there were three old women who wanted a pancake to eat. The first one brought an egg, the second one milk, and the third one grease and flour. When the thick, fat pancake was done, it pulled itself up in the pan and ran away from the three old women. It ran and ran, steadfastly,

steadfastly into the woods. There it came upon a little hare, who cried, "Thick, fat pancake, stop! I want to eat you!"

The pancake answered, "I have run away from three old women. Can I not run away from Hoppity Hare as well?" And it ran steadfastly, steadfastly into the woods.

Then a wolf came running toward him, and cried, "Thick, fat pancake, stop! I want to eat you!"

The pancake answered, "I have run away from three old women and Hoppity Hare. Can I not run away from Waddly Wolf as well?" And it ran steadfastly, steadfastly into the woods.

Then a goat came hopping by, and cried, "Thick, fat pancake, stop! I want to eat you!"

The pancake answered, "I have run away from three old women, Hoppity Hare, and Waddly Wolf. Can I not run away from Longbeard Goat as well?" And it ran steadfastly, steadfastly into the woods.

Then a horse came galloping by, and cried, "Thick, fat pancake, stop! I want to eat you!"

The pancake answered, "I have run away from three old women, Hoppity Hare, Waddly Wolf, and Longbeard Goat. Can I not run away from Flatfoot Horse as well?" And it ran steadfastly, steadfastly into the woods.

Then a sow came running up, and cried, "Thick, fat pancake, stop! I want to eat you!"

The pancake answered, "I have run away from three old women, Hoppity Hare, Waddly Wolf, Longbeard Goat, and Flatfoot Horse. Can I not run away from Oink-Oink Sow as well?" And it ran steadfastly, steadfastly into the woods.

Then three children came by. They had neither father nor mother, and they said, "Dear pancake, stop! We have had nothing to eat the entire day!" So the thick, fat pancake jumped into the children's basket and let them eat it up.

*Source:* Carl and Theodor Colshorn, "Vom dicken fetten Pfannekuchen," *Märchen und Sagen* (Hannover: Verlag von Carl Rümpler, 1854), no. 57, pp. 168–69. The Colshorns' source: "oral, from Salzdahlum."

*Commentary*

American readers will immediately recognize this tale as a variant of "The Gingerbread Boy," a favorite since its first publication in 1875. Generically known as "The Runaway Pancake" (A-T 2025), this tale most often has a tragic conclusion (for the pancake, at least), ending with the escapee being eaten by a wily fox or a hungry pig. Thus one of the tale's several functions may be to carefully, and in a nonthreatening manner, warn children about potentially life-threatening dangers that lurk outside the home. The version from Germany given here softens the traditional ending by having the pancake volunteer to be eaten by hungry and deserving children.

## ENDLESS STORY

### *"It Was a Dark and Stormy Night" (England and United States)*

It was a dark and stormy night, and a band of villainous robbers sat around their campfire, when their captain stood up and said, "Antonio, tell us a story," so Antonio stood up and said, "It was a dark and stormy night, and a band of villainous robbers sat around their campfire, when their captain stood up and said, 'Antonio, tell us a story,' so Antonio stood up and said..."

*Source:* Recalled from personal memory.

### *Commentary*

This formula story (A-T 2320) has been collected throughout England and America. It is sometimes told in verse, and its setting also can be a ship's deck. Some storytellers let the tale form a recursive loop, as told here, while others change the name of the internal storyteller each time around. Janet and Allan Ahlberg turned this tale within a tale into a children's book, titled, of course, *It Was a Dark and Stormy Night* (1993).

The hackneyed opening, "It was a dark and stormy night," is the first phrase of the novel *Paul Clifford* by Edward Bulwer-Lytton. The phrase has been parodied endlessly in the *Peanuts* cartoon strip and is a much-used starting point for school writing assignments.

## ETIOLOGIC TALE

### *"Why the Bear Is Stumpy-Tailed" (Norway)*

One day the bear met the fox, who came slinking along with a string of fish he had stolen.

"Where did you get those from?" asked the bear.

"I've been out fishing and caught them, Mr. Bear," said the fox.

So the bear wanted to learn to fish as well, and he asked the fox how he should go about it.

"It will be easy for you," answered the fox. "You'll quickly learn how. Just go out onto the ice, chop a hole in it and stick your tail down into it, and then you must hold it there as long as you can. Don't mind if your tail hurts a little; that's just the fish biting. The longer you hold it there the more fish you'll catch. Then suddenly pull it out sideways!"

Yes, the bear did what the fox had said to do, and held his tail a long, long time down in the hole, until it was tightly frozen in. Then he pulled it out sideways, and it snapped off short. And that is why he goes about stumpy-tailed to this very day.

*Source:* Peter Christen Asbjørnsen and Jørgen Moe, *Popular Tales from the Norse,* trans. George Webbe Dasent (London: George Routledge and Sons, n.d.), p. 210. Translation revised.

### Commentary

Animal tales are popular in all cultures, with the animal characters typically symbolizing different types of human behavior. These tales often appear in cycles. Shorter adventures, such as the type 2 tale related here, can be told either separately or as continuing episodes linked into one longer narrative. Thus each incident draws on and supplements other episodes in the storyteller's repertory, whether or not they are part of the current performance. Before a story begins, we already know from other familiar tales that the fox is a sly, amoral trickster and that the bear is a brutish but easily duped lout.

The preceding tale pretends to tell us why certain things in nature are as they are, and thus it intrudes ever so lightly into the realm of myth. But myths offer serious explanations, bringing the gods themselves into play, whereas "Why the Bear Is Stumpy-Tailed" is entirely playful, obviously a lighthearted fiction.

## EXEMPLUM

### "Of the Remembrance of Benefits" (Gesta Romanorum)

There was a knight who devoted much of his time to hunting. It happened one day, as he was pursuing this diversion, that he was met by a lame lion, who showed him his foot. The knight dismounted, and drew from it a sharp thorn; and then applied an unguent to the wound, which speedily healed it. A while after this, the king of the country hunted in the same wood, and caught that lion, and held him captive for many years. Now, the knight, having offended the king, fled from his anger to the very forest in which he had been accustomed to hunt. There he betook himself to plunder, and spoiled and slew a multitude of travelers. But the king's sufferance was exhausted; he sent out an army, captured, and condemned him to be delivered to a fasting lion. The knight was accordingly thrown into a pit, and remained in terrified expectation of the hour when he should be devoured. But the lion, considering him attentively, and remembering his former friend, fawned upon him; and remained seven days with him destitute of food. When this reached the ears of the king, he was struck with wonder, and directed the knight to be taken from the pit. "Friend," said he, "by what means have you been able to render the lion harmless?"

"As I once rode along the forest, my lord, that lion met me lame. I extracted from his foot a large thorn, and afterward healed the wound, and therefore he has spared me."

"Well," returned the king, "since the lion has spared you, I will for this time ratify your pardon. Study to amend your life."

The knight gave thanks to the king, and ever afterwards conducted himself with all propriety. He lived to a good old age, and ended his days in peace.

Application: My beloved, the knight is the world; the lame lion is the human race; the thorn, original sin, drawn out by baptism. The pit represents penitence, whence safety is derived.

*Source: Gesta Romanorum*, trans. Charles Swan (London: George Bell and Sons, 1877), no. 104, pp. 180–82.


*Commentary*

An exemplum is literally an example of positive or negative behavior, narrated in a didactic tale. The *Gesta Romanorum* (Deeds of the Romans) is a collection of some 283 exempla, legends, and fables, compiled by an anonymous cleric about 1330 in England as a sourcebook for sermons and other religious purposes. Each piece concludes with an "application," which—as illustrated here—does not always relate directly to the text itself.

The preceding depiction of exemplary behavior, with its ensuing blessing, is a variant of the tale of "Androcles and the Lion" (A-T 156), found in the folklore of most European countries, with its genealogy going back to the Aesopic fables of Phaedrus and other stories from Greek and Roman antiquity. George Bernard Shaw turned this material into a drama, *Androcles and the Lion* (first performed in 1912).

Androcles and the lion. Illustration by John D. Batten. Joseph Jacobs, *European Folk and Fairy Tales* (New York: G.P. Putnam's Sons, 1916), p. 107.

## FABLE

*"The Monkey and the Camel" (Aesop)*

At a gathering of all the beasts the monkey gave an exhibition of dancing, and entertained the company vastly. There was great applause at the finish, which excited the envy of the camel and made him desire to win the favor of the assembly by the same means. So he got up from his place and began dancing, but he cut such a ridiculous figure as he plunged about, and made such a grotesque exhibition of his ungainly person, that the beasts all fell upon him with ridicule and drove him away.

*Source: Æsop's Fables,* trans. V.S. Vernon Jones (London: W. Heinemann, 1912), p. 131.

*Commentary*

This Aesopic tale exemplifies the three defining qualities of the fable: animal actors, brevity, and didacticism. The animals, of course, are animals in name only. Here, as in most fables, they represent human behavior: in this instance the envious imitation of others and the unwillingness to be true to one's own nature. Brevity, another defining quality of the fable, is also well represented in the preceding fable, which comprises only three well-crafted sentences. Didacticism, the fable's third requirement, is also present here, although not in the form of an appended "moral of the story." The lesson here is self-evident: "Be yourself." No literary or psychological purpose would be filled by restating the obvious.

## FACETIA

### *"The Peasant Who Wanted to Marry a Girl" (Poggio)*

A peasant from Pergola wanted to marry his neighbor's young daughter. When he saw her, he said that she was too young and immature. "She is more mature than you think," replied her father. "She has already given birth to three children by our parish priest."

*Source: The Facetiae of Poggio,* vol. 2 (Paris: Isidore Liseux, 1879), no. 154.

*Commentary*

Gian Francesco Poggio Bracciolini, usually referred to simply as Poggio, is typical of the jest writers of the late Middle Ages and the Renaissance. Although he wrote in Latin, his style and subject matter remained close to ordinary people. In fact, the word *vulgar* (a synonym for *ordinary*) applies to typical facetiae, relying as they so often do on scatological and sexual humor as well as anticlerical sentiment.

## FAIRY TALE

### *"The Fairies" (Charles Perrault)*

Once upon a time there was a widow who had two daughters. The elder was often mistaken for her mother, so like her was she both in nature and in looks. Both of them were so disagreeable and arrogant that no one could live with them.

The younger girl, who was a true likeness of her father in the gentleness and sweetness of her disposition, was also one of the most beautiful girls imaginable. The mother doted on the elder daughter naturally enough, since she resembled her so closely; and she disliked the younger one just as intensely. She made her eat all her meals in the kitchen and work from morning till night.

One of the poor child's many duties was to go twice a day and draw water from a spring a good half mile away, bringing it back in a large pitcher. One day when she was at the spring an old woman came up and begged for a drink.

"Why, certainly, good mother," said the beautiful girl. Rinsing the pitcher, she drew some water from the cleanest part of the spring and handed it to her, lifting up the pitcher so that she might drink more easily.

Now this old woman was a fairy, who had taken the form of a poor peasant woman to see just how far the girl's good nature would go. "You are so beautiful," she said, when she had finished drinking, "and so polite, that I am determined to bestow a gift upon you. I grant you," the fairy continued, "that with every word you speak, a flower or a precious stone shall fall from your mouth."

When the beautiful girl arrived at home, her mother scolded her for staying so long at the spring.

"I beg your pardon, mother," said the poor child, "for having taken so long," and as she spoke these words, two roses, two pearls, and two large diamonds fell from her mouth.

"What am I seeing?" cried her mother. "I do believe that I saw pearls and diamonds dropping out of your mouth? What have you been doing, my daughter?" (This was the first time she had ever called her her daughter.)

The poor child related what had happened, scattering countless diamonds as she spoke.

"Indeed!" cried her mother. "I must send my own daughter there. Come here, Fanchon. Look what comes out of your sister's mouth whenever she speaks! Wouldn't you like to be able to do the same thing? All you have to do is to go and draw some water at the spring, and when a poor woman asks you for a drink, give it to her very nicely."

"You want to see me going to the spring?" replied the ill-mannered girl.

"I am telling you that you are to go," replied the mother, "and this very instant!"

Very sulkily the girl went out taking with her the best silver flask in the house. No sooner had she reached the spring than she saw a magnificently dressed lady, who came out of the woods towards her and asked for a drink.

This was the same fairy who had appeared to her sister, but she was now disguised as a princess in order to see how far this girl's bad manners would go.

"Do you think I have come here just to get you a drink?" said the rude girl arrogantly. "Do you think I brought a silver flask here just to give madam a drink? Yes, that's just what I think! Have a drink, if you must!"

"You are not very polite," replied the fairy, showing no anger. "Very well! In return for your lack of courtesy I grant that for every word you speak a snake or a toad shall drop out of your mouth."

As soon as her mother saw her returning she cried out, "Well, daughter!"

"Well, mother?" replied the rude girl. As she spoke two vipers and two toads fell from her mouth.

"Heavens!" cried the mother. "What do I see? Her sister is the cause of this. She will pay for it!"

Off she ran to beat her, but the poor child ran off and escaped into the woods nearby. The king's son met her on his way home from hunting, and noticing how beautiful she was, he asked her what she was doing there all alone, and why she was crying.

"Alas, sir, my mother has driven me from home."

As she spoke, the king's son saw five or six pearls and as many diamonds fall from her mouth. He begged her to tell him how this came about, and she told him the whole story.

The king's son fell in love with her, and considering that such a gift as had been bestowed upon her was worth more than any dowry that he might receive from someone else, he took her to his father's royal palace, where he married her.

As for her sister, she made herself so hateful that her own mother drove her out of the house. No one would take in the miserable girl, so at last she went into a corner of the woods and died.

Moral:
> Diamonds and gold coins may
> Work some wonders in their way;
> But a gentle word is worth
> More than all the gems on earth.

Another Moral:
> Though—when otherwise inclined—
> It's a trouble to be kind,
> Often it will bring you good
> When you least believed it could.

*Source:* Charles Perrault, "Les Fées," trans. A.E. Johnson (1921). Morals translated by S.R. Littlewood (1912). Translations revised.

*Commentary*

Although the term *fairy tale* has become synonymous with the more precise phrase *magic tale,* the former term originally applied only to a tale about fairies. "The Fairies" by Charles Perrault combines both concepts by letting a fairy (there seems to be only one of them, in spite of the plural form in the title) be the source of magic in his story, a variant of an extremely popular folktale found nearly everywhere in the world and known generically as "The Kind and the Unkind Girls" (A-T 480). This tale always features magic rewards and punishments, but these do not normally emanate from fairies.

All of Perrault's tales are didactic, and in "The Fairies" the morals are especially easy to derive: Kind and selfless acts result in happiness and prosperity; whereas unkind behavior brings misery, even death. In addition to supernatural rewards and punishments, Perrault's tale illustrates another quality often found in fairy tales: the symbolic use of precious stones or metals. Logically considered, having pearls and diamonds fall from one's mouth with every utterance would soon prove to be a gift with as little lasting value as the gold touch of King Midas. But fairy tales rely on a logic different from the mathematics and science of this world. In fairy tales pearls, diamonds, and gold represent unqualified good, even if practical considerations might suggest otherwise.

## FOOL'S TALE

### *"How the Kadambawa Men Counted Themselves" (Sri Lanka)*

Twelve Kadambawa men cut fence sticks, tied them into twelve bundles, then set them upright and leaned them together. Then one of the men said, "Are our men all here? We must count and see."

So a man counted them, but he counted only eleven men, omitting himself. "There are only eleven men, but there are twelve bundles of fence sticks," he said.

Then another man said, "Maybe you have made a mistake," and counted them again in the same way. "There are eleven men and twelve bundles of fence sticks. There is a man missing," they said, and they went into the jungle to look for him.

While they were in the jungle looking, a man from another village heard them shouting. He came to them and asked why they were shouting.

The men said, "Twelve of our men came to cut fence sticks. There are twelve bundles of sticks but only eleven men. One man is missing."

This man saw that there were twelve men, so he said, "Let each of you pick up your own bundle of fence sticks."

So each of the twelve men picked up his own bundle of sticks, and thus they all returned to their village.

*Source:* Henry Parker, *Village Folk-Tales of Ceylon,* vol. 1 (London: Luzac and Company, 1910), no. 44, p. 258. Type 1287.


### Commentary

Fools feature prominently in folktales around the world, with their inability to count themselves providing one of the favorite episodes (A-T 1287). The fools of these tales fit into two main categories: those who are genuinely stupid and those who only feign stupidity in order surreptitiously to achieve some goal. The popularity of each category is easy to understand. We relish hearing of the mishaps of genuine simpletons, because such characters make us look good by comparison. Especially children, who in real life are reminded repeatedly of their inferiority to grownups, delight in the discovery of adults who make mistakes that they themselves would avoid, even if these adults are only fictitious characters in made-up tales. If the foolishness is only feigned, then the story becomes a trickster tale, with the person held to be a fool exploiting this misunderstanding to his or her own benefit.

In the preceding tale from Sri Lanka the fools seem to be of the former variety, genuinely stupid. However, essentially the same story is told of those who use their apparent stupidity as a tool to manipulate their superiors. A famous example from England is the legend of the wise men of Gotham. According to tradition, when messengers of King John (who reigned from 1199 to 1216) came to Gotham in Nottinghamshire, in preparation for a royal visit, the villagers, not wanting to bear the expense of the king's planned sojourn, feigned stupidity to convince the king's men that the place was rife with idiots and thus unfit for royalty. Their tricks included unsuccessful attempts to count themselves, attempting to drown an eel, trying to capture a cuckoo by building a fence around its nest, and carrying buckets filled with light into a windowless and dark house. Their pretended foolishness had the desired effect, and the king went elsewhere. However, from that day forth Gothamites have had a reputation for stupidity, and not always of the purposeful, feigned variety.

Note on the text: Parker's translation follows his Sinhalese sources so closely that English syntax is violated in almost every sentence. I have cautiously attempted to bring his narrative closer to idiomatic English.

# FRAME STORY

*Frame Story to the* 1,001 Nights

Sultan Schahriar had a wife whom he loved more than all the world. It was therefore with the deepest shame and sorrow that he accidentally discovered, after several years, that she had deceived him completely, and her whole conduct turned out to have been so bad, that he felt himself obliged to have her put to death. Furthermore, he was quite sure that all women were as wicked as the sultana, so every evening he married a fresh wife and had her put to death the following morning.

The grand vizier, whose task it was each day to find a new bride for the sultan, was himself the father of two daughters. The elder was called Scheherazade and the younger Dinarzade. Dinarzade had no particular gifts, but her elder sister, in addition to being unexcelled in beauty, was clever and courageous. It is said that she had read a thousand books of stories, and to hear her speak was like listening to music. One day, when the grand vizier was talking to Scheherazade, she said to him, "Father, will you grant me a favor?"

"I can refuse you nothing," he replied, "that is just and reasonable."

"Then listen," said Scheherazade. "I am determined to stop this barbarous practice of the sultan's."

"It would be an excellent thing to do," returned the grand vizier, "but how do you propose to accomplish it?"

"My father," answered Scheherazade, "it is you who have to provide the sultan daily with a fresh wife, and I implore you to allow the honor to fall upon me."

"Have you lost your senses?" cried the grand vizier, starting back in horror. "What has put such a thing into your head? You ought to know by this time what it means to be the sultan's bride!"

"Yes, my father, I know it well," she replied, "and I am not afraid to think of it. If I fail, my death will be a glorious one, and if I succeed I shall have done a great service to my country."

"It is of no use," said the grand vizier. "I shall never consent."

But the maiden absolutely refused to attend to her father's words, and at length, in despair, the grand vizier was obliged to give way, and went sadly to the palace to tell the sultan that the following evening he would bring him Scheherazade.

The sultan received this news with the greatest astonishment. "How have you made up your mind," he asked, "to sacrifice your own daughter to me?"

Scheherazade, Dinarzade, and the sultan. Illustration by H.J. Ford (1898). Andrew Lang, *The Arabian Nights Entertainment* (London: Longmans, Green, and Company, 1898), p. 3.

"Sire," answered the grand vizier, "it is her own wish. Even the sad fate that awaits her could not hold her back."

So the sultan told the grand vizier he might bring his daughter as soon as he liked. The vizier took back this news to Scheherazade, who received it as if it had been the most pleasant thing in the world. Then she went to prepare herself for the marriage, and begged that her sister Dinarzade should be sent for, to speak to her.

When they were alone, Scheherazade addressed her thus: "My dear sister, I want your help in a very important affair. My father is going to take me to the palace to celebrate my marriage with the sultan. When his highness receives me, I shall beg him, as a last favor, to let you sleep in our chamber, so that I may have your company during the last night I am alive. If, as I hope, he grants me my wish, be sure that you wake me one hour before dawn, and speak to me in these words, 'My sister, if you are not asleep, I beg you, before the sun rises, to tell me one of your charming stories.' Then I shall begin, and I hope by this means to deliver the people from the terror that reigns over them."

Dinarzade replied that she would do with pleasure what her sister wished.

When the usual hour arrived, the grand vizier conducted Scheherazade to the palace, and left her alone with the sultan, who bade her raise her veil and was amazed at her beauty. But seeing her eyes full of tears, he asked what was the matter. "Sire," replied Scheherazade, "I have a sister who loves me as tenderly as I love her. Grant me the favor of allowing her to sleep this night in the same room, as it is the last we shall be together." Schahriar consented to Scheherazade's petition, and Dinarzade was sent for.

One hour before daybreak Dinarzade awoke, and exclaimed, as she had promised, "My dear sister, if you are not asleep, tell me, I pray you, before the sun rises, one of your charming stories. It is the last time that I shall have the pleasure of hearing you."

Scheherazade did not answer her sister, but turned to the sultan. "Will your highness permit me to do as my sister asks?" said she.

"Willingly," he answered. So Scheherazade began.

*Source:* Abstracted from Andrew Lang, *The Arabian Nights Entertainment* (London: Longmans, Green and Company, 1898), pp. 1–5.

*Commentary*

As is well known, Scheherazade did not finish the tale before sunrise, so the sultan let her live another day and another night in order to hear the story's conclusion. Each night she completed the previous night's tale and began another, thus delaying her death by another day. So it continued for 1,001 nights, by which time the sultan had fallen in love with her and abandoned his cruel plan. Thus every story in the *1,001 Nights' Entertainment,* also known as the *Arabian Nights,* is a tale within a tale. In fact, a number of Scheherazade's characters are themselves storytellers, who relate tales within the framework of Scheherazade's tale. Such stories within stories within stories are not unusual in ancient folktale compilations, especially those from the Orient. The resulting layers of interconnected plots become a game in their own right, with part of the listener's or reader's pleasure deriving from the untangling of the narratives, like solving a riddle or finding one's way through a maze.

## GHOST STORY

### *"The Golden Arm" (England)*

There was once a man who traveled the land all over in search of a wife. He saw young and old, rich and poor, pretty and plain, and could not meet with one to his mind. At last he found a woman young, fair, and rich, who possessed the supreme, the crowning glory of having a right arm of solid gold. He married her at once, and thought no man so fortunate as he was. They lived happily together, but, though he wished people to think otherwise, he was fonder of the golden arm than of all his wife's gifts besides.

At last she died. The husband appeared inconsolable. He put on the blackest black, and pulled the longest face at the funeral. But for all that he got up in the middle of the night, dug up the body, and cut off the golden arm. He hurried home to secrete his recovered treasure, and thought no one would know.

The following night he put the golden arm under his pillow, and was just falling asleep, when the ghost of his dead wife glided into the room. Stalking up to the bedside it drew the curtain, and looked at him reproachfully. Pretending not to be afraid, he spoke to the ghost, and said, "What have you done with your cheeks so red?"

"All withered and wasted away," replied the ghost, in a hollow tone.

"What have you done with your red rosy lips?"

"All withered and wasted away."

"What have you done with your golden hair?"

"All withered and wasted away."

"What have you done with your *golden arm?*"

"You have it!"

*Source:* Sabine Baring-Gould, appendix, *Notes on the Folk Lore of the Northern Counties of England,* by William Henderson (London: Longmans, Green, and Company, 1866), no. 14, pp. 338–39. Language modernized.

### *Commentary*

Sabine Baring-Gould appends the following description of a storyteller's performance to his text of this tale: "The dialog progresses in horror, till at the close, the ghost's exclamation is shrieked out at the top of the narrator's voice, the candle extinguished, and the young auditors duly panic stricken. No one desires to know what became of the avaricious husband." From this statement it should be clear that this ghost story's appeal lies in its ability to frighten its listeners.

The ghost returns for her golden arm. Illustration by John D. Batten. Joseph Jacobs, *English Fairy Tales* (London: David Nutt, 1898), p. 138.

We still delight in being frightened, as evidenced by the continued success of gothic novels, horror movies, and roller coasters. If the frightening experience has a well-defined and predictable end, the adrenaline rush that accompanies the proverbial sigh of relief brings us cathartic pleasure, not terror. Ghost stories have played this role for centuries.

Ghost stories serve other, more serious functions as well. "The Golden Arm," a type 366 folktale, depicts the theft of a corpse's property. Such tales, however trivial they appear today, may have their origins in myths designed to prevent grave desecration and the looting of goods buried with the dead for their use in a next world. Furthermore, ghost stories of all types are reminders that spirits of the departed can and do maintain communication with the living. As such, these tales can have deep religious meaning.

## INCANTATION

*"Merseburg Incantation" (Germany)*

Phol and Wodan rode into the woods,
There Balder's foal sprained its foot.
It was charmed by Sinthgunt, her sister Sunna;
It was charmed by Frija, her sister Volla;
It was charmed by Wodan, as he well knew how:
"Bone-sprain, like blood-sprain, like limb-sprain:
Bone to bone; blood to blood;
Limb to limb—like they were glued."

*Source:* A manuscript from the tenth century.


*Commentary*

Many nineteenth-century folklorists, including Jacob and Wilhelm Grimm, held the view that most oral folktales were remnants of ancient rituals and myths. The preceding incantation is a case in point. Recorded in the tenth century, but from textual evidence composed before the year 750, this piece contains both a story and the exact words of a healing ritual. The story is simple: Two Germanic gods (Phol is apparently another name for the god Balder) rode into the woods, where Balder's horse sprained its foot. Four goddesses attempted to heal the horse with magic charms, but they failed. Only Wodan was successful, and the precise words of his magic charm are given, presumably enabling those who faithfully commit this tale to memory to heal their lame horses as well.


## JEST

*"The Baneyrwal and His Drowned Wife" (Pakistan)*

There was once a sudden flood in the Indus, which washed away numbers of people, and, among others, the wife of a certain Baneyrwal. The distracted husband was wandering along the banks of the river, looking for the dead body, when a countryman accosted him thus, "Oh friend, if, as I am informed, your wife has been carried away in the flood, she must have gone down the stream with the rest of the poor creatures; yet you are going up the stream."

"Ah, sir," answered the wretched Baneyrwal, "you did not know that wife of mine. She always took an opposite course to everyone else. And even now that she is drowned, I know full well that, if other bodies have floated down the river, hers *must* have floated up."

*Source:* Charles Swynnerton, *Indian Nights' Entertainment; or, Folk-Tales from the Upper Indus* (London: Elliot Stock, 1892), no. 35. Language cautiously modernized.

### Commentary

On the surface, the message of this famous jest, known generically as "Seeking a Contrary Wife Upstream" (A-T 1365A), is encapsulated in its punch line: A contrary woman (the drowned person is always female) will not change her ways, even after death. But another interpretation is also possible. The text offers no proof that the woman actually floated upstream, only that her husband *thought* that she had done so. Examined under this light, the tale is not about an impossibly stubborn woman, but rather about an incredibly stupid man. This option of double interpretation has contributed to this simple tale's longevity and wide distribution. Variants are found in some of our oldest folktale collections—for example, the *1,001 Nights* and the *Facetiae* of Poggio—and in diverse cultures from India to Scandinavia.

Note on the text: A Baneyrwal is an inhabitant of Baneyr, a tribal region along the Afghan-Pakistani border.

## JOKE

### "Willy Brandt and Walter Ulbricht" (German Democratic Republic)

What is the difference between Willy Brandt and Walter Ulbricht?— Brandt collects jokes that people tell about him, and Ulbricht collects people that tell jokes about him.

*Source:* Personal recollection, Arnstadt, German Democratic Republic, 1974.

### Commentary

Folklorists use the terms *jest* and *joke* more or less synonymously, usually with *jest* referring to older samples of the genre and *joke* referring to more recent ones. This joke about joke telling is typical of those that circulate in totalitarian regimes, where governments harshly seek to protect themselves against ridicule. But such attempts are usually self-defeating, just as it is nearly always counterproductive to warn 12-year-old boys against telling "dirty" jokes. The taboo itself is what makes such a story funny, not the joke's nominal subject. Note also that the preceding joke follows the form of a riddle, with a play on words forming both the riddle's answer and the joke's punch line.

Note on the text: Willy Brandt and Walter Ulbricht were the heads of the Federal Republic of Germany (West Germany) and the German Democratic Republic (East Germany), respectively, in the early 1970s.

## LEGEND

### "Mally Dixon" (England)

Stories of fairies appearing in the shape of cats are common in the North of England. Mr. Longstaffe relates that a farmer of Staindrop, in Durham, was one night crossing a bridge, when a cat jumped out, stood before him, and looking him full in the face, said:

> Johnny Reed! Johnny Reed!
> Tell Madam Momfort
> That Mally Dixon's dead.

The farmer returned home, and in mickle wonder recited this awfu' stanza to his wife, when up started their black cat, saying, "Is she?" and disappeared for ever. It was supposed she was a fairy in disguise, who thus went to attend a sister's funeral, for in the North fairies do die, and green shady spots are pointed out by the country folks as the cemeteries of the tiny people.

*Source:* James Halliwell-Phillips, *Popular Rhymes and Nursery Tales* (London: John Russell Smith, 1849), p. 51.

### Commentary

By folklorists' convention, a legend is a narrative that claims to be true. Storytellers often enhance the credibility of such accounts by including specific names of people and places in their stories. Note, however, that in this tale, the person identified as Mr. Longstaffe is not the individual who experienced the miraculous event. The story was related by the proverbial "friend of a friend" (referred to as a FOAF by modern folklorists), not by an actual participant, a process long observed by collectors of legends.

The dividing line between the genres legend and fairy tale is extremely fluid, in part because of the high degree of belief given to fairy lore in many cultures of the not-too-distant past. For example, variants of the preceding tale are classified both as folktales of type 113A and as migratory legends of type 6070B. In general, a folklorist would lean toward the migratory legend classification for narratives that are very sparsely told and toward the folktale classification for narratives that have more literary adornments, such as the cat's direct quotation in "Mally Dixon," as well as the storyteller's obvious intent to build tension into his narrative, revealing the mystery of the fairy's funeral only as a climactic punch line.

## LIE

*"Ash Lad Who Made the Princess Say, 'You're a Liar'" (Norway)*

Once upon a time there was a king who had a daughter, and she was such a liar that there was no one else like her. So he proclaimed that if anyone could tell her such a story as to make her say, "You're a liar," he should have her to wife, and half the kingdom as well. Many tried, for everyone wanted to have the princess and half the kingdom. But they all failed.

Then three brothers resolved to try their luck. The older two set out first, but they fared no better than the others. Then Ash Lad set forth, and he met the princess in the cowshed.

"Good day," he said, "and thank you for your hospitality."

"Good day" she said, "and the same to you. Your cowshed isn't as big as ours," she said, "for when a shepherd stands at either end of ours, and they blow their ram's horns, the one can't hear the other."

"Oh, yes!" said Ash Lad. "Ours is much bigger; for if a cow gets with calf at one end of ours, by the time she gets to the other end she will have the calf."

"You don't say!" said the princess. "But you don't have as big an ox as ours. See him there! When a man sits on each horn, they can't touch each other with a ten-foot pole."

"Twaddle!" said Ash Lad. "We have an ox so big, that when a man sits on each horn, and each one blows a trumpet, they can't hear each other."

"You don't say!" said the princess. "But you don't have as much milk as we do," she said. "We milk into large pails, then carry them in and pour them into large cauldrons and make large cheeses."

"Oh, we milk into large cauldrons and pour them into brewing vats and make cheeses as large as a house. We had a gray mare to tread the cheese, but it foaled in the cheese, and after we had been eating the cheese for seven years we came upon a gray horse. One day I was going to ride it to the mill when its backbone broke, but I knew how to fix it. I took a spruce tree and put it in for a backbone, and it was the only backbone it had from then on. But the tree grew until it became so tall that I climbed right up into heaven on it. And when I got there, the Virgin Mary was sitting and spinning barley broth into bristle ropes. Then suddenly the spruce tree broke off, and I couldn't get down again; so the Virgin Mary lowered me down by one of the ropes. I landed in a fox's den, and who was sitting there but my mother and your father, patching shoes. And just as I stepped in, my mother gave your father such a box on the ear that the scurf flew off him."

"You're a liar!" said the princess. "My father has never been scurvy!"

*Source:* Peter Christen Asbjørnsen and Jørgen Engebretsen Moe, "Askeladden som fikk prinsessen til å løgste seg," *Samlede eventyr,* vol. 1 (Oslo: Den norske Bokklubben, 1982), pp. 243–45.

### Commentary

"Lie" is one of the dictionary definitions of *fairy tale,* but even the most imaginative of fairy tales normally present at least a pretense of reality. Not so with these tales within a tale, which unashamedly revel in their untruth. Ironically, the princess accepts the storyteller's exaggerations and nonsense until he casts aspersions at her father, at which point she calls the hero a liar, giving him victory in the contest, and thus her hand in marriage.

## LITERARY FAIRY TALE

### "The Emperor's New Clothes" (Hans Christian Andersen)

Many years ago there lived an emperor who loved beautiful new clothes so much that he spent all his money on being finely dressed. His only interest was in going to the theater or in riding about in his carriage where he could show off his new clothes. He had a different costume for every hour of the day. Indeed, where it was said of other kings that they were at court, it could only be said of him that he was in his dressing room!

One day two swindlers came to the emperor's city. They said that they were weavers, claiming that they knew how to make the finest cloth imaginable. Not only were the colors and the patterns extraordinarily beautiful, but in addition, this material had the amazing property that it was to be invisible to anyone who was incompetent or stupid.

"It would be wonderful to have clothes made from that cloth," thought the emperor. "Then I would know which of my men are unfit for their positions, and I'd also be able to tell clever people from stupid ones." So he immediately gave the two swindlers a great sum of money to weave their cloth for him.

They set up their looms and pretended to go to work, although there was nothing at all on the looms. They asked for the finest silk and the purest gold, all of which they hid away, continuing to work on the empty looms, often late into the night.

"I would really like to know how they are coming with the cloth!" thought the emperor, but he was a bit uneasy when he recalled that anyone who was unfit for his position or stupid would not be able to see the material. Of course, he himself had nothing to fear, but still he decided to send someone else to see how the work was progressing.

"I'll send my honest old minister to the weavers," thought the emperor. He's the best one to see how the material is coming. He is very sensible, and no one is more worthy of his position than he.

So the good old minister went into the hall where the two swindlers sat working at their empty looms. "Goodness!" thought the old minister, opening his eyes wide. "I cannot see a thing!" But he did not say so.

The two swindlers invited him to step closer, asking him if it wasn't a beautiful design and if the colors weren't magnificent. They pointed to the empty loom, and the poor old minister opened his eyes wider and wider. He still could see nothing, for nothing was there. "Gracious," he thought. "Is it possible that I am stupid? I have never thought so. Am I unfit for my position? No one must know this. No, it will never do for me to say that I was unable to see the material."

"You aren't saying anything!" said one of the weavers.

"Oh, it is magnificent! The very best!" said the old minister, peering through his glasses. "This pattern and these colors! Yes, I'll tell the emperor that I am very satisfied with it!"

"That makes us happy!" said the two weavers, and they called the colors and the unusual pattern by name. The old minister listened closely so that he would be able to say the same things when he reported back to the emperor, and that is exactly what he did.

The swindlers now asked for more money, more silk, and more gold, all of which they hid away. Then they continued to weave away as before on the empty looms.

The emperor sent other officials as well to observe the weavers' progress. They too were startled when they saw nothing, and they too reported back to him how wonderful the material was, advising him to have it made into clothes that he could wear in a grand procession. The entire city was alive in praise of the cloth. "Magnifique! Nysseligt! Excellent!" they said, in all languages. The emperor awarded the swindlers with medals of honor, bestowing on each of them the title Lord Weaver.

The swindlers stayed up the entire night before the procession was to take place, burning more than sixteen candles. Everyone could see that they were in a great rush to finish the emperor's new clothes. They pretended to take the material from the looms. They cut in the air with large scissors. They sewed with needles but without any thread. Finally they announced, "Behold! The clothes are finished!"

The emperor came to them with his most distinguished cavaliers. The two swindlers raised their arms as though they were holding something and said, "Just look at these trousers! Here is the jacket! This is the cloak!" and so forth. "They are as light as spider webs! You might think that you didn't have a thing on, but that is the good thing about them."

"Yes," said the cavaliers, but they couldn't see a thing, for nothing was there.

"Would his imperial majesty, if it please his grace, kindly remove his clothes," said the swindlers. "Then we will fit you with the new ones, here in front of the large mirror."

The emperor took off all his clothes, and the swindlers pretended to dress him, piece by piece, with the new ones that were to be fitted. They took hold of his waist and pretended to tie something about him. It was the train. Then the emperor turned and looked into the mirror.

"Goodness, they suit you well! What a wonderful fit!" they all said. "What a pattern! What colors! Such luxurious clothes!"

"The canopy to be carried above your majesty awaits outside," said the grandmaster of ceremonies.

"Yes, I am ready!" said the emperor. "Don't they fit well?" He turned once again toward the mirror, because it had to appear as though he were admiring himself in all his glory.

The chamberlains who were to carry the train held their hands just above the floor as if they were picking up the train. As they walked they pretended to hold the train high, for they could not let anyone notice that they could see nothing.

The emperor walked beneath the beautiful canopy in the procession, and all the people in the street and in their windows said, "Goodness, the emperor's new clothes are incomparable! What a beautiful train on his jacket. What a perfect fit!" No one wanted it to be noticed that he could see nothing, for then it would be said that he was unfit for his position or that he was stupid. None of the emperor's clothes had ever before received such praise.

"But he doesn't have anything on!" said a small child.

"Goodness, let us hear the voice of an innocent child!" said the father, and whispered to another what the child had said.

"A small child said that he doesn't have anything on!"

Finally everyone was saying, "He doesn't have anything on!"

The emperor shuddered, for he knew that they were right, but he thought, "The procession must go on!" He carried himself even more proudly, and the chamberlains walked along behind carrying the train that wasn't there.

*Source:* Hans Christian Andersen, "Keiserens nye klæder" (1837). Andersen's source was a Spanish story recorded by Don Juan Manuel.

## Commentary

The two names from the nineteenth century most associated with fairy tales are Grimm and Andersen. Their approaches were completely different. The Grimm brothers collected folktales from various sources (both oral and written), then edited them cautiously, rarely introducing major changes into a tale's structure or plot. On the other hand, Hans Christian Andersen's tales are for the most part pure invention. He does borrow bits and pieces from traditional folklore, but the final products are his own literary creations. Such is the case with "The Emperor's New Clothes," a justly famous story of trickery, hypocrisy, self-doubt, and unwarranted pride, all exposed in the end by an innocent but perceptive child. Folklore versions of this material are classified as type 1620 tales, and they typically deal with a trickster who promises a magic garment that can ascertain whether its wearers were conceived within wedlock, rather than determining their competence, as in the Andersen story.

## MAGIC TALE

*"The Frog King; or, Iron Heinrich" (Jacob and Wilhelm Grimm)*

| First edition, 1812 | Final edition, 1857 |
|---|---|
| Once upon a time there was a princess who went out into a forest and sat next to a cool well. | In olden times, when wishing still did some good, there lived a king whose daughters were all beautiful, but the youngest was so beautiful that the sun itself, who, indeed, has seen so much, marveled every time it shone upon her face. In the vicinity of the king's castle there was a large, dark forest, and in this forest, beneath an old linden tree, there was a well. In the heat of the day the princess would go out into the forest and sit on the edge of the cool well. |

**First edition, 1812**

She took great pleasure in throwing a golden ball into the air and catching it, but once it went too high. She held out her hand with her fingers curved to catch it, but it fell to the ground and rolled and rolled right into the water.

Horrified, the princess followed it with her eyes, but the well was so deep that she could not see its bottom.

Then she began to cry bitterly, "I'd give anything, if only I could get my ball back: my clothes, my precious stones, my pearls, anything in the world."
At this a frog stuck his head out of the water and said, "Princess, why are you crying so bitterly?"

"Oh," she said, "you ugly frog, how can you help me? My golden ball has fallen into the well."

The frog said, "I do not want your pearls, your precious stones, and your clothes, but if you'll accept me as a companion and let me sit next to you and eat from your plate and sleep in your bed, and if you'll love and cherish me, then I'll bring your ball back to you."

**Final edition, 1857**

To pass the time she would take a golden ball, throw it into the air, and then catch it. It was her favorite plaything. Now one day it happened that the princess's golden ball did not fall into her hands, that she held up high, but instead it fell to the ground and rolled right into the water.
The princess followed it with her eyes, but the ball disappeared, and the well was so deep that she could not see its bottom.
Then she began to cry. She cried louder and louder, and she could not console herself.

As she was thus lamenting, someone called out to her, "What is the matter with you, princess? Your crying would turn a stone to pity."
She looked around to see where the voice was coming from and saw a frog, who had stuck his thick, ugly head out of the water. "Oh, it's you, old water-splasher," she said. "I am crying because my golden ball has fallen into the well."
"Be still and stop crying," answered the frog. I can help you, but what will you give me if I bring back your plaything?"
"Whatever you want, dear frog," she said, "my clothes, my pearls and precious stones, and even the golden crown that I am wearing."

The frog answered, "I do not want your clothes, your pearls and precious stones, nor your golden crown, but if you will love me and accept me as a companion and playmate, and let me sit next to you at your table and eat from your golden plate and drink from your cup and sleep in your bed, if you will promise this to me, then I'll dive down and bring your golden ball back to you."

**First edition, 1812**

The princess thought, "What is this stupid frog trying to say? After all, he does have to stay here in the water. But still, maybe he can get my ball. I'll go ahead and say yes," and she said aloud, "Yes, for all I care. Just bring me back my golden ball, and I'll promise everything." The frog stuck his head under the water and dove to the bottom.

He returned a short time later with the golden ball in his mouth and threw it onto the land.

When the princess saw her ball once again, she rushed toward it, picked it up, and was so happy to have it in her hand again, that she could think of nothing else than to run home with it. The frog called after her, "Wait, princess, take me with you like you promised," but she paid no attention to him.

The next day the princess was sitting at her table when she heard something coming up the marble steps: plip, plop.

Then there came a knock at the door, and a voice called out, "Princess, youngest, open the door for me!"

She ran and opened the door. It was the frog, whom she had put completely out of her mind.

Frightened, she slammed the door shut and returned to the table.

**Final edition, 1857**

"Oh, yes," she said, "I promise all of that to you if you will just bring the ball back to me." But she thought, "What is this stupid frog trying to say? He just sits here in the water with his own kind and croaks. He cannot be a companion to a human."

As soon as the frog heard her say "yes" he stuck his head under and dove to the bottom.

He paddled back up a short time later with the golden ball in his mouth and threw it onto the grass.

The princess was filled with joy when she saw her beautiful plaything once again, picked it up, and ran off.

"Wait, wait," called the frog, "take me along. I cannot run as fast as you." But what did it help him, that he croaked out after her as loudly as he could? She paid no attention to him, but instead hurried home and soon forgot the poor frog, who had to return again to his well.

The next day the princess was sitting at the table with the king and all the people of the court, and was eating from her golden plate when something came creeping up the marble steps: plip, plop, plip, plop.

As soon as it reached the top, there came a knock at the door, and a voice called out, "Princess, youngest, open the door for me!"

She ran to see who was outside. She opened the door, and the frog was sitting there.

Frightened, she slammed the door shut and returned to the table.

| First edition, 1812 | Final edition, 1857 |
|---|---|
| The king saw that her heart was pounding and asked, "Why are you afraid?" | The king saw that her heart was pounding and asked, "My child, why are you afraid? Is there a giant outside the door who wants to get you?" |
| "There is a disgusting frog out there," she said, "who got my golden ball out of the water. I promised him that he could be my companion, but I didn't think that he could leave his water, but now he is just outside the door and wants to come in." | "Oh, no," she answered, "it is a disgusting frog." "What does the frog want from you?"<br><br>"Oh, father dear, yesterday when I was sitting near the well in the forest and playing, my golden ball fell into the water. And because I was crying so much, the frog brought it back, and because he insisted, I promised him that he could be my companion, but I didn't think that he could leave his water. But now he is just outside the door and wants to come in." |
| Just then there came a second knock at the door, and a voice called out: | Just then there came a second knock at the door, and a voice called out: |

Youngest daughter of the king,
Open up the door for me,
Don't you know what yesterday,
You said to me down by the well?
Youngest daughter of the king,
Open up the door for me.

| The king said, "What you have promised, you must keep. Go and let the frog in." She obeyed, and the frog hopped in, then followed her up to her chair. | The king said, "What you have promised, you must keep. Go and let the frog in." She went and opened the door, and the frog hopped in, then followed her up to her chair. |
| After she had sat down again, he called out, "Lift me up onto your chair and let me sit next to you." | He sat there and called out, "Lift me up next to you." |
| The princess did not want to, but the king commanded her to do it. | She hesitated, until finally the king commanded her to do it. |
| When the frog was seated next to her he said, "Now push your golden plate closer. I want to eat from it." | When the frog was seated next to her he said, "Now push your golden plate closer, so we can eat together." |
| She had to do this as well. | She did it, but one could see that she did not want to. |

**First edition, 1812**

When he had eaten all he wanted, he said, "Now I am tired and want to sleep. Take me to your room, make your bed, so that we can lie in it together."

The princess was horrified when she heard that. She was afraid of the cold frog and did not dare to even touch him, and yet he was supposed to lie next to her in her bed; she began to cry and didn't want to at all.

Then the king became angry and commanded her to do what she had promised.

There was no helping it; she had to do what her father wanted, but in her heart she was bitterly angry. She picked up the frog with two fingers, carried him to her room, and climbed into bed, but instead of laying him next to herself, she threw him bang! against the wall.

"Now you will leave me in peace, you disgusting frog!"

But when the frog came down onto the bed, he was a handsome young prince, and he was her dear companion, and she held him in esteem as she had promised, and they fell asleep together with pleasure.

The next morning the prince's faithful Heinrich arrived in a splendid carriage drawn by eight horses, decorated with feathers and glistening with gold.

**Final edition, 1857**

The frog enjoyed his meal, but for her every bite stuck in her throat. Finally he said, "I have eaten all I want and am tired. Now carry me to your room and make your bed so that we can go to sleep."

The princess began to cry and was afraid of the cold frog and did not dare to even touch him, and yet he was supposed to sleep in her beautiful, clean bed.

The king became angry and said, "You should not despise someone who has helped you in time of need."

She picked him up with two fingers, carried him upstairs, and set him in a corner. As she was lying in bed, he came creeping up to her and said, "I am tired, and I want to sleep as well as you do. Pick me up or I'll tell your father."

With that she became bitterly angry and threw him against the wall with all her might.

"Now you will have your peace, you disgusting frog!"

But when he fell down, he was not a frog, but a prince with beautiful friendly eyes. And he was now, according to her father's will, her dear companion and husband. He told her how he had been enchanted by a wicked witch, and that she alone could have rescued him from the well, and that tomorrow they would go together to his kingdom. Then they fell asleep.

The next morning, just as the sun was waking them, a carriage pulled up, drawn by eight horses. They had white ostrich feathers on their heads and were outfitted with chains of gold. At the rear stood the young king's servant, faithful Heinrich.

| First edition, 1812 | Final edition, 1857 |
|---|---|
| He had been so saddened by the prince's transformation that he had had to place three iron bands around his heart to keep it from bursting in sorrow. | He had been so saddened by the prince's transformation that he had had to place three iron bands around his heart to keep it from bursting in sorrow. |
| The prince climbed into the carriage with the princess. His faithful servant stood at the rear to drive them to his kingdom. | The carriage was to take the king back to his kingdom. Faithful Heinrich lifted them both inside and took his place at the rear. He was filled with joy over the redemption. |
| After they had gone a short distance, the prince heard a loud crack from behind. | After they had gone a short distance, the prince heard a crack from behind, as though something had broken. |
| He turned around and said: | He turned around and said: |
| "Heinrich, the carriage is breaking apart." | "Heinrich, the carriage is breaking apart." |
| "No, my lord, the carriage it's not, But one of the bands surrounding my heart, That suffered such great pain, When you were sitting in the well, When you were a frog." | "No, my lord, the carriage it's not, But one of the bands surrounding my heart, That suffered such great pain, When you were sitting in the well, When you were a frog." |
| Once again, and then once again the prince heard a cracking sound and thought that the carriage was breaking apart, but it was the bands springing from faithful Heinrich's heart because his master was now redeemed and happy. | Once again, and then once again the prince heard a cracking sound and thought that the carriage was breaking apart, but it was the bands springing from faithful Heinrich's heart because his master was now redeemed and happy. |
| *Source:* "Der Froschkönig," *Kinder- und Hausmärchen,* 1st ed., vol. 1 (Berlin: Realschulbuchhandlung, 1812), no. 1. | *Source:* "Der Froschkönig," *Kinder- und Hausmärchen,* 7th ed., vol. 1 (Göttingen: Verlag der Dieterichschen Buchhandlung, 1857), no. 1. |

The Grimms' source of this tale is not precisely known, but they apparently heard it while guests of the family Wild in Kassel. Members of this family provided many of their best folktale texts, and in 1825 Wilhelm Grimm married one of the daughters, Henriette Dorothea (Dortchen) Wild.

## Commentary

"The Frog King" by the brothers Grimm, number one in all of their editions, is the quintessential magic tale. It fully deserves its primary position, containing as it does perhaps the most meaningful symbolic expressions of the joys and anxieties of young womanhood of any traditional tale known today.

A bottomless well, a lost golden ball, an authoritarian father, and a despicable frog demanding to eat and sleep with a beautiful princess are among the images and symbols that have made this story a perennial favorite for folklore interpreters. But few, in my opinion, have elucidated the most significant symbolic moment in the tale, the moment when the frustrated princess—acting against her father's wishes and in violation of her own promise—hurls the frog against the wall instead of giving him access to her bed. Most interpretations of this passage dwell on the evolution of the young woman's attitude toward cohabitation from one of repulsion to one of pleasure, but they seldom mention the significance of the timing of this important change. The frog's metamorphosis comes at exactly the moment when the princess throws him against the wall, thus breaking a promise (made under duress, but nonetheless a promise) and openly refusing to obey her father. It is not her acceptance of traditional values but rather her rejection of these standards through her violent assertion of sexual independence that leads to the tale's happy ending.

Not everyone, of course, would be comfortable with such a chain of events. Indeed, the first translation of this famous story to appear in English (translated by Edgar Taylor in 1823) altered the Grimms' conclusion. Instead of throwing the frog against the wall, Taylor's princess allows him to sleep for three nights "upon the pillow of her own little bed," an act of passive acceptance that converts him into a handsome prince. In any event, whether by force (as recorded by the Grimms) or by submission (as claimed by their English translator), the heroine of "The Frog King" quite literally re-forms her future husband.

Pairing the Grimms' first edition of this tale with their final version provides insight into the editing process that they applied to most of their tales. Although the two brothers shared more or less equally the collecting of folktales and their initial publication, Wilhelm, the more poetic and less rigorously scientific of the two, was the moving force behind the subsequent revisions of the tales. As can be seen in "The Frog King," the revisions (most of which were introduced with the second edition of 1819) give the tales more of a contrived literary style, in contrast to the unadorned simplicity of the first edition.

Furthermore, a number of passages were rewritten in order to bring them closer to the bourgeois expectations of the nineteenth-century public. For example, the 1812 text states, "he was supposed to lie next to her in her bed," which was revised to "he was supposed to sleep in her beautiful, clean bed." This is a small, but significant change, for the emphasis moves from the princess's objection to the frog lying "next to her" to the frog lying "in her beautiful, clean bed." The first version describes a violation of her person, whereas the second is only a violation of her clean bed.

Another example is offered with the 1812 phrase "they fell asleep together with pleasure," which was changed to "they fell asleep," the words "together" and "with pleasure" being omitted, even though the prince "was now, according to her father's will, her dear companion and husband." This latter phrase, absent in the 1812 version, somehow legitimizes their spending the night in her bedroom, whether or not they sleep "together" and "with pleasure." Such a justification, almost certainly absent in their oral source, also was deemed unnecessary in the first edition, but helped to give later editions respectability among nineteenth-century book buyers.

## MEMORATE

### "Old Pat Dirane and the Fairies" (John M. Synge)

Old Pat Dirane continues to come up every day to talk to me, and at times I turn the conversation to his experiences of the fairies. He has seen a good many of them, he says, in different parts of the island, especially in the sandy districts north of the slip. They are about a yard high with caps like the "peelers" pulled down over their faces. On one occasion he saw them playing ball in the evening just above the slip, and he says I must avoid that place in the morning or after nightfall for fear they might do me mischief.

He has seen two women who were "away" with them, one a young married woman, the other a girl. The woman was standing by a wall, at a spot he described to me with great care, looking out towards the north. Another night he heard a voice crying out in Irish, "mhathair ta me marbh" ("O mother, I'm killed"), and in the morning there was blood on the wall of his house, and a child in a house not far off was dead.

Yesterday he took me aside, and said he would tell me a secret he had never yet told to any person in the world. "Take a sharp needle," he said, "and stick it in under the collar of your coat, and not one of them will be able to have power on you."

*Source:* John M. Synge, *The Aran Islands* (Dublin: Maunsel and Company, 1907), pt. 1.

*Commentary*

Everyone tells stories of personal experiences, but not necessarily well. A grandparent's opening phrase "When I was your age..." or "I remember when..." understandably causes youngsters to want to be elsewhere. Not everyone reminisces accurately or relates interestingly, but when the storyteller is a master wordsmith like John M. Synge, and his reminiscences are from an inherently fascinating time and place (here the Aran Islands off the west coast of Ireland), then the narrative has an undeniable charm. Such is the case with this memorate, a specialized term used by folklorists to designate an anecdote based on personal experience. Synge, although a gifted playwright, makes no attempts here to adorn his account with literary trappings or to provide it with a dramatic structure; instead he simply recalls the events of his personal encounter with a true believer in fairies.

## MIGRATORY LEGEND

*"The Devil's Bridge" (Switzerland)*

A Swiss herdsman who often visited his girlfriend had either to make his way across the Reuss River with great difficulty or to take a long detour in order to see her. It happened that once he was standing on a very high precipice when he spoke out angrily, "I wish that the devil were here to make me a bridge to the other side!"

In an instant the devil was standing beside him, and said, "If you will promise me the first living thing that walks across it, I will build a bridge for you that you can use from now on to go across and back."

The herdsman agreed, and in a few moments the bridge was finished. However, the herdsman drove a chamois across the bridge ahead of himself, and he followed along behind.

The deceived devil ripped the animal apart and threw the pieces from the precipice.

*Source:* Jacob Grimm and Wilhelm Grimm, "Teufelsbrücke," *Deutsche Sagen,* vol. 1 (Berlin: Nicolaische Buchhandlung, 1816), no. 337.

*Commentary*

The comments accompanying the legend "Mally Dixon" recorded earlier in the chapter about the fluidity of the dividing line between the genres legend and fairy tale also apply here. A migratory legend, as the name suggests, is a legend that travels easily from one locale to another. "The Devil's Bridge" is such a story. Local storytellers claim that dozens of bridges throughout the British Isles, Scandinavia, and continental Europe were created by the devil in return for the sacrifice of the first being to cross over. However, in virtually all instances the devil is cheated out of his intended human victim when an animal is driven or lured across the bridge. Because this legend, as it is normally told, shares many attributes of a fairy tale (for example, the victory of an ordinary hero over a supernatural ogre) and a dramatic structure with a well-defined beginning, middle, and end, it is also classified as a folktale (A-T 1191).

Note on the text: The Reuss River flows from the high Alps near the Saint Gottard Pass into Lake Urn near the Swiss city of Altdorf.

## MYTH

### *"Why People Die Forever" (Blackfoot Indian)*

One time Old Man said to Old Woman, "People will never die."

"Oh!" said Old Woman, "that will never do; because, if people live always, there will be too many people in the world."

"Well," said Old Man, "we do not want to die forever. We shall die for four days and then come to life again."

"Oh, no!" said Old Woman, "it will be better to die forever, so that we shall be sorry for each other."

"Well," said Old Man, "we will decide this way. We will throw a buffalo chip into the water. If it sinks, we will die forever; if it floats, we shall live again."

"Well," said Old Woman, "throw it in."

Now, Old Woman had great power, and she caused the chip to turn into a stone, so it sank. So when we die, we die forever.

*Source:* Clark Wissler and D.C. Duvall, *Mythology of the Blackfoot Indians,* vol. 2, pt. 1 (New York: Anthropological Papers of the American Museum of Natural History, 1908), p. 21.

### *Commentary*

Of all the folktale genres, myth is the most problematic, for over the centuries the word has collected numerous meanings, many of them at variance with the others. Definitions of myth literally range from the sublime to the ridiculous. A myth can be a story associated with religious beliefs (for example, a creation myth) or a fanciful and fallacious theory (such as the myth of racial differences).

However, folklorists are more or less united in defining myth as a traditional story that explains, often in symbolic terms, fundamental issues of humanity. The preceding native American story certainly fits this definition, explaining as it does the mortality of humankind. However, this tale lacks the self-conscious seriousness of most traditional myths. The storyteller seems to revel in the irony of the claim that our primeval parents decided by throwing buffalo dung into water whether future humans would live forever. The ironic playfulness of this account draws it at least partially away from the world of religious myth and into the realm of folktales.

Note on the text: The Blackfoot people of today live primarily in Montana and Alberta.

## NONSENSE TALE

### "Sir Gammer Vans" (England)

Last Sunday morning at six o'clock in the evening as I was sailing over the tops of the mountains in my little boat, I met two men on horseback riding on one mare: so I asked them, "Could they tell me whether the little old woman was dead yet who was hanged last Saturday week for drowning herself in a shower of feathers?" They said they could not positively inform me, but if I went to Sir Gammer Vans he could tell me all about it.

"But how am I to know the house?" said I.

"Ho, 'tis easy enough," said they, "for 'tis a brick house, built entirely of flints, standing alone by itself in the middle of sixty or seventy others just like it."

"Oh, nothing in the world is easier," said I.

"Nothing can be easier," said they. So I went on my way.

Now this Sir G. Vans was a giant, and a bottle maker. And as all giants who are bottle makers usually pop out of a little thumb bottle from behind the door, so did Sir G. Vans.

"How d'ye do?" says he.

"Very well, I thank you," says I.

"Have some breakfast with me?"

"With all my heart," says I.

So he gave me a slice of beer, and a cup of cold veal; and there was a little dog under the table that picked up all the crumbs.

"Hang him," says I.

"No, don't hang him," says he; "for he killed a hare yesterday. And if you don't believe me, I'll show you the hare alive in a basket."

Sir Gammer Vans. Illustration by John D. Batten. Joseph Jacobs, *More English Fairy Tales* (New York and London: G.P. Putnam's Sons, n.d., first published 1894), p. 43.

So he took me into his garden to show me the curiosities. In one corner there was a fox hatching eagle's eggs; in another there was an iron apple tree, entirely covered with pears and lead; in the third there was the hare which the dog killed yesterday alive in the basket; and in the fourth there were twenty-four hipper switches threshing tobacco, and at the sight of me they threshed so hard that they drove the plug through the wall, and through a little dog that was passing by on the other side. I, hearing the dog howl, jumped over the wall; and turned it as neatly inside out as possible, when it ran away as if it had not an hour to live.

Then he took me into the park to show me his deer: and I remembered that I had a warrant in my pocket to shoot venison for his majesty's dinner. So I set fire to my bow, poised my arrow, and shot amongst them. I broke seventeen ribs on one side, and twenty-one and a half on the other; but my arrow passed clean through without ever touching it, and the worst was I lost my arrow: however, I found it again in the hollow of a tree. I felt it; it felt clammy.

I smelt it; it smelt honey. "Oh, ho," said I, "here's a bee's nest," when out sprang a covey of partridges. I shot at them; some say I killed eighteen; but I am sure I killed thirty-six, besides a dead salmon which was flying over the bridge, of which I made the best apple pie I ever tasted.

*Source:* Joseph Jacobs, *More English Fairy Tales* (New York and London: G.P. Putnam's Sons, n.d., first published 1894), pp. 43–45.

### Commentary

Similar to the Norwegian lying tale "Ash Lad Who Made the Princess Say, 'You're a Liar'" discussed earlier in the chapter, this nonsense tale delights in its flight from reality. Even the title hero's name is a contradiction. The word *gammer*, a corruption of *grandmother*, means *old woman*. Sir Gammer Vans's pronouncements are worse than lies; they are non sequiturs and logical impossibilities, but therein lies the story's charm, especially for young listeners, who will take great pleasure in discovering for themselves the adult storyteller's mistakes. Such tales of contradictions and extremes are classified under type 2014. The episode of the hunter's lucky shot is classified under type 1890.

## NOVELLA

### "Griselda" (Giovanni Boccaccio)

Gualtieri, the Marquis of Saluzzo, spent so much time at hunting and other sports that he gave no thought about marrying and establishing a family. His friends and subjects, fearing that old age would overtake him before he acquired an heir, pressured him to take a wife. Finally, more to silence his critics than to satisfy any desire that he might have for matrimony, he resolved to court a beautiful, but poor young woman from a neighboring village. Her family's low station in life would spite those who had so urgently insisted that he marry, and her beauty, he thought, would make living with her at least bearable.

Gualtieri informed Griselda—that was the young woman's name—of his intention to marry her, and asked her if she would accept him as a husband, to love, honor, and obey, for better or for worse, and never criticize him nor question his authority. She readily agreed, and their wedding was celebrated forthwith.

Griselda appeared to be a worthy addition to Gualtieri's noble household, but the marquis, unsure of the depth of her character, decided to test her loyalty and her patience. Thus, soon after the birth of their first child—it was a

Griselda gives up her daughter. Woodcut from an eighteenth-century English chapbook. John Ashton, ed., *Chap-Books of the Eighteenth Century* (London: Chatto and Windus, 1882), p. 177.

beautiful girl—he informed her that his subjects were unhappy with the child and that it was to be put to death. Without hesitation she acceded to her husband's demands and surrendered the child. However, instead of killing the baby girl, Gualtieri had her spirited away and tended in a secret place.

Some time later Griselda gave birth to a son, and her husband, intent on carrying his test still further, berated her and insisted that her child be put to death. She again yielded to his demands without complaint, and as before, he took the child to a secret place where he was well cared for.

Still unsatisfied, Gualtieri devised a final test. He publicly denounced Griselda, claiming that the pope had granted him dispensation to divorce her and to take a more deserving wife. Griselda, wearing only a shift, was sent back to her father. All these indignities she bore without complaint.

As the day approached when Gualtieri, as it was supposed, was to take a new bride, he asked Griselda to return to his palace, for no one knew better how to prepare for guests than did she. Griselda returned to her former residence, now as a cleaning woman and servant, to make preparations for her former husband's wedding.

Gualtieri had his and Griselda's daughter, who was now twelve years old, dressed in bridal clothes, and he presented her to Griselda, who could not have known that this was her own child. "What do you think of my new bride?" he asked.

Griselda replied without guile, "If her wisdom matches her beauty, then the two of you will be very happy together."

At last recognizing Griselda's sincerity, faithfulness, and patience, Gualtieri revealed to her the trials that he had devised to test her loyalty. With tears of joy, she received her children and once again assumed her position as Gualtieri's ever patient and obedient wife.

*Source: The Decameron* (written between 1348 and 1353), day 10, tale 10. Retold and shortened.

### Commentary

The 100 novellas of Boccaccio's *The Decameron* can be called naturalistic fairy tales, for they too typically depict amazing happenings, although unlike their fairy-tale counterparts they rarely rely on the supernatural. These compact tales have served as patterns for writers of short fiction into our own era. Boccaccio's plots (often drawn from folktales) have easily found their way back into the repertories of oral storytellers. Such is the case with "Griselda" (A-T 887), a tale of unchallenged male dominance that was among the most popular stories in medieval and Renaissance Europe. Another famous literary treatment is Geoffrey Chaucer's "The Clerk's Tale" from the *Canterbury Tales* (written between ca. 1380 and 1400). The story is also found in ballads and chapbooks throughout Europe. Readers of Boccaccio's version, which as the last tale in his collection serves as a sort of capstone, should not be led to think that its message of female humiliation and servitude typifies *The Decameron* as a whole. To the contrary, many of Boccaccio's female characters are high-spirited and independent women who pay but little heed to the traditional restrictions of a male-dominated society.

## NURSERY TALE

### "The Three Bears" (England)

Once upon a time there were Three Bears, who lived together in a house of their own, in a wood. One of them was a Little, Small, Wee Bear; and one was a Middle-Sized Bear; and the other was a Great, Huge Bear. They had each a pot for their porridge: a little pot for the Little, Small, Wee Bear; and a middle-sized pot for the Middle Bear; and a great pot for the Great, Huge Bear. And they had each a chair to sit in: a little chair for the Little, Small,

Wee Bear; and a middle-sized chair for the Middle Bear; and a great chair for the Great, Huge Bear. And they had each a bed to sleep in: a little bed for the Little, Small, Wee Bear; a middle-sized bed for the Middle Bear; and a great bed for the Great, Huge Bear.

One day, after they had made the porridge for their breakfast, and poured it into their porridge pots, they walked out into the wood while the porridge was cooling, that they might not burn their mouths by beginning too soon to eat it. And while they were walking, a little girl, named Silver-Hair, came to the house. First she looked in at the window, and then she peeped in at the keyhole; and, seeing nobody in the house, she lifted the latch. The door was not fastened, because the Bears were good Bears, who did nobody any harm, and never suspected that anybody would harm them. So little Silver-Hair opened the door and went in, and well pleased she was when she saw the porridge on the table. If she had been a good little girl, she would have waited till the Bears came home, and then, perhaps, they would have asked her to breakfast, for they were good Bears,—a little rough or so, as the manner of Bears is, but for all that, very good natured and hospitable.

So first she tasted the porridge of the Great, Huge Bear, and that was too hot for her; and then she tasted the porridge of the Middle Bear, and that was too cold for her; and then she went to the porridge of the Little, Small, Wee Bear, and tasted that; and that was neither too hot nor too cold, but just right; and she like it so well, that she ate it all up.

Then little Silver-Hair sat down in the chair of the Great, Huge Bear, and that was too hard for her; and then she sat down in the chair of the Middle Bear, and that was too soft for her; and then she sat down in the chair of the Little, Small, Wee Bear, and that was neither too hard nor too soft, but just right. So she seated herself in it, and there she sat till the bottom of the chair came out, and down she came plump upon the ground.

Then little Silver-Hair went upstairs into the bed chamber in which the Three Bears slept. And first she lay down upon the bed of the Great, Huge Bear, but that was too high at the head for her; and next she lay down upon the bed of the Middle Bear, and that was too high at the foot for her; and then she lay down upon the bed of the Little, Small, Wee Bear; and that was neither too high at the head nor at the foot, but just right. So she covered herself up comfortably, and lay there till she fell fast asleep.

By this time the Three Bears thought their porridge would be cool enough; so they came home to breakfast. Now little Silver-Hair had left the spoon of the Great Huge Bear standing in his porridge.

"**SOMEBODY HAS BEEN AT MY PORRIDGE!**" said the Great, Huge Bear, in his great, rough, gruff voice. And when the Middle Bear looked at his, he saw that the spoon was standing in it too.

"SOMEBODY HAS BEEN AT MY PORRIDGE!" said the Middle Bear, in his middle voice.

Then the Little, Small, Wee Bear looked at his, and there was the spoon in the porridge pot, but the porridge was all gone.

*"Somebody has been at my porridge, and has eaten it all up!"* said the Little, Small, Wee Bear, in his little, small, wee voice.

Upon this the Three Bears, seeing that someone had entered their house, and eaten up the Little, Small, Wee Bear's breakfast, began to look about them. Now little Silver-Hair had not put the hard cushion straight when she rose from the chair of the Great, Huge Bear.

"**SOMEBODY HAS BEEN SITTING IN MY CHAIR!**" said the Great, Huge Bear, in his great, rough, gruff voice.

And little Silver-Hair had squatted down the soft cushion of the Middle Bear.

"SOMEBODY HAS BEEN SITTING IN MY CHAIR!" said the Middle Bear, in his middle voice.

And you know what little Silver-Hair had done to the third chair.

*"Somebody has been sitting in my chair, and has sat the bottom of it out!"* said the Little, Small, Wee Bear, in his little, small, wee voice.

Then the Three Bears thought it necessary that they should make further search; so they went upstairs into their bed chamber. Now little Silver-Hair had pulled the pillow of the Great, Huge Bear out of its place.

"**SOMEBODY HAS BEEN LYING IN MY BED!**" said the Great, Huge Bear, in his great, rough, gruff voice.

And little Silver-Hair had pulled the bolster of the Middle Bear out of its place.

"SOMEBODY HAS BEEN LYING IN MY BED!" said the Middle Bear, in his middle voice.

And when the Little, Small, Wee Bear came to look at his bed, there was the bolster in its place; and the pillow in its place upon the bolster; and upon the pillow was little Silver-Hair's pretty head,—which was not in its place, for she had no business there.

*"Somebody has been lying in my bed,—and here she is!"* said the Little, Small, Wee Bear, in his little, small, wee voice.

Little Silver-Hair had heard in her sleep the great, rough, gruff voice of the Great, Huge Bear; but she was so fast asleep that it was no more to her than the

The wee little bear discovers an intruder in his bed. Illustration by Arthur Rackham. Flora Annie Steel, *English Fairy Tales* (London and New York: Macmillan, 1918), p. 21.

roaring of wind or the rumbling of thunder. And she had heard the middle voice of the Middle Bear, but it was only as if she had heard someone speaking in a dream. But when she heard the little, small, wee voice of the Little, Small, Wee Bear, it was so sharp and so shrill that it awakened her at once. Up she started; and when she saw the Three Bears on one side of the bed she tumbled out at the other, and ran to the window. Now the window was open, because the Bears, like good, tidy Bears as they were, always opened their bed-chamber window when they got up in the morning. Out little Silver-Hair jumped; and away she ran into the wood, and the Three Bears never saw anything more of her.

*Source: Old Mother Hubbard's Fairy Tale Book* (Glasgow: David Bryce and Son, ca. 1860), pp. 117–28.

### Commentary

"The Three Bears" is one of the English-speaking world's all-time favorite children's tales, although it is virtually unknown elsewhere. Demonstrably a traditional tale, "The Three Bears" was first published in 1837 by Robert Southey. The following decades saw the printing of numerous versions, where the intruder is variously depicted as a little old woman (Southey), a fox (Joseph Jacobs), and a girl with silver hair (several tales, including the preceding example). In *Aunt Friendly's Nursery Book* (ca. 1868) she is called "Golden Hair." Not until about 1904 with the publication of *Old Nursery Stories and Rhymes,* illustrated by John Hassall, was she given the now-familiar name "Goldilocks."

The story's appeal for young listeners is understandable. They can readily identify with the girl's innocent misbehavior and undoubtedly experience a sort of catharsis when she escapes unpunished. The repetitive dialogue is easy to follow, and the different voices (in printed versions always marked by different typefaces) produce a dramatic effect especially appreciated by children.

## PARABLE

### *"The Parable of the Mustard Seed" (India)*

Kisagotami is the name of a young girl, whose marriage with the only son of a wealthy man was brought about in true fairy-tale fashion. She had one child, but when the beautiful boy could run alone, it died. The young girl, in her love for it, carried the dead child clasped to her bosom, and went from house to house of her pitying friends asking them to give her medicine for it.

But a Buddhist mendicant, thinking "She does not understand," said to her, "My good girl, I myself have no such medicine as you ask for, but I think I know of one who has."

"O tell me who that is," said Kisagotami.

"The Buddha can give you medicine; go to him," was the answer.

She went to Gautama, and doing homage to him said, "Lord and master, do you know any medicine that will be good for my child?"

"Yes, I know of some," said the teacher.

Now it was the custom for patients or their friends to provide the herbs which the doctors required, so she asked what herbs he would want.

"I want some mustard seed," he said; and when the poor girl eagerly promised to bring some of so common a drug, he added, "You must get it from some house where no son, or husband, or parent, or slave has died."

"Very good," she said, and went to ask for it, still carrying her dead child with her.

The people said, "Here is mustard seed, take it."

But when she asked, "In my friend's house has any son died, or husband, or a parent or slave?" they answered, "Lady, what is this that you say; the living are few, but the dead are many."

Then she went to other houses, but one said, "I have lost a son"; another, "We have lost our parents"; another, "I have lost my slave."

At last, not being able to find a single house where no one had died, her mind began to clear, and summoning up resolution, she left the dead body of her child in a forest, and returning to the Buddha paid him homage.

He said to her, "Have you the mustard seed?"

"My lord," she replied, "I have not; the people tell me that the living are few, but the dead are many."

Then he talked to her on that essential part of his system—the impermanence of all things, till her doubts were cleared away, and, accepting her lot, she became a disciple and entered the first path.

*Source:* T.W. Rhys Davids, *Buddhism: Being a Sketch of the Life and Teachings of Gautama, the Buddha* (London: Society for Promoting Christian Knowledge, 1907), pp. 133–34.

*Commentary*

Parables have been used by religious teachers of all faiths to explain and promote higher principles. These stories provide a this-worldly context for abstract values. Typically such narratives do not claim to be true accounts of actual events, but rather plausible stories that describe typical human behavior, present moral choices, and depict consequences, thus helping the listeners to clarify their own beliefs and to set their own courses.

## PARODY

### *"The Hare" (Wilhelm Busch)*

The hare sat contentedly in the cabbage patch eating. Nearby a little white lamb was grazing. Then suddenly the wicked wolf came and carried the little lamb away. The hare saw it all. Jumping up, he ran to the farmer and cried, "Oh dear, oh dear, the wicked wolf carried away your little lamb!" So the farmer picked up a stout cudgel, and while saying, "Thank you, my dear hare!" he struck him dead. Then with a laugh he muttered, "Now my cabbage is safe."

And anyone who asks, "What is the moral of the story?" is just as stupid as the hare.

*Source:* Wilhelm Busch, *Stipstörchen für Äuglein und Öhrchen* (Munich: Verlag von Bassermann, 1880). Freely translated from rhymed verse.

*Commentary*

Wilhelm Busch, whose stories in pictures and words are forerunners to the comic strip, was a master of satire, both visual and verbal. His drawings are caricatures, and his language witty (his best-known works are all in rhymed verse). The preceding piece imitates an Aesopic fable, with the rhymed versions of La Fontaine first coming to mind. But in place of the understated elegance and charm that cloak a fable by La Fontaine, here we have intentional rustic clumsiness. And instead of providing the traditional moral, Busch sarcastically questions the reader's intelligence for expecting any such pronouncement.

## PROVERB

*"Every Fairy Tale" (Germany)*

Every fairy tale has someone who believes it.

*Source:* Karl Friedrich Wilhelm Wander, *Sprichwörter-Lexikon: Ein Hausschatz für das deutsche Volk,* vol. 3 (Leipzig: F.A. Brockhaus, 1867), col. 455.

*Commentary*

Proverbs, it can be argued, are the world's shortest folktales, typically consisting of only a single sentence. Because of their brevity, proverbs often depend on double meanings for their impact. Here we have a proverb about fairy tales, a phrase with more than one meaning, both in English and in the original German. A fairy tale (German *Märchen*) is both a literary genre and a lie. Thus the preceding proverb can mean either, "Every lie will be believed by someone"; or, "Every story (however magical and fantastic) will be accepted as the truth by someone."

## RELIGIOUS TALE

*"The Genesis of the Hid-Folk" (Iceland)*

Once upon a time, God Almighty came to visit Adam and Eve. They received him with joy, and showed him everything they had in the house. They also brought their children to him, to show him, and these he found promising and full of hope.

Then he asked Eve whether she had no other children than these whom she now showed him.

She said, "None."

But it so happened that she had not finished washing them all, and, being ashamed to let God see them dirty, had hidden the unwashed ones. This God knew well, and said therefore to her, "What man hides from God, God will hide from man."

These unwashed children became forthwith invisible, and took up their abode in mounds, and hills, and rocks. From these are the elves descended, but we men from those of Eve's children whom she had openly and frankly shown to God. And it is only by the will and desire of the elves themselves that men can ever see them.

*Source:* Jón Arnason, *Icelandic Legends,* trans. George E.J. Powell and Eiríkur Magnússon (London: R. Bentley, 1864), pp. 19–20.

### Commentary

This tale, explaining the creation of elves and their relationship to humans, borders on a myth; but its playful aspects bring it back to the realm of folktale (A-T 758). Like many other religious tales circulating outside of authorized theological channels, this story combines canonized beliefs (characters from the Bible), popular superstitions (belief in elves), and almost burlesque humor (Eve trying to hide her unwashed children from God). The tale, combining aspects of myth, legend, and jest, illustrates the difficulties of genre definition.

## RIDDLE

### "Oedipus Solves the Riddle of the Sphinx" (Greece)

Laius, king of Thebes, was warned by an oracle that there was danger to his throne and life if his new-born son should be allowed to grow up. He therefore committed the child to a herdsman with orders to destroy him; but the herdsman, moved with pity, yet not daring entirely to disobey, tied up the child by the feet and left him hanging to the branch of a tree. In this condition the infant was found by a peasant, who carried him to his master and mistress, King and Queen of the Corinthians, by whom he was adopted and called Oedipus, or Swollen-foot.

After reaching manhood Oedipus consulted the oracle at Delphi concerning his parentage, and was told that he should not return to his homeland, for should he do so he would kill his father and commit incest with his mother. Believing he was a Corinthian, Oedipus immediately turned his chariot in

The Sphinx, from an Italian tomb painting (ca. 700–475 B.C.).
Richard Huber, *Treasury of Fantastic and Mythological Creatures*
(New York: Dover, 1981), plate 9. Dover Pictorial Archive Series.

the opposite direction in order to escape from the oracle's curse. Underway he encountered Laius, accompanied by a single attendant. They met in a narrow road, and when Oedipus refused to yield, the king's attendant killed one of his horses. Filled with rage, Oedipus slew both Laius and the attendant without knowing that he had thus killed his own father.

Shortly after this event the city of Thebes was afflicted with a monster which infested the highroad. It was called the Sphinx. It had the body of a lion and the head of a woman. It lay crouched on the top of a rock, and stopped all travelers who came that way, proposing to them a riddle, with the condition that those who could solve it should pass safely by, but those who failed should be killed. No one had yet succeeded in solving it, and all had been slain. Oedipus, undaunted by these alarming accounts, boldly advanced to the trial.

The Sphinx asked him, "What animal goes on four feet in the morning, at noon on two, and in the evening on three?"

Oedipus replied, "Man, who in childhood crawls on hands and knees, in adulthood walks erect, and in old age walks with the aid of a staff."

The Sphinx was so mortified at the solving of her riddle that she cast herself down from the rock and perished.

The gratitude of the people for their deliverance was so great that they made Oedipus their king, giving him in marriage their widowed queen Jocasta. Oedipus, ignorant of his parentage, thus married his own mother, having already unwittingly killed his own father. These horrors remained undiscovered, till at length Thebes was afflicted with famine and pestilence, and the oracle being consulted, the double crime of Oedipus came to light. Jocasta put an end to her own life, and Oedipus, seized with madness, tore out his eyes and wandered away from Thebes, and after a period of miserable wandering, he found the termination of his wretched life.

*Source:* Thomas Bulfinch, *The Age of Fable* (first published 1855), ch. 16. Text slightly amended. Bulfinch's principal source: Apollodorus (falsely attributed), *Library,* bk. 3, secs. 48–56 (second century A.D.).

### Commentary

Riddles are closely related to folk narratives, and many traditional storytellers were also gifted riddlers. It is thus quite natural that numerous folktales are built around riddles, as, for example, the famous tale of Oedipus (A-T 931). Here Oedipus solves the fateful riddle apparently without foreknowledge and without trickery. In other riddling tales the hero's own experiences lead to the solution of a riddle or enable him to set a riddle that another person cannot solve (typically a princess, whose hand he thus wins). Oedipus, in contrast, solves the Sphinx's riddle with pure brain power, or possibly through the intervention of fate, for the riddle in this tale is merely a means to an end, the end being the tragic but predicted marriage of Oedipus to his own mother.

## ROMANTIC TALE

### "How the Wicked Sons Were Duped" (Kashmir)

A very wealthy old man, imagining that he was on the point of death, sent for his sons and divided his property among them. However, he did not die for several years afterwards; and miserable years many of them were. Besides the weariness of old age, the old fellow had to bear with much abuse and cruelty from his sons. Wretched, selfish ingrates! Previously they vied with one another in trying to please their father, hoping thus to receive more money, but now they had received their patrimony, they cared not how soon he left them—nay, the sooner the better, because he was only a needless trouble and expense. This, as we may suppose, was a great grief to the old man.

One day he met a friend and related to him all his troubles. The friend sympathized very much with him, and promised to think over the matter, and call in a little while and tell him what to do. He did so; in a few days he visited the old man and put down four bags full of stones and gravel before him.

"Look here, friend," said he. "Your sons will get to know of my coming here today, and will inquire about it. You must pretend that I came to discharge a long-standing debt with you, and that you are several thousands of rupees richer than you thought you were. Keep these bags in your own hands, and on no account let your sons get to them as long as you are alive. You will soon find them change their conduct towards you. Salám. I will come again soon to see how you are getting on."

When the young men got to hear of this further increase of wealth they began to be more attentive and pleasing to their father than ever before. And thus they continued to the day of the old man's demise, when the bags were greedily opened, and found to contain only stones and gravel!

*Source:* J. Hinton Knowles, *Folk-Tales of Kashmir* (London: Kegan Paul, Trench, Trübner, and Company, 1893), pp. 241–42.

### Commentary

The word *romantic,* when defining a literary genre, has little to do with the boy-meets-girl romances of popular novels and films. Instead, the word, derived from an Old French term, denotes a story marked by unexpected turns. The unexpected turn in "How the Wicked Sons Were Duped" (A-T 982) is, of course, how the wicked sons were duped. The tale's surprise ending comes as no surprise to the reader, who is privy to the secret from its inception, but only to the selfish sons when they learn that their expected second inheritance is worthless.

The plot suggests a number of moral conclusions, especially for old people. Among these are: Do not prematurely give away your life's savings. And: Deception and trickery are acceptable means of acquiring benefits that are due to you, if you cannot get them otherwise.

## SAINT'S LEGEND

### "The Dragon" (Germany)

In ancient times a fiery dragon came to the area above the village of Ebringen and disappeared into a cave on the southern slope of Schönberg Mountain. The heathen population revered the dragon as a god, to whom from time to time a human sacrifice had to be presented for its nourishment. Finally the lot fell on the charming and youthful daughter of the prince who resided at Schneeburg Castle.

At the same time there lived at the foot of Schönberg Mountain a young knight who had secretly converted to Christianity. When he learned of the horrible fate awaiting the prince's daughter he bravely resolved to kill the all-powerful dragon. Well armored and with a mighty spear in his right hand, he mounted his valiant steed and, trusting in his god, he advanced toward the hellish beast.

Greedily awaiting the fearlessly advancing attacker, the monster lay before his cave, his jaws opened and fuming with poison. The proud and foaming steed reared up, but powerful arms swiftly and surely held the reigns and aimed the spear. Hissing, the death-delivering projectile flew into the monster's open throat.

The prince and the people received the news of the young knight's brave and liberating deed with jubilation. And with jubilation they praised the battle god who had granted such great power to the warrior. To commemorate the deed, stone crosses were erected on the houses in Ebringen, above which the dragon had formerly flown. Some of these stone crosses still exist on gables in the village. The daring knight, whose name was George, was now revered as a saint, and thus the place where he lived was later called Saint George.

St. George slays the dragon. Illustration by Arthur Rackham. Flora Annie Steel, *English Fairy Tales* (London and New York: Macmillan, 1918), p. 1.

Until a short time ago, an annual festival was held there every April 23, the saint's day, and peasants from the region would ride their horses around the church three times, asking Saint George's protection for their horses.

*Source:* J. Waibel and H. Flamm, "Der Drache," *Badisches Sagenbuch: Sagen Freiburgs und des Breisgaus* (Freiburg im Breisgau: J. Waibel, 1899), pp. 74–75.

### Commentary

The word *legend* formerly referred to a tale about a Christian saint, and from the Middle Ages onward such tales were an important part of European literature and folklore. Many legends of saints contradict one another or are so steeped in magic and fantasy (miracles, reincarnations, and mythical beasts) that even the faithful find them incredible.

No saint has prompted greater storytelling activity than Saint George, one of the most durable legendary heroes in the Western world. According to tradition, he was born in England in the fourth century and served in the imperial army in Asia Minor. He has been the patron saint of England since the Middle Ages and is among the greatest saints for the Eastern Orthodox Christian Churches. His famous duel with the dragon is set in various Holy Land locations plus North Africa, and diverse European countries, including Germany, as evidenced by the preceding narrative.

Dragons, an obvious symbol for evil in many religious traditions, play prominent roles in fairy tales as well. Tales about dragon slayers are classified as type 300 and are found around the world.

## TALL TALE

### "Baron Münchhausen and the Frozen Horn" (Germany)

It was my misfortune to be traveling from Russia to my homeland in Germany during one of the coldest winters ever to befall Europe. The sun itself was so frostbitten that even to the present day it is suffering from the consequences. Traveling by post carriage, we came to a narrow passageway between tall thorn hedges. I urged the coachman to sound his horn so that any carriage approaching us from the opposite direction could hear the signal and avoid a collision. He raised the horn to his lips and blew into the horn with all his might, but to no avail, for not a single sound came out.

The consequence of this unexplainable event was that a carriage coming from the opposite direction met us in the narrow passageway and could not get past. I jumped from my carriage and immediately unhitched the horses. Then I lifted the carriage, complete with all the baggage, onto my shoulders and jumped with it over the hedge, which was about nine feet high. In retrospect this was no small achievement, considering how heavy the carriage was. Then I jumped back into the road behind the other carriage. Hurrying back to our horses, I picked up one under each arm and jumped over the hedge twice more. We hitched them up and arrived safely at the inn where we were to take shelter for the night. Recovering from our adventure, the coachman hung his horn near the kitchen fire, and I took a seat across from him.

Gentlemen, listen to what happened next! Suddenly we heard a tra-ra-ra! To our surprise we now discovered why the coachman had been unable to blow his horn. The sounds had frozen solidly inside his horn and were just now thawing out and sounding forth loudly and clearly. We heard a Prussian march in addition to a number of other pieces, including the evening song "All the Woods Are Quiet Now." This final piece brought an end to our thaw-entertainment, and this is also the end of the story of my trip to Russia.

*Source:* Gottfried August Bürger, trans., *Wunderbare Reisen zu Wasser und Lande des Freyherrn von Münchhausen* (Göttingen: Dieterich, 1786), ch. 5.

Slightly shortened. Bürger's source: Rudolf Erich Raspe, *Baron Munchausen's Narrative of His Marvellous Travels and Campaigns in Russia* (Oxford, 1785).

*Commentary*

Travel accounts that mix fantasy and exaggeration with fact are found in the literature and folklore of all cultures. Whether such tales present themselves as "make-believe" or as authentic experiences, the framework of the journey provides a credible link between the listener's everyday world and the narrator's account. Homer's *Odyssey,* the Greek *Alexander Romance,* the tales of Sinbad the Sailor from the *1,001 Nights, Gulliver's Travels* by Jonathan Swift, the travel novels by Jules Verne, and *The Wonderful Wizard of Oz* by L. Frank Baum are typical—each in its own manner—of fantastic travel accounts.

A particularly successful collection of stories that superimpose fanciful adventures onto believable journeys comprises the tall tales of "the Liar Baron," Karl Friedrich Hieronymus Freiherr von Münchhausen, also known as Baron von Münchhausen, or Baron Munchausen. A number of the baron's exploits, which have many analogues in folklore and in the anecdote literature of previous ages, were published in a German periodical between 1781 and 1783. In 1785 Rudolf Erich Raspe, a German exile living in England, incorporated the stories into a continuous account, publishing them anonymously under the title *Baron Munchausen's Narrative of His Marvellous Travels and Campaigns in Russia.* Gottfried August Bürger brought the tales back to their German homeland with his translation of 1786.

The man who tethered his horse to a stake protruding from deep snow, then discovered—after the snow melted—that he actually had used the top of a church steeple for a hitching post (A-T 1960Z); weather so cold that a musical instrument played outdoors had to be brought inside and thawed out before one could hear it (A-T 1889F); the hunter who shot a deer with cherry stones, then saw the same deer—a few years later—with a cherry tree growing from its head (A-T 1889C)—these are but a few of the baron's adventures. Such self-revealing lies combine unpretentious wit with elaborate irony. One exaggeration builds upon another until the structure collapses under its own weight. The hardiness and longevity of these tall tales and others of their kind prove that we don't always resent being lied to.

The liar baron's stories (whether they came from his pen or from another source) have prospered especially well in frontier and rural America. In fact, it would be difficult to find a collection of American folk narratives that does not contain a generous portion of fish stories, hunter's lies, farmer's exaggerations, and other tall tales.

## TRICKSTER TALE

### "The Tiger and the Shadow" (Malaya)

There was a saltlick in the jungle to which all the beasts of the forest resorted, but they were greatly afraid by reason of an old tiger which killed one of them every day. At length, therefore, Plando the mouse-deer said to the tiger, "Why not permit me to bring you a beast every day, to save you from hunting for your food?"

The tiger consented, and Plando went off to make arrangement with the beasts. But he could not persuade any of them to go, and after three days he set off, taking nobody with him but Kuwis the smallest of the flying squirrels.

On their arrival Plando said to the tiger, "I could not bring you any of the other beasts because the way was blocked by a fat old tiger with a flying squirrel sitting astride its muzzle."

On hearing this the tiger exclaimed, "Let us go and find it and drive it away."

The three therefore set out, the flying squirrel perched upon the tiger's muzzle and the mouse-deer sitting astride upon its hind quarters. On reaching the river, the mouse-deer pointed to the tiger's likeness in the water and exclaimed, "Look there! That is the fat old tiger that I saw."

On hearing this, the tiger sprang into the river to attack his own shadow [reflection], and was drowned immediately.

*Source:* Walter Skeat, *Fables and Folk-Tales from an Eastern Forest* (Cambridge: Cambridge University Press, 1901), pp. 28–29. Skeat's source: "This tale is from Ulu Kedah."

### Commentary

Trickster tales are found in all cultures. Their all-too-human characters are often cast as animals, a device that gives the storyteller at least some distance from the plot, and thus some protection from the persecution that might follow if powerful humans saw themselves targeted in the tales. The powerful are indeed the victims in most trickster tales, while the tricksters themselves nearly always represent the weak and the oppressed. The appeal of such stories is self-evident, for here the expected advantages of wealth and position turn against their holders, often fatally, and in the end a little person triumphs.

The fable of the ruthless beast who is tricked into attacking his own reflection (A-T 92) is told around the world, from China to the American South.

Note on the text: Skeat spells the hero's name *P'lando*.

## UNFINISHED TALE

### *"The Treasure" (Italy)*

Once upon a time there was a prince who studied and racked his brains so much that he learned magic and the art of finding hidden treasures. One day he discovered a treasure in a bank, let us say the bank of Ddisisa. "Oh," he says, "now I am going to get it out." But to get it out it was necessary that ten million million ants should cross one by one the river Gianquadara (let us suppose it was that one) in a bark made of the half shell of a nut. The prince puts the bark in the river and begins to make the ants pass over. One, two, three,—and he is still doing it.

Here the person who is telling the story pauses and says, "We will finish this story when the ants have finished passing over."

*Source:* Thomas Frederick Crane, *Italian Popular Tales* (Boston and New York: Houghton, Mifflin, and Company, 1885), no. 39, p. 156.

### *Commentary*

This tale (A-T 2300) has an obvious kinship to the endless stories (A-T 2320) discussed elsewhere in this chapter. These trick tales play an obvious role in a storyteller's repertory: to bring story-time to a close, for not even the most patient listener will pay attention very long to the continuing loops and endless repetitions inherent in such tales.

## URBAN LEGEND

### *"Russian Soldiers" (Austria)*

My friend Horst Grillmayer has a friend who had Russian soldiers quartered in his house during the occupation, and they had never seen a bathroom. They thought the toilet was a well, and drew water from it for drinking, and they used the bathtub for a coal bin. But the funniest thing was to watch one of them try to ride a bicycle. Not a one of them could keep his balance, and they were always getting their feet caught in the spokes.

*Source:* Personal recollection, Steyr, Austria, 1959.

### *Commentary*

Once again it was the proverbial "friend of a friend" (FOAF) who experienced the events that form the basis of a story known by many but difficult or impossible to verify. Tales about ethnic minorities unable to cope with the accoutrements of an ostensibly superior culture are common (for example, the many tasteless Polish jokes currently circulating in America, or the Irish jokes of a generation or two earlier). Especially popular are tales, often told as true accounts, about "technically challenged" individuals who injure themselves while misusing or who are frightened by modern mechanical devices (A-T 1319A*).

## Four

# Scholarship and Approaches

### PLATO AND SOCRATES

From the earliest times storytellers, their audiences, and interpreters have theorized about the nature, the extended meanings, and the impact of made-up tales. Plato, through the words of Socrates in *The Republic* (360 B.C.), criticizes adults for telling casual tales to children, tales that might instill beliefs that would prove untrue when the children mature. Even if such tales attempt to teach higher truths through symbols, a young person—says Plato's Socrates—cannot judge what is allegorical and what is literal; therefore fantasy tales should not be told to children.

This premise is possibly the oldest recorded example of folktale scholarship. A distinguished philosopher postulates a theory, cites examples, and draws a generalizing conclusion. Variations on Plato's position concerning the potential dangers of fantasy literature have surfaced repeatedly—even to the present time—with myths, fairy tales, comic books, and television successively and repeatedly coming under attack.

For the most part Plato's rejection of fantasy literature for children has not found favor among folktale interpreters, who more often have sought to show how the qualities of such stories can promote desirable behavior, both for children and adults. These qualities may be hidden behind a screen of symbolism, which gives scholars and interpreters a double function: to point out a tale's important and possibly hidden details, and then to explain the meaning of those details in literal language.

## GESTA ROMANORUM

One example of an early European story collector who thus integrated a body of folklore and literature into an ideological system is the anonymous English cleric who in about 1330 compiled the *Gesta Romanorum* (Deeds of the Romans). Confirming his personal faith, he saw a Christian allegory in each tale of this collection. He neither asks who may have first told a given tale nor what may have been the original author's intentions. His only interest is how the tales will edify and enlighten his contemporaries within a Christian context.

Approximately 30 of the 283 entries in the *Gesta Romanorum* are folktales with an oral tradition apart from written literature. One story in particular, known generically as "An Ungrateful Beast Is Tricked Back into Captivity" (A-T 155), has a very wide dissemination as a folktale. Versions of this tale have been collected on virtually every continent. The example from the *Gesta Romanorum* differs from other international versions only in small details. Titled here "Of Nature and the Returns of Ingratitude," its summary follows:

An emperor who was hunting in a certain wood came upon a serpent that some shepherds had captured and bound to a tree. Moved by pity he released the serpent, which immediately began to bite him. "Why do you repay good with evil?" asked the emperor, to which the serpent replied, "I cannot act against my nature, and by my nature I am an enemy to man." They walked along arguing their case until they came upon a philosopher, whom they asked to judge between them. "I cannot judge the matter," said the philosopher, "until I see things as they stood before the man intervened." To demonstrate how the events had started, the serpent allowed himself to be bound to the tree once again. "Can you free yourself?" asked the philosopher. "I cannot," replied the serpent. "Then die," said the philosopher. "That is my sentence. You always were ungrateful to man, and you always will be." So saying, he sent the emperor on his way, admonishing him never again to repeat his folly. "Remember," said the philosopher in parting, "that the serpent is only influenced by his natural propensities."

The anonymous editor then appends to this story an "application," which tells his readers how they are to interpret this fantasy tale. He explains: "The emperor is any good ecclesiastic, the wood is the world, and the serpent is the devil. The shepherds are the prophets, patriarchs, Christian preachers, etc. The philosopher is a discreet confessor."

This is one of the most widespread folktales in the world. Versions have been collected throughout Europe, Africa, Asia, and the Americas. The fourteenth-century churchman who built this story into the *Gesta Romano-*

*rum* did not find it difficult to turn it into an allegory, with each character and element symbolizing some larger aspect of Christianity. The text lends itself to such an interpretation, but essentially the same tale also has been told throughout the centuries by Buddhists, Hindus, Jews, Muslims, and secularists, all of whom have seen different meanings behind it—or no symbolic meaning at all, instead simply enjoying the story for the sake of its clever plot.

Long-lived and widely distributed tales of many types share this quality with "An Ungrateful Beast Is Tricked Back into Captivity," having the capacity to speak at many levels to audiences of different backgrounds. Such diversity of appeal goes far to explain the longevity and diffusion of most traditional folktales. A story that resonates with both genders, all ages, and different socioeconomic and educational levels—often for quite different reasons—has a greater chance of being remembered and retold than does a tale with a narrower audience appeal.

This rather self-evident observation leads to a bold conclusion: Even folktale interpreters who contradict one another can be justified in their conclusions, each one having selected a different aspect of the tale for examination. An old saw claims that everything can be proven through the Bible and Shakespeare. Folktales can readily be added to that list of authorities.

## DEGRADED MYTHS

The first systematic scholars of folktales were Jacob and Wilhelm Grimm. Today their names are familiar around the world because of their collection *Kinder- und Hausmärchen* (Children's and Household Tales), but the brothers (especially Jacob) were also insightful and prolific scholars in linguistics and medieval studies. Both held professorships at the University of Göttingen in Germany, but they were dismissed, along with five other colleagues—the so-called Göttingen Seven—for waging a formal protest against a constitutional violation of Ernst August, King of Hannover. The Grimm brothers received many offers for new positions, finally accepting professorships at the University of Berlin.

Although modern folklorists have criticized the Grimms for the liberties they took in formulating tales in their own words, rather than reporting them verbatim as they received them from informants, their folkloric methods were in many regards pioneering. Unlike their predecessors (or most of their immediate followers) they recorded the names of their informants, listed variants, and drew comparisons with analogues found in literature and in the folklore of other countries.

As folktale scholars their principal interest was less in the interpretation of tales and more in the investigation of origins. The Grimms' observation that numerous elements of their tales were very ancient led them to the conclusion that many folktales, magic tales in particular, were surviving fragments of primeval myths. They also recognized that various motifs, sometimes entire plots, were told in widely separated places. Drawing on their (especially Jacob's) pioneering research in comparative philology, they concluded that these primeval myths had been common to a unified Indo-European people, the same folk that once spoke the original Indo-European language from which most languages spoken between India and northwestern Europe demonstrably evolved.

Anticipating and contradicting later theories, they postulated that these erstwhile myths had neither migrated from some distant land of origin (diffusion) nor been created independently and concurrently by imaginative storytellers speaking different languages and representing diverse cultures (polygenesis). Instead, they theorized, the myths from which fairy tales devolved were universal (at least throughout the Indo-European language area) and of such great antiquity as to be considered timeless. They recognized that fairy-tale creation was an ongoing process, with some elements of even traditional tales being relatively new. They also accepted the position that some tales migrate from one culture to another, although they thought that such instances were unusual.

Many European folktales contain motifs that support the Grimms' view that such tales are degraded myths. For example, a famous episode from Germanic mythology, recorded in the Old Norse *Saga of the Volsungs,* tells how Brynhild (apparently one of the Valkyries who were charged with deciding who would survive and who would perish on the field of battle) struck down a warrior whom Odin had promised victory. As punishment the Norse god stabbed her with a sleeping thorn. She remained in a trancelike sleep until awakened by the hero Sigurd (elsewhere called Siegfried). Fairy-tale lovers will immediately see in this myth elements of the familiar fairy tales "Sleeping Beauty" (A-T 410) and "Little Snow-White" (A-T 709).

Another important example is provided by the tale "Frau Holle" (Grimm 24), where an underground benefactress magically rewards a kind and industrious girl, then punishes her unkind and lazy stepsister. Well into the nineteenth century legends circulated throughout Germany depicting miracles performed by a supernatural being named Frau Holle (or a linguistic variation thereof). Apparently Frau Holle was an important goddess among the ancient Germans, but one who by the nineteenth century was remembered only through legends and fairy tales.

The vast subject of fairy lore provided the Grimms with further examples of degraded myths. Their interest in the hidden people is documented promi-

Cover illustration from a nineteenth-century textbook on Norse mythology, with the name Othinn (Odin, Wotan) spelled in runes. Rasmus B. Anderson, *Norse Mythology*, 7th ed. (Chicago: Scott, Foresman, 1907), cover illustration. First edition and copyright 1875.

nently in their 1826 translation (with a lengthy introductory essay) of *Fairy Legends and Traditions of the South of Ireland* by Thomas Crofton Croker. Jacob also wrote extensively about the underground people in his *Deutsche Mythologie* (German Mythology, first edition 1835). There is ample evidence that active belief in fairies, elves, and other such hidden people was widespread and sincere throughout the British Isles, Scandinavia, and northern Europe, even into the twentieth century.

Many fairy tales, now using the term in its literal sense, reinforce the Grimms' view that magic tales told as household entertainment do indeed hearken back to rituals and myths that formerly were cornerstones of religious belief. Three of the Grimms' tales (grouped under the collective title "The Elves" as number 39) describe human encounters with elves, which can be (and have been) related either as true experiences or as fantasy tales. It is not illogical to conclude, as did the Grimms, that in some instances the former degraded into the latter.

The relationship between myth and folktale continues to be studied to the present day. A few of the many scholars who have made contributions in this comparative work are James G. Frazer, Bronislaw Malinowski, Joseph Campbell, and Mircea Eliade.

## SOLAR MYTHOLOGISTS

The Grimms' mythological views were well received in England, especially as interpreted by Max Müller, a German-born Sanskrit scholar who emigrated to England and became a distinguished Oxford professor. His essay "Comparative Mythology" (1856) advanced the theory that a process called "disease of language" gave rise to new myths when the original names of deities were forgotten, mispronounced, or mistranslated by succeeding generations. As a prime example he offered the Sanskrit and Greek deity names Dyâus and Zeus, each a sky god. The similarities between their names suggested to Müller that both were mutations from a primeval Indo-European sky deity.

Furthermore, folktale motifs dealing with sun, moon, stars, sky, clouds, winds, and the like were seen as distorted descendents from ancient sky-god myths. Müller's claims were immensely influential, dominating English folktale scholarship for the next quarter century. It was not difficult for solar or celestial mythologists (as they came to be known) to find evidence for their claims. For example, they saw in the predilection of fairy tales for the numbers 7 and 12 symbolic battles between light and dark (7 day-night cycles per week and 12 moon cycles per year).

Furthermore, they immediately jumped upon any fairy tale that used celestial names or concepts in its text—for example, Giambattista Basile's version of "Sleeping Beauty" (A-T 410), which he titles "Sun, Moon, and Thalia," the first two words being the names that Thalia, the sleeping beauty, gives to the twins that are born to her while she sleeps. Similarly, the heroine in Charles Perrault's version of the same tale, "Sleeping Beauty in the Wood," names her first children Dawn and Day. If heroines name their children after the sun, the moon, the dawn, and the day, then surely their stories evolved from myths depicting the struggle between night and day, or so dictated the logic of the solar mythologists. Nor did they need names like Sun, Moon, Dawn, and Day to conclude that virtually every fairy tale, whatever the apparent plot, was actually about the primeval conflict between light and dark.

This chapter in folklore scholarship offers lessons to students in all fields. Stith Thompson, arguably the twentieth century's most eminent folktale scholar, looking back at the record of the solar mythologists, summarizes: "Proceeding from a few major premises, which they seem to have found entirely by introspection, they built up a structure so fantastic that the modern reader who ventures to examine it begins to doubt his own sanity" (*The Folktale,* p. 371).

The view that all Indo-European folklore derived from a primeval and unified belief system was immensely satisfying to nineteenth-century European intellectuals. However, as the century advanced two of the Grimm brothers' theories concerning the propagation of folktales came under increasing criticism. As previously mentioned, they held that neither polygenesis (the independent invention of essentially the same tale in different places) nor diffusion (the migration of a tale to outlying regions, following its creation at once specific place) accounted for the fact that similar tales were found at widely separated locations. Instead, they held that such tales had devolved from a common myth. The Grimms' collection and publication efforts prompted scholars and amateurs throughout Europe to compile similar works, typically focused on a single national or ethnic group. This collection activity amassed substantial evidence that folk and fairy tales do indeed migrate, and that diffusion, in one form or another, is the best explanation for their dispersal.

## THE INDIAN SCHOOL

If folktales migrate, then the question naturally arises as to where the stories were first told and when and by what routes they came to their current homes. The German Sanskrit scholar Theodor Benfey, through his study of comparative grammar and his translation and analysis of *The Panchatantra,* concluded that India was the principal source of Europe's folktales, with the exception of Aesopic fables, which demonstrably originated in Greece. He theorized that the migration of Indian tales to Europe began as a consequence of Alexander the Great's invasion of India (fourth century B.C.) and reached a high point during the Middle Ages by way of Arabic intermediaries.

However, folktale collections published subsequent to Benfey's pronouncements failed to establish the close relationship between Indian and European folktales that he postulated. Indeed, only about half of the tales in *The Panchatantra*—which according to Benfey should have been the mother lode of European folktales—are commonly found in Europe. And many of these are animal fables, which demonstrably migrated in antiquity from the Mediterranean area to India, not the other way around. Nonetheless, Benfey's scholarship brought him followers throughout Europe, including W.A. Clouston in Scotland, Emmanuel Cosquin in France, and Reinhold Köhler in Germany. Even if Benfey and his followers overstated their case, there is still evidence that many European fairy tales did indeed originate in India.

## ANTHROPOLOGICAL APPROACHES

Folktale study in Great Britain, beginning in the late 1870s, was increasingly dominated by a group of scholars centered around the Folk-Lore Society, founded in 1878. Trained as historians, classicists, medievalists, and the like, they shared disdain for the solar mythologists and enthusiasm for the developing academic disciplines of cultural anthropology and folklore. Many were involved in the discovery, documentation, and interpretation of British, Celtic, Saxon, and Norse antiquities, ranging from stone monuments to holiday customs. Their findings were published in the society's quarterly journal *Folk-Lore* as well as by a number of publishing houses—for example, David Nutt—that came to specialize in folklore monographs.

The ever-expanding British Empire gave them access to cultures around the world, resulting in a large number of published folktale collections from remote areas, including Australia, India, Ceylon (Sri Lanka), Africa, and many more. They were also active in their own islands, producing exemplary folktale collections from the Orkneys to Land's End and throughout Ireland.

Their interests were eclectic and their approaches nondogmatic. The common denominator of their work was cultural anthropology. Among the members of this group were Edward Clodd, Laurence Gomme, Edwin Sidney Hartland, Joseph Jacobs, Andrew Lang, Alfred Nutt, and E.B. Tylor.

Illustration by John D. Batten from an advertisement for fairy tales from the British Empire by Joseph Jacobs, published by David Nutt (1896). Advertising matter appended to Mrs. K. Langloh Parker, *Australian Legendary Tales* (London: David Nutt, 1896).

Working in the same academic climate as those researchers was James G. Frazer, a Cambridge cultural anthropologist. His reputation was established with the publication of *The Golden Bough* in 1890. This monumental work, which over a number of years expanded to 12 volumes, synthesized and compared religious and magic rituals of primitive cultures from around the world and from ancient times to the nineteenth century. Frazer concluded that fairy tales, nursery rhymes, and other kinds of folklore were remnants of ancient narratives that once accompanied and explained fertility rites, a view not far removed from the one held by the Grimms.

The influence of the nineteenth-century anthropological school continues through the work of such recent British folklorists as Katherine M. Briggs,

Iona and Peter Opie, and Ruth L. Tongue. Folktale scholars from other countries pursuing similar anthropology-based research include Richard M. Dorson (North America), Lutz Röhrich (Germany), and Linda Dégh (Hungary).

## THE FINNISH SCHOOL

As the nineteenth century drew to a close a new method of folktale research began to establish itself in Europe, known variously as the geographic-historic method, the comparative method, the Finnish school (after the nationality of some of its most prestigious practitioners), or the Finnish-Scandinavian-American school (an effort to include all of its principal players). The main thrust of this movement was to accurately document as many appearances of a given folktale type as possible, faithfully recording the text exactly as received, and noting the date and location of its recital or publication. In the case of oral transmission, scholars collected details about the storytelling situation and relevant information about the storyteller, such as age, gender, position within the community, and the like.

The Finnish school received its impetus, appropriately, from investigations conducted by Julius Krohn into the sources and analogues of individual stories and songs imbedded within the great Finnish national epic *The Kalevala*. This epic was assembled by Elias Lönnrot from folklore collected in Finland's Kaleva district between 1828 and 1842 and published between 1835 and 1849. Lönnrot's final product, although based on authentic folk narratives and songs, was nonetheless his own poetic creation. Julius Krohn, by tracing the migration of individual songs and analyzing the differences between variants, attempted to recreate the original version of each piece.

Kaarle Krohn, the son of Julius, began in 1886 to apply these same comparative methods to more prosaic folktales then current in his native Finland: fables about the bear and the fox. In 1898 Kaarle Krohn was appointed professor of Finnish and comparative folklore at the University of Helsinki, thus becoming the world's first professor of folklore. Krohn's contemporary Antti Aarne was an even more prolific scholar. In a period of about 15 years he produced about one major monograph per year analyzing individual tale types.

The intellectual center of the Finnish school was the society Folklore Fellows. This group is known for its series of monographs, mostly on folktales, established in 1910 and still being published. Reflecting the changes in international scholarship standards (and not only in folklore studies), prior to the First World War most of the Folklore Fellows' publications were in German; the period between the two world wars saw a more-or-less even distribution between German and English; and since 1945 its publications have been predominantly in English.

Finnish school practitioners were greatly aided in their work by the publication of the monumental *Anmerkungen zu den Kinder- und Hausmärchen der Brüder Grimm* (Commentary to the Children's and Household Tales of the Brothers Grimm, 5 vols., 1913–1932) assembled by the German medievalist Johannes Bolte and his partner Georg Polívka, a Slavicist from Prague. In this work they documented analogues and variants of the individual tales in the Grimms' collection, drawing on medieval and Renaissance sources as well as folklore from eastern and western Europe.

Because the Grimms' collection, with its more than 200 tales, encompassed all the major genres of folk narrative and a broad sampling of folktale types (as they would later come to be defined), Boltes and Polívka's study functioned as a descriptive catalog of European folktales, thus giving a valuable tool to researchers wishing to draw comparisons between different versions of a particular tale. Students of comparative folklore still find *Bolte-Polívka* (as the work is often abbreviated) an indispensable resource.

An important by-product of the Finnish school was a number of type and motif indexes, most prominently *The Types of the Folktale* started by Antti Aarne in 1910, with enlarged editions following in 1928 and 1960, authored by the American folklorist Stith Thompson. Thompson is also the creator of the massive *Motif-Index of Folk-Literature: A Classification of Narrative Elements in Folktales, Ballads, Myths, Fables, Mediaeval Romances, Exempla, Fabliaux, Jest-Books, and Local Legends* (1955). These two works cover primarily folk literature between India and northwestern Europe. Type and motif indexes, patterned after such models, have since been compiled for many other regions of the world.

The Finnish school's legacy is very substantial. Their insistence on authentic texts, not arbitrarily rewritten by editors, and on the careful documentation of the place, year, and other details surrounding a tale's discovery has become the norm for folklore research. However, their attempts to definitively identify places of origin and to recreate original texts by mapping out the locations of all known variants of a given tale are not always convincing. There is no reliable way of knowing whether collected stories accurately represent the actual life history of a tale with all its migrations. In many instances too much of the storytelling record has been lost to allow one to project reliable patterns from the few surviving data points.

## PSYCHOLOGICAL APPROACHES

Some scholarship that emanated from the Finnish school might be compared to the research of a paleontologist who dedicated himself or herself to the discovery, mapping, cleaning, and sorting of ancient bones, and then the reconstruction of skeletons from those bones, but who afterward made little effort to interpret the meaning of the finished product. In a sense, the Finnish school provided later scholars with the raw materials (authentic, annotated texts) and the tools (type and motif indexes) with which to carry out their work of interpretation.

Professional scholars and amateurs alike have been interpreting folktales for all of recorded history. Plato's censure of fantasy tales for children, as outlined at the beginning of this chapter, is an act of interpretation. When medieval editors added aphorisms to Aesopic fables, restating "the moral of the story," they were practicing interpretation, as was the compiler of the *Gesta Romanorum* when he discovered a Christian allegory behind each of his tales.

Of all modern interpretive methods, none has been more prevalent than the psychological approach. Two distinct (but not mutually exclusive) directions are possible: The interpreter can analyze the psychology behind a storyteller's creative process, including the recollection of old tales, the invention of new ones, and the performance itself. Or the interpreter can analyze the psychological motivation of the fairy-tale characters.

## Fairy Tales and Dreams

Observers of the human psyche and of creative processes have long noted similarities between dreams and fairy tales. Like poets and philosophers before him, Sigmund Freud theorized that the same psychic energy that generates dreams may play a role in the creation of fantasy tales. Thus both fairy tales and dreams are important windows into the unconscious.

For Freud the force behind dreams (the dream-work) derives from repressed fears and desires (often sexual) that are best able to express themselves once a sleeping person's inhibitions relax. Even then, the dream-work often disguises tabooed or particularly painful material through the use of symbolic images, thus making the dream somewhat more acceptable, even to a sleeping person. An important task of psychoanalysis, according to Freud, is to reveal the literal meaning of such symbols and to determine what event in the patient's past gave rise to the fears or fantasies that they represent.

Traditional storytellers, as is well documented, often slip into an altered state of consciousness as their tales unwind—almost as though the stories were driving them, not the other way about. If hypnotism and association exercises (two other methods used by Freud), like dreams, provide access into the inner mind, then storytelling, especially of fantasy tales, may also reflect mental activity that under other circumstances is unconscious. Freud himself recognized this, outlining in a well-known essay, "Märchenstoff in Träumen" (Fairy-Tale Subject Matter in Dreams, 1913), a number of specific cases

Children en route to dreamland or fairyland. Peter Christen Asbjørnsen, *Fairy Tales from the Far North,* translated by H.L. Brækstad
(New York: A.L. Burt Company, 1897), frontispiece.

where elements in his patients' dreams resembled the images and motifs of familiar fairy tales.

Some traditional fairy tales reflect their relationship to dreams within their own texts. For example, the leading character in "Master Pfriem" (Grimm 178) dreams that he dies and goes to heaven. The entire tale is the contents of his dream. More recent authors and filmmakers have made frequent use of this technique. The magical plot of *Alice's Adventures in Wonderland* turns out to be a dream, which the reader discovers only in the book's final pages. Similarly, the miraculous, surrealistic events in the filmed version (although not in the book) of *The Wizard of Oz* are a dream, with some characters, grotesquely disguised, crossing over between the two worlds. Walt Disney, the most prolific and influential storyteller of the twentieth century, understood the relationship between dreams and fairy tales. His studio has often been called a "dream factory." Similarly, Steven Spielberg's studio is named Dream-Works.

Dreams are featured as sources of foreknowledge and motivation in countless folktales and myths. One famous example is the story of the man who became rich through a dream (A-T 1645) found in the *1,001 Nights* and also told as a local legend throughout Europe.

"The Peddler of Swaffham" from England is typical. After dreaming that good fortune would befall him at London Bridge, the peddler traveled to that place, and there related his dream to a shopkeeper. The Londoner ridiculed the stranger for having made such a long journey merely because of a dream, adding that he too recently had dreamed of buried treasure but was too sensible to pursue such a fantasy. He then described the treasure's location, as revealed in his dream. From the shopkeeper's description, the peddler recognized his own orchard. He hurried home and found the treasure.

This widespread tale is doubly ironic. First, two dreams had to be combined to find the buried treasure; and second, the protagonist discovered the treasure in his own garden, but he had to leave home before he could do so.

## Oedipus and Electra Complexes

Another aspect of Freudian psychiatry that has been influential in fairy-tale research is his theory that between the ages of about three and five (when fairy tales are particularly appealing) every child is sexually attracted to his or her parent of the opposite gender, and hence jealous of the parent of the same gender. Freud gave the name Oedipus complex to a boy's infatuation with his mother and associated animosity toward his father. The female counterpart is called Electra complex. Most children, theorized Freud, outgrow these tendencies at a young age, but some do not, and for these individuals what was a natural condition grows into a mental illness that requires treatment through psychoanalysis.

Much ink has been spent pointing out supposed examples of Oedipus and Electra complexes in fairy tales (always hidden behind symbols, of course). To the skeptic some of these studies seem as belabored and improbable as the sun-myth claims of an earlier generation. However, not all such claims can be easily dismissed. Following is one example of a tale where a Freudian interpretation seems fully justified.

"Iron Hans" (Grimm 136) opens when a king incarcerates a wild man in a cage, prohibiting anyone from releasing him, under penalty of death. The king's eight-year-old son is playing near the cage when he loses control of his golden ball, and it falls into the cage. The wild man refuses to give the ball back to the boy, unless the latter will unlock his cage. The boy says that he does not know where the key is hidden. "It is under your mother's pillow," replies the wild man. The boy finds the key and opens the door, and the wild man escapes. Fearing his father, the boy begs the wild man to return. The wild man comes back and carries the boy into the woods. Many trials follow, but the hero is victorious, and in the end marries a princess. Among the guests at his wedding are his mother and father, and also a mysterious foreign king who introduces himself as the former wild man. "I had been transformed into a wild man," he explains, "but you redeemed me."

This complicated tale lends itself to different interpretations, certainly including one from a Freudian perspective. The wild man clearly symbolizes a force that the father wants to control, possibly his son's emerging sexuality. The boy releases the force, partially by accident and partially by intention, discovering its key under his own mother's pillow. After undergoing ordeals and trials the boy is ready for marriage, and the wild man, now tame and respectable, comes to his wedding. Also present are the hero's parents, suggesting a full reconciliation, although at one stage the boy was deathly afraid of his own father.

## Surrealism

Freud's theories of the unconscious influenced artists and thinkers in many different fields. One such group, the so-called surrealists, had a strong connection to fairy tales. According to André Breton, their principal spokesman, surrealistic art connected the unconscious and the conscious realms, thus creating a reality that was beyond the actuality of either realm considered separately.

The distortions and seemingly unnatural juxtapositions that have come to be known as hallmarks of surrealistic painting and literature are common in traditional fairy tales, a fact that was noted more than a century before Freud by the German poet Novalis: "A fairy tale is actually like a dream image—without context—an ensemble of miraculous things and happenings—for example, a musical fantasy—the harmonic progressions of an Aeolian harp—nature herself" (*Schriften*, vol. 3, p. 454).

A prominent example of such surrealistic dreamlike imagery in a fairy tale is found in "Hans-My-Hedgehog" (Grimm 108). The title hero, a half-boy, half-hedgehog creature, rejected by his father, leaves home playing a set of bagpipes and riding upon a rooster that has been shod by a blacksmith. Thus mounted and armed he captures himself a bride. I omit many important details, but one dramatic and surrealistic image remains long after the story has been told: a half-human, half-hedgehog creature astride a rooster and playing the bagpipes. This image calls out for symbolic interpretation, even from younger readers and listeners.

Like many traditional tales, its very longevity and wide distribution indicate that there is more than one reason for the story's appeal, but certainly a Freudian explanation will make sense for at least some members of its audience.

### Archetypes

Carl Jung was another pioneering psychiatrist who used fairy tales in his research. His essays and lectures—for example, "Zur Psychologie des Geistes" (On the Psychology of the Spirit, 1945)—frequently cite fairy tales and demonstrate the author's extensive knowledge of European folklore. Jung's concept of the archetype has found many followers among fairy-tale interpreters. Jung theorized that similar experiences of humans over countless generations have created a "collective unconscious," which has somehow become genetically imbedded in the psyches of all humans. This reveals itself through archetypes—patterns and images experienced in personal dreams and fantasies, and also found in icons, myths, rituals, and fairy tales inherited from the past.

Scholars who have used either Freudian or Jungian psychology as a basis for fairy-tale studies are too numerous to enumerate here. Some prominent names, especially those influential in the English-speaking world, in approximate chronological order, are Ernest Jones, Géza Róheim, Erich Fromm, Julius Heuscher, Bruno Bettelheim, Marie-Louise von Franz, and Alan Dundes.

*Structuralism*

The word *pattern* appears frequently in discussions of archetypes. Structuralism, a movement that examines the relationships between patterns in language, narratives, rituals, visual art, and the like, emerged from the disciplines of psychology and anthropology. According to Claude Lévi-Strauss, a leading spokesman for this movement, the structures revealed by these investigations reflect the inherent structure of the human mind. Drawing examples from his own fieldwork among the indigenous peoples of Brazil and other preliterate cultures, Lévi-Strauss analyzed a wide range of human acts, including mythology, art, kinship rules, and eating customs.

In 1928 the Russian scholar Vladimir Propp published *Morphology of the Folktale,* an innovative theoretical study of 100 selected magic tales from the classic folktale collection of Aleksandr Afanasyev. Propp's work had little international impact until 1958, when it was first translated into English, but since then it has proven very influential. Propp's definition of morphology, a term borrowed from biology, is straightforward: "a description of the tale according to its component parts and the relationship of these components to the whole" (*Morphology of the Folktale,* p. 19). With the aid of charts and lists, Propp demonstrates that although at a first reading Afanasyev's magic tales (A-T 300–749) appear very diverse in their form, upon closer investigation they exhibit an amazing uniformity. The backbone of Propp's magic-tale skeleton is a list of 31 "functions," beginning with "One of the members of a family absents himself from home" and concluding with "The hero is married and ascends the throne" (ch. 3). According to Propp's analysis, Afanasyev's magic tales (and by implication, others as well) are virtually always constructed from a selection of these 31 elements. Furthermore, the relationships of the elements to each other demonstrate a marked similarity from tale to tale.

Another pioneering structuralist is the Dutch scholar André Jolles, whose book *Einfache Formen* (Simple Forms, 1929) identifies nine elemental literary forms and describes their structures. Jolles theorized that the basic structures of these genres, characterized by brevity and simplicity, are in a sense natural and irresistible, deriving as they do from structures within the human mind. Jolles's simple forms are saint's tale, legend, myth, riddle, proverb, exemplum, memorate, fairy tale, and joke.

## SOCIOLOGICAL APPROACHES

Although the issues of sociology—relationships between organized groups of human beings—have been studied since Greek antiquity, it emerged as a separate academic discipline only in the late nineteenth century. Its early expansion coincided with the development of cultural anthropology as a field of study, which—as shown earlier in this chapter—prompted a substantial amount of folktale interest, especially in England.

As is the case with psychological folklore studies, sociologists have found at least two areas of interest in folktales. First, there is the sociology *of* storytelling, collection, and publication. Such studies investigate the mechanisms behind the gathering of an audience for the purpose of hearing stories, the processes used by collectors and editors in finding and preparing final texts for publication, and changes made from one edition to the next in response to public expectations. Second, there is sociology *in* folktales, that is, the use of folktale texts as case studies of social relationships.

Although folk and fairy tales nearly always feature individuals (not groups) in their search for fulfillment, many different social organizations serve as backdrops, providing substantial raw data for sociological analysis. The family is by far the most important social organization in fairy tales. Parent-child relationships, problems associated with large families, sibling cooperation and rivalry, arranged marriages, conflicts arising from the death or remarriage of a parent or spouse, care of aging parents: these are the issues of countless fairy tales and also prime study topics for sociologists of family life.

Also visible, but less central, are governing institutions represented by work overseers, landowners, rent collectors, constables, bailiffs, judges, and kings. As a rule the further removed such officials are from a commoner, the less specific are the depictions. For example, kings and queens feature prominently in most fairy tales, but they serve more as abstract ultimate goals than as functioning heads of state. The expected reward for a fairy-tale hero or heroine is to become king or queen, but rarely are any details given as to what that entails.

Religion permeates the folklore of most cultures. Words like *pious* or *virtuous* often describe the leading characters, with the understood definitions of such words dependent upon the local faith. Religious hypocrisy is targeted in legends, anecdotes, and jests in all cultures. Folktales around the world ridicule unworthy priests, rabbis, mullahs, and fakirs. Such tales provide sociologists of religion much material for analysis.

Sociological research in the aforementioned fields and others has proven very fruitful. Recent scholars in this area (without differentiation according to subspecialty) include Cristina Bacchilega, Ruth B. Bottigheimer, Linda Dégh, Richard M. Dorson, Donald Haase, Lutz Röhrich, Kay F. Stone, James M. Taggart, Maria Tatar, Marina Warner, and Jack Zipes.

Two subspecialties in particular have attracted many folktale interpreters: Marxism and feminism.

*Marxism*

In spite of its dramatic failure as a practical economic and political system, Marxism still provides a theoretical basis for some schools of literary interpretation, including those involved in folk and fairy-tale interpretation. On the surface, traditional fairy tales should provide fertile ground for Marxist literary critics. Fairy-tale protagonists typically come from the lowest social group, the proletariat, and as the tale progresses they nearly always engage in a conflict with the rich and the powerful, ultimately gaining victory through cunning and magic.

However, with rare exceptions, these struggles are not class conflicts, but rather individual battles. The final victory is virtually never that of an exploited class over a privileged class, but rather of one hero over one tyrant. In the end all social organizations remain intact: family, community, religion, and royalty. A swineherd becomes king, or a kitchen maid becomes queen—individual, not class victories—but all else in the society remains essentially the same.

Thus traditional fairy tales, taken as a whole, provide scant pickings for Marxist scholars, but that is not to say that individual episodes and tale types do not provide credible examples of class consciousness and the critique of bourgeois and upper-class values, as championed by Marxism.

One such example is the tale known generically as "The Rich Peasant and the Poor Peasant" (A-T 1535), told throughout Europe since the Middle Ages and represented in the Grimms' collection as "The Little Peasant" (61).

These tales typically begin when a rich peasant ruthlessly kills an animal belonging to a poor peasant. To cut his losses the poor peasant takes the animal's hide to market, hoping to sell it. Under way he convinces another wealthy peasant that the pelt is magic and sells it to him for an exorbitant price. Back at home his rich neighbor asks about the source of his new wealth. "That's the price I received for the pelt at the market," he answers, more-or-less honestly. Hoping for a great profit, the rich peasant then slaughters his entire herd of cattle, but he receives only scorn when he tries to sell their hides at the market.

Several other episodes follow, in which the poor peasant betters priests, public officials, and, of course, his principal adversary, the rich neighbor. In the end he convinces the rich peasant and others of his ilk that reflections of clouds are actually sheep grazing in an underwater pasture. They jump into the lake to collect the sheep and are all drowned. The poor peasant takes possession of their goods.

This is a tale about rich versus poor, but class consciousness per se is not at its center. It is, rather, one man's conflict with his ruthless neighbors. In the end he is rich and they are dead, but social institutions that allowed or even promoted the initial inequities are still in place. There are no guarantees or indications that the once-poor and now-rich peasant will behave any better than did his adversary the once-rich and now-dead peasant. In fact, some versions of this tale depict the poor hero sacrificing other members of his class—even his own mother—to gain his personal ends (for example, "Big Peter and Little Peter" by Peter Christen Asbjørnsen and Jørgen Moe).

## Feminism

Folktales provide substantial raw material for gender-related studies. Unlike much traditional literature, household folktales typically were created and transmitted by women. A substantial body of evidence supports this claim. For example, most, if not all, European languages have expressions akin to *Mother Goose* associated with such tales, but masculine counterparts are scarce or nonexistent. As a matter of record, the majority of the Grimms' informants were female.

Whether created and performed by male or female storytellers, traditional folktales feature many unforgettable women. Granted, the modest and patient heroine who passively waits for a prince to awaken her or to rescue her from an ogre is a fairy-tale stereotype; and a large number of traditional folktales do ridicule women for talking too much, spending too freely, or attempting to dominate their husbands—all labels produced and promoted by patriarchal societies. However, folk and fairy tales also feature innumerable active, clever, and resourceful female characters. They outwit male opponents in setting and solving riddles (A-T 875), set traps for would-be sexual harassers (A-T 1730), steal food from stingy husbands or masters (A-T 1407, 1741), outmaneuver despotic husbands and lovers (A-T 311, 955), take revenge on jealous husbands (A-T 882), and establish sexual independence for themselves outside of marriage (A-T 1423).

In short, there is a vast pool of raw material for gender-oriented studies. The proverbial "battle of the sexes" is played out in countless traditional tales, sometimes with predictable, tradition-dictated results, but often with surprising, even revolutionary turns.

In many instances the same tale type is told with different conclusions, indicating that individual storytellers have dared to mold stories to their own needs and views instead of always conforming to a received standard. Possibly the best example of this is offered by the various versions of "The Frog King" (A-T 440). In most traditions the princess turns the frog into a prince by kissing him or by sleeping with him for three nights. In other words, she converts him by doing what *he* wants, by accepting him as he is. A minority position has also been recorded, the first tale in the Grimms' *Kinder- und Hausmärchen*. Here (the complete text is reproduced in chapter 3) the princess refuses to allow the frog into her bed, but rather throws him against the wall, apparently intending to kill him. Precisely this self-assertive act, performed in direct violation of her father's will, converts the frog into a prince.

Thus the different versions of this tale present one problem but two solutions. The problem is a woman's arranged marriage with an unattractive man. One solution is to accept him as he is, and everything will be all right. The other solution is for the heroine to take matters into her own hands and assert herself, and everything will be all right. Fairy tales, in their rich diversity, offer feminists examples of dominated and manipulated women, but also of liberated and self-directing women.

## AESTHETIC APPROACHES

A final method of interpreting folk and fairy tales is to apply to them the same standards that one would apply to any literary or artistic creation: Are they aesthetically pleasing? This approach combines many or even most of the previously discussed methods, because a fairy tale (like a poem, a novel, or a film) can be satisfying for different reasons: musicality of language, vividness of imagery, perceptive observation of human behavior, and many more.

Typically practitioners of this kind of fairy-tale interpretation are less interested in a given story's genealogy than in its impact on today's readers. Questions about our emotional involvement with the characters become more important than where the story came from and how it evolved into its present form. Scholars studying folktales for their aesthetic qualities often combine their folklore interests with traditional literary studies, including children's literature and literary fairy tales for adults. Representative scholars in this area include Steven Swann Jones, Max Lüthi, James M. McGlathery, Wolfgang Mieder, Roger Sale, and Jack Zipes.

It is appropriate to end this discussion of literature and fairy tales with a purposefully enigmatic and fragmentary statement by Novalis: "Fairy tales are the canon of literature. Everything poetical must be like a fairy tale. Poets worship coincidence" (*Schriften,* vol. 3, p. 449).

## WORKS CITED

*Gesta Romanorum: or, Entertaining Moral Stories; Invented by the Monks as a Fireside Recreation, and Commonly Applied in Their Discourses from the Pulpit.* London: Bell, 1877.

Novalis (penname for Friedrich von Hardenberg). *Novalis Schriften: Die Werke Friedrich von Hardenbergs.* Ed. Richard Samuel. Stuttgart: Kohlhammer, 1960.

Propp, Vladimir. *The Morphology of the Folktale.* Trans. Laurence Scott. 2nd ed. Austin: U of Texas P, 1968. First published 1928 in Russian.

Thompson, Stith. *The Folktale.* Berkeley: U of California P, 1977. First published 1946.

# Five
## Contexts

**ONCE UPON A TIME**

The charm of folk and fairy tales permeates our culture. Magical images from our favorite stories stay with us throughout our lives, providing shared experiences that cross national, ethnic, and social boundaries. A naïve little girl talking to a wolf in the forest; two children eating from a gingerbread house; a princess kissing a frog; a sleeping beauty—each of these images conjures up memories from childhood and releases a host of associations. This familiar ground is exploited by advertisers, used by joke makers, and manipulated by artists in many fields; and such has been the case for centuries. Our language itself is enriched with words and sayings from folk and fairy tales, as illustrated by the following list:

- Big bad wolf
- Bluebeard
- Cinderella team
- Crying wolf
- Don't count your chickens before they are hatched.
- Fairy godmother
- Fairy-tale ending
- Fairy-tale wedding
- Flying carpet

- Fool's paradise
- Goose that laid the golden eggs
- Happily ever after
- Kiss a frog
- Let the genie out of the bottle.
- Lion's share
- Magic lamp
- Magic word
- Midas touch
- Never-never land

The lion's share. Illustration from a nineteenth-century edition of Aesop's fables. *Fables of Aesop* (Boston: Lee and Shepard, n.d. [ca. 1850]), p. 22.

- Old wives' tale
- Once upon a time
- Open sesame
- Pound of flesh
- Prince Charming
- Silver bullet

- Sour grapes
- Ugly duckling
- Wicked stepmother
- Wolf in sheep's clothing
- Wolf whistle

## LITERARY FABLES

Among the oldest folktales still told are fables, especially those attributed to Aesop, the legendary Greek storyteller. These brief moralizing stories, often featuring animals and inanimate objects as characters, have been reformulated, parodied, and built into larger works by literary and visual artists from Roman antiquity to the present. Because of their inherent didactic nature, artists with a cause have turned to them repeatedly. One such writer was the anonymous compiler of the so-called *Gesta Romanorum* (Deeds of the Romans), written in

England about 1330. Of the 283 "deeds" recorded here, about a dozen are animal fables, each with an appended moral. And because the author was a Catholic cleric, "the moral of the story" is always to abide by some specified Christian precept.

Soon after the introduction of movable-type printing in about 1455, collections of Aesopic fables were published in most European languages, with the individual tales reformulated—sometimes in verse, sometimes in prose—to meet the expectations of new and changing audiences. Between 1668 and 1694 Jean de La Fontaine, an exemplary representative of the Age of Enlightenment, recreated some 240 Aesopic fables in French verse. Even to this day many readers know the so-called Aesop's fables primarily through La Fontaine's witty renditions. The didactic nature of the fable, its pragmatic this-worldly view, and its roots in classical antiquity appealed to many other gifted European writers of this era. Three additional authors who wrote fables in the style of Aesop are John Locke and John Gay from England and Gotthold Ephraim Lessing from Germany.

Many writers in the twentieth century have written imitations and parodies of traditional fables for their own social-critical purposes, but no one more successfully than the American humorist James Thurber in his witty and ironic *Fables for Our Time* (1940).

## FOLKLORE IN LITERATURE

Historians of literature often neglect the influence of orally transmitted songs and narratives on the output of writers in preliterate eras. Functional literacy is a product of many factors, including education, availability of affordable reading material, and social environment. Well into the nineteenth century a substantial portion of ordinary people had only rudimentary reading skills, at best, and even then had but scant access to reading material. For these people orally transmitted tales filled a compelling need.

Great writers recognize good stories when they hear them, often mining raw material from them for their own creations. Giovanni Boccaccio, Geoffrey Chaucer, and William Shakespeare—to name three master writers from earlier periods—all incorporated folktales into their work. They may have seen other authors' adaptations of certain stories, but they were also influenced by tales heard as oral presentations.

### Boccaccio

Bridging the Middle Ages and the Renaissance, Boccaccio's *The Decameron,* written between 1348 and 1353, is one of the world's greatest collections of stories. The framework is simple: To escape the ravages of the Black Death, seven women and three men abandon the city of Florence and take shelter in a country estate. To make their exile more pleasant each of the 10 refugees tells one story every day. *The Decameron* records the narratives of 10 days—100 stories, about 30 of which are demonstrably based on folktales. However, Boccaccio's 10 narrators tell only a few stories of fantasy and magic (for example, 3:8, 5:8, 10:9), favoring instead earthy anecdotes about tricksters, errant priests, rascally husbands, and mischievous wives. Variants of these stories are known in many cultures, but no one formulates them more cleverly or relates them more eloquently than does Boccaccio.

### Chaucer

A northern European counterpart to *The Decameron* is Chaucer's *The Canterbury Tales,* written between 1387 and 1400 in the language known today as Middle English. The frame story describes a band of pilgrims traveling from London to Canterbury. To entertain one another they tell stories. As was the case with Boccaccio, Chaucer's narrators tell stories that in large part were already familiar (in fact, some tales are found in both collections). Furthermore, like his Italian forebear, Chaucer exhibits unusual psychological perception and uncommon wit and style in his narration.

### Shakespeare

Writing some 200 years after Chaucer, Shakespeare shared his predecessor's keen ability to observe people of all types and classes, and like the author of *The Canterbury Tales,* Shakespeare too incorporated much folk material into his literature. Following is a selection of folktale plots and motifs used by Shakespeare.

The basic story line of *All's Well That Ends Well* is derived from the widespread folktale known generically as "A Wife, in Disguise, Seduces Her Own Husband" (A-T 891). Boccaccio used this same tale in his *Decameron* (3:9), which was Shakespeare's immediate source. In both Boccaccio's and Shakespeare's versions a count is forced to marry a woman whom he considers to be unworthy of him. He abandons her immediately, declaring that he will accept her as a wife only if she can present him with a ring that he never removes from his finger and with a child that he has fathered, although he refuses to be near her. She achieves these seemingly impossible tasks by secretly following him to his new place of residence, then substituting herself in the bed of a young woman whom he has been trying to seduce. Later the truth of these assignations is disclosed, and the count restores his wife to full recognition.

Another Shakespeare play based on a folktale and with a close analogue in Boccaccio's *Decameron* (2:9) is *Cymbeline*. Both versions follow quite closely the widespread traditional European folktale "Wager on a Wife's Fidelity" (A-T 882). The basic plot remains the same, whether the tale is told by an anonymous oral storyteller, Boccaccio, or Shakespeare. The names from *Cymbeline* are used in the following summary: A deceitful man named Iachimo bets his friend Posthumus that he can seduce the latter's wife Imogen. Trusting his wife's fidelity, Posthumus accepts the wager. Hidden in a large trunk, Iachimo has himself smuggled into Imogen's bedroom, where he not only observes the room's furnishings and sees a mole under Imogen's breast, but also succeeds in stealing a bracelet from the sleeping woman. Armed with this intimate information and the bracelet, Iachimo convinces Posthumus of his wife's infidelity. In a jealous rage Posthumus orders his wife's death, but in good fairy-tale tradition (think of "Little Snow-White"), the servant trusted with her execution spares her life, and she takes refuge with a family of forest dwellers. Ensuing circumstances bring Iachimo's deception to light; he is duly punished and Posthumus and Imogen are happily reunited.

The main plot of *King Lear* is based on a folktale known generically as "Love Like Salt" (A-T 923). A father (here King Lear) asks his daughters how much they love him and is insulted when the youngest (here Cordelia) replies with a modest but sincere expression of devotion. Traditionally the youngest daughter answers, "I love you like salt." Shakespeare's Cordelia responds that she can promise her father only half her love, the other half being reserved for her future husband. Jealous King Lear, like his folktale counterparts, disowns his daughter for her supposed lack of filial love. Unlike traditional folktales, Shakespeare's drama concludes as a tragedy, and does not end happily with a reconciliation between the estranged father and daughter.

*The Merchant of Venice* contains a number of folktale motifs, most famously the "pound of flesh" (A-T 890) demanded of Antonio by the villainous moneylender Shylock as security for a loan. When Antonio cannot meet the repayment deadline, the cruel Shylock, knife in hand, approaches the debtor to extract the pound of flesh. However, when warned that he will be in violation of the law and will forfeit his own life if he takes one ounce too little or too much, or even if he spills any blood while cutting out the contractually agreed upon flesh, Shylock sees the impossibility of keeping within the letter of the law and surrenders his claim.

The most famous (or, from a feminist perspective, infamous) of Shakespeare's plays based on folklore is *The Taming of the Shrew,* a version of the very widespread folktale "Taming a Shrewish Wife" (A-T 901). Reflecting values that today are difficult to defend, this play depicts an unending chain of abuse inflicted by Petruchio on his strong-willed bride Katharina, in his attempt to transform her "from a wild Kate to a Kate conformable as other household Kates."

A happier play, by today's standards, is the comedy *A Midsummer Night's Dream,* which from beginning to end is a veritable fairy tale. Apart from the burlesque play-within-a-play, *The Most Lamentable Comedy and Most Cruel Death of Pyramus and Thisbe,* a story from Roman mythology, *A Midsummer Night's Dream* is not based on any single traditional tale. However, the work is filled with fairy lore and magic-tale motifs: mischievous fairies, herbs that cause invisibility, love potions, transposed heads, shape-shifting, and changelings.

## ANTHROPOMORPHIC STORIES

### Children's Fables

Letting animals, plants, and things take on human attributes has a special appeal for children, who in their play quite naturally pretend that pets and objects are people. Traditional storytellers and writers of children's stories alike have long taken advantage of this observation. Two nineteenth-century authors deserve special notice. Leo Tolstoy incorporated both traditional and original material into fables and fairy tales for primers and readers that he wrote in the 1870s to teach Russian peasants' children how to read. The American Joel Chandler Harris was from a different world, but he drew on the same traditional material in his *Uncle Remus* stories, written between 1879 and the author's death in 1908. Featuring the trickster Brer Rabbit and set in the pre–Civil War American South, these animal tales contain many episodes also found in Aesopic fables. African American folklore provided much of Harris's raw material, which suggests that Africa may have played a substantial role in the development and transmission of Aesopic fables from the earliest times. According to some sources the man Aesop was a darkskinned native of Ethiopia.

The first decades of the twentieth century, especially in England and America, saw the publication of a number of children's animal books whose quality would give them active readership into the twenty-first century. In 1901 Beatrix Potter privately printed *The Tale of Peter Rabbit,* the first of her many small-format, illustrated books with animal characters. Her charming watercolors and unadorned language tell the story of a mischievous rabbit's narrow escape from Mr. McGregor's garden. A cautionary tale, told carefully and in an unthreatening manner, this perennial favorite is not about rabbits but about human children who disobey their parents. It forms a counterpart to "Goldilocks and the Three Bears," with each story telling of an intrusion into a forbidden realm and ending with a narrow escape.

Rudyard Kipling's *Just So Stories for Little Children* (1902), with the author's own illustrations, parody traditional etiologic tales. With far-fetched logic bordering on nonsense he explains various animals' features—for example, "How the Camel Got His Hump" and "How the Leopard Got His Spots." Kenneth Grahame's classic of children's fiction, *The Wind in the Willows* (1908), features Mole, Rat, Badger, and Toad in very human roles. A.A. Milne dramatized the novel as *Toad of Toad Hall* (1930). Following the tradition of Grahame, Potter, and Kipling—although by general consensus not meeting their standard of excellence—is the series of tales *Old Mother West Wind* (beginning 1910) by the American author Thornton W. Burgess.

*The Story of Doctor Dolittle* (1920) was the first of Hugh Lofting's many popular books celebrating an eccentric country doctor who, aided by his ability to speak their language, treats and befriends animals as well as humans. A number of movie versions have been made, including one starring Rex Harrison (1967) and one starring Eddie Murphy (2002). A.A. Milne's *Winnie-the-Pooh* (1926) introduced the world to Christopher Robin and his menagerie of stuffed animals. This book blurs the distinction between children's and adult's literature. Although written for and about children, *Winnie-the-Pooh* is widely read by adults.

In mid-century the tradition of fable-inspired children's literature continued with Robert Lawson's *Rabbit Hill* (1944) and the exemplary books by E.B. White. The hero of White's *Stuart Little* (1945) is a mouse born of human parents, obviously patterned after the Tom Thumb of traditional fairy tales (A-T 700). In *Charlotte's Web* (1952), White's recognized masterpiece, the leading characters are Wilbur, a runt pig, and his friend and protector, a barn spider named Charlotte. His third children's book, *The Trumpet of the Swan* (1970), features a swan who overcomes his disadvantage of being speechless by learning to play the trumpet.

### Political Fables

Children's fables often have serious messages tucked cautiously between their lines. Writers of adult fantasy fiction need not tread so lightly, as evidenced by some twentieth-century fabulists. In 1912 George Bernard Shaw turned the ancient Aesopic fable *Androcles and the Lion* (A-T 156) into a witty and impious critique of religion in general and Christianity in particular. George Orwell's political fable *Animal Farm* (1945) is a biting anti-utopian satire. On the surface, *Watership Down* (1972) by Richard Adams is an adventure novel about a community of rabbits facing the destruction of their warren by land developers, but most readers will see in it an allegory of human relationships to one another and to their natural environment. In 1978 *Watership Down* was made into a critically acclaimed animated movie.

Not all modern-day fabulists have chosen prose fiction as their medium. Comic strips, with their strong visual element, lend themselves to the satiric use of animal characters that typify Aesopic fables. Walter Kelly, the creator of the *Pogo* comic strip, represents modern fables in this medium as well as anyone. For Kelly, like the ancient Greek and Indian fabulists, the story was in the message, and Kelly's message was one of liberal, pro-environmentalist politics. *Pogo* comic strips began their long run in 1948. Kelly died in 1973, and the strip continued, with other artists and writers, until 1993. Even today conservationists quote the little opossum's sad observation as he looks over his garbage-littered Okefenokee Swamp: "We have met the enemy and he is us."

### Mickey Mouse

The final name in this section is arguably the twentieth century's best-known storyteller, Walt Disney. His most memorable creation, the inimitable Mickey Mouse, is in many ways a descendent of Aesop's talking creatures. Mickey debuted in 1928 as the star of *Steamboat Willie,* the first animated cartoon with sound. Disney's moralizing is always gentle, avoiding extremes and controversies. Mickey, who—like many fairy-tale heroes—has no special talents, shows that good luck will follow those who are sincere and kind, and who do not take themselves too seriously. In traditional fables various animals symbolize different human qualities: the fox is sly, the bear is brutish and slow-witted, and so forth. Mickey Mouse, too, represents a particular type of human: He is everyone.

## LITERARY FAIRY TALES

### Old, Old Stories

Andrew Lang, in the preface to his *Lilac Fairy Book* (1910), observed that "nobody can write a *new* fairy tale; you can only mix up and dress up the old, old stories." Since the mid-eighteenth century European creative writers have been mixing up and dressing up the old, old stories. Done well, the results are aesthetically and psychologically satisfying, but they are still recognizable as old, old stories.

The fantasy world of traditional magic tales has an appeal that transcends time and space. These tales take place in an otherworldly realm where wishes come true, where right prevails, and where special rules supercede the expected laws of nature. This realm is akin both to the fairyland of countless legends as well as to the spirit world of various religions. It is an existence that inexplicably runs parallel to ordinary life. On rare occasions the two worlds merge, allowing ordinary mortals to experience, even to cross over into, the other world.

## Objections of Realists

In spite of the great popular appeal of such magic realms, in many instances fueled by a sincere desire to believe that they actually exist, the literary establishment has not always been friendly toward works depicting the supernatural. In particular, the European Age of Enlightenment during the seventeenth and eighteenth centuries saw in magic stories an abandonment of reason and a potentially dangerous flirtation with medieval superstition. Similarly, many of the more puritanical religious movements rejected the writing and reading of such fantasy tales as being at best a frivolous waste of time and at worst an acceptance of pagan occultism. These arguments, in some circles, have survived into the twenty-first century, as evidenced by certain religion-based objections leveled against the Harry Potter books.

## Dickens and Irving

In his novel *Hard Times* (1854) Charles Dickens wrote a biting criticism of hyperrealists whose philosophy of childhood education leaves no room for fantasy or make-believe. The characters Thomas Gradgrind ("a man of realities, facts, and calculations") and schoolmaster Mr. McChoakumchild represent the worst aspects of such a philosophy. Dickens himself, although known for realistic portrayals in his own fiction, defended fairy tales as children's literature. Three of his five Christmas books depict supernatural occurrences: *A Christmas Carol in Prose* (1843), *The Chimes: A Goblin Story* (1844), and *The Cricket on the Hearth: A Fairy Tale of Home* (1845).

Writing in America a generation earlier, Washington Irving used belief in the supernatural more for a humorous effect. Three of the stories in his *Sketch Book of Geoffrey Crayon, Gent* (1819–1820) are based on German folktales. Two of them are parodies, appearing to depict supernatural events, which in the end are revealed as elaborate hoaxes: "The Legend of Sleepy Hollow" (based on the headless huntsman legends) and "The Spectre Bridegroom" (patterned after a folktale of type 365). The third story, "Rip Van Winkle," is a genuine fairy tale (type 766). It describes a colonial American's encounter with some mysterious little people. After drinking some of their liquor he falls asleep and does not awaken for 20 years.

### Romanticism

Romanticism, a cultural movement encompassing roughly the period between 1790 and 1850 in Europe, reversed the Age of Enlightenment's trend against the use of fantasy elements in literature and other arts. The fairy tale established itself during these decades as a serious literary genre, especially in Germany, where such writers as Johann Karl August Musäus, Johann Wolfgang Goethe, Ludwig Tieck, Clemens Brentano, Friedrich de la Motte Fouqué, E.T.A. Hoffmann, and Wilhelm Hauff created innovative works with lasting influence. These were not merely children's bedtime stories, but works of art intended primarily for adults, and with substantial aesthetic and psychological impact.

The Danish writer Hans Christian Andersen was greatly influenced by the German Romantics. Although often compared to the Grimm brothers' tales, Andersen's stories are quite different. The Grimms were collectors and editors, whereas Andersen was primarily a creative writer. Of his approximately 150 tales only a dozen are based directly on traditional folklore, the others being of his own invention. The Grimms published folktales; Andersen created literary fairy tales, many of which have become international favorites.

### The Victorian Era

Following this literary fairy-tale tradition in Britain was the Scottish writer George MacDonald, whose *Phantastes, a Faerie Romance for Men and Women* (1858) describes a dreamlike visit to fairyland. This work, as indicated by the title, was intended for adults. MacDonald later wrote a number of allegorical fairy tales for children, still considered masterpieces. Among his best such works are *At the Back of the North Wind* (1871), *The Princess and the Goblin* (1872), and *The Princess and Curdie* (1873).

Other writers of this era who made lasting contributions to fantasy children's literature include John Ruskin, William Makepeace Thackeray, Charles Kingsley, and Charles L. Dodgson. Ruskin wrote one of the first fantasy books for children, *King of the Golden River* (1851). He was an influential champion

H.C. Andersen's "The Mermaid." Illustration by Charles Robinson (1905). *Fairy Tales from Hans Christian Andersen* (London: J.M. Dent, 1905), frontispiece.

of gothic revival in architecture, an appropriate position for a lover of fairy tales with their many motifs inherited from the Middle Ages. Thackeray's Christmas book *The Rose and the Ring* (1855) is a witty set of ironic sketches based on traditional fairy tales. Kingsley's *The Water-Babies: A Fairy Tale for a Land-Baby* (1863), a heavily moralistic story, features an abused chimney sweep who falls into a river where he discovers a magic underwater world.

Charles L. Dodgson, writing under the penname Lewis Carroll, created arguably the two greatest children's fantasy books in the English language: *Alice's Adventures in Wonderland* (1865) and its sequel *Through the Looking Glass* (1871). Borrowing from traditional legends about fairyland, the author describes a fanciful existence parallel to this world, a wonderland of delightful confusion. Furthermore, unlike most children's literature of the Victorian era, Lewis Carroll's books show no hint of didacticism, allowing children the freedom to read for pleasure and not for training.

Italy, a country with a rich folk and fairy-tale tradition, made a new contribution to international children's fantasy literature in the 1880s with the novel *Pinocchio: Storia di un burattino* (Pinocchio: The Story of a Puppet) by Carlo Lorenzini, using the penname Carlo Collodi. The mischievous puppet's adventures appeared serially between 1881 and 1882 in a Rome newspaper, then were published as a book in 1883. The story's worldwide popularity was further enhanced with the animated Disney movie *Pinocchio* (1940).

Many additional authors working at the end of the nineteenth century and the beginning of the twentieth century wrote fantasy stories and fairy tales for children as well as for adults. Such writers from America include Louisa May Alcott, Jane Goodwin Austin (not to be confused with the English novelist Jane Austen), Maud Ballington Booth, Gelett Burgess, Howard Pyle, and Frank Stockton. From Great Britain were Hilaire Belloc, Dinah Maria Mulock Craik, Juliana Horatia Ewing, Jean Ingelow, and Andrew Lang. Although remembered today primarily as a folklorist and compiler of the popular fairy-tale collections, Lang was also an author in his own right, especially of literary fairy tales. Robert Louis Stevenson, best known for adventure novels, also wrote numerous fantasy stories for children based mostly on the *1,001 Nights.*

W.W. Jacobs, the English short-story writer, also belongs to this group, if only for his memorable horror story "The Monkey's Paw" (1902), a modern and sinister version of the very widespread "Three Wishes" folktale (A-T 750A). The Irish poet, playwright, and novelist Oscar Wilde, famous (or infamous) because of his controversial lifestyle and his witty dramas, also authored two volumes of children's fairy tales: *The Happy Prince, and Other Tales* (1888) and *A House of Pomegranates* (1891).

## The Twentieth Century

The turn of the century saw two otherworldly fantasy pieces for children with lasting impact: *The Wonderful Wizard of Oz* (1900) by the American author L. Frank Baum and *Peter Pan* (1904) by the Scottish playwright James Barrie. In 1911 Barrie rewrote this immensely popular play as a novel with the title *Peter and Wendy.* Baum has the distinction of being the first American author of a full-length fantasy novel for children. He wrote many additional children's books, including numerous sequels to *The Wonderful Wizard of Oz,* but none were as successful as this one pivotal book. Furthermore, there is a general consensus among historians of children's literature that the classic 1939 film *The Wizard of Oz,* starring Judy Garland, tells the story even better than did its original author.

The lines between fantasy tales based on old fairy tales and those based on futuristic science are often blurred. In some instances the same writers experiment with the alternative worlds offered by each genre. The literary output of H.G. Wells offers a case in point. His novels *The Time Machine* (1895) and *The War of the Worlds* (1898), among others, are pioneering examples of modern science fiction, but he also wrote numerous magic tales of high quality.

Similarly, C.S. Lewis authored classic books both of science fantasy—*Out of the Silent Planet* (1938), *Perelandra* (1943), *That Hideous Strength* (1945)— and of magic fantasy—the *Chronicles of Narnia* (7 vols., 1950–1956). In the first of the *Narnia* books, *The Lion, the Witch, and the Wardrobe,* four siblings have been sent to an old country house to escape the London air raids during World War Two. The youngest sister investigates a large wardrobe sitting in an otherwise empty room and discovers that it serves as an entryway into another world, the land of Narnia, inhabited by fauns, dwarfs, talking animals, and— of course—a threatening witch. A film version of this novel is in production and is scheduled for release in 2005.

In the mid-twentieth century, fantasy literature for children was dominated by two names: C.S. Lewis and his close friend J.R.R. Tolkien, who for a time were colleagues together on the English faculty at Oxford University. Professionally, Tolkien was a specialist in Anglo-Saxon language and literature. His books *The Hobbit* (1937) and the trilogy *The Lord of the Rings* (completed in 1949, but first published in 1954–1955) were written in large part as a personal diversion. Set in "Middle-Earth" in the mythical past, these books feature a complex community of elves, dwarfs, and hobbits. The "secondary world" (a term used by Tolkien in his 1939 lecture "On Fairy-Stories") created here has much in common with the magic realm of traditional fairy tales. Furthermore, the names, characterizations, and situations encountered there all ring true, in large part because of the author's expertise in linguistics, fairy lore, legendry, and mythology.

Tolkien has attracted an almost cultlike group of followers, a phenomenon further promoted by video games and films. The animated movie *The Lord of the Rings* (1978) still has a loyal following. A quarter century later three high-budget extravaganzas followed: *The Fellowship of the Ring* (2001), *The Two Towers* (2002), and *The Return of the King* (2003). They succeed as dramatic, special-effect action films, but not as a faithful depiction of Tolkien's Middle-Earth.

Alan Garner, while a student at Oxford, met both C.S. Lewis and J.R.R. Tolkien but claims that he has read neither the *Chronicles of Narnia* nor *The Lord of the Rings*. Nonetheless, his fantasy fiction, based largely on British legends, is often compared with Tolkien's trilogy. The most popular successor of Tolkien and Lewis in the fantasy-literature realm is J.K. Rowling with her enormously successful series of Harry Potter books, beginning with *Harry Potter and the Sorcerer's Stone* (1998). As of 2003 five books and two films have appeared, all enormously successful. According to the author, a total of seven books is projected.

Robin McKinley, an American author now living in England, specializes in fantasy fiction for young adult women. An avid fan of Tolkien, she repeatedly draws on traditional legends and fairy tales for inspiration and raw material. Among her most popular novels are two different versions of "Beauty and the Beast": *Beauty* (1978) and *Rose Daughter* (1997). *Deerskin* (1993) derives from the type 510B family of folktales—for example, Perrault's "Donkeyskin" and the Grimms' "All-Kinds-of-Fur." Her *Spindle's End* (2000) is a variation of "Sleeping Beauty" (A-T 410).

### Romance Novels

Literally hundreds of romance novels have been written using fairy-tale themes. Harlequin, the most famous name in this popular genre, announced its own series *Lovers and Legends,* beginning in 1993, with this explanation: "Fairy tales and legends are basic human stories, retold in every age, in their own way. Romance stories, at their heart, are the happily ever after of every story we listened to as children." Other series titles from various publishers include *Once upon a Dream, Once upon a Kiss, Once upon a Time Romances, Faerie Tale Romances, Fairy Tale Series,* and *Legendary Lovers.*

## OPERA, BALLET, AND PROGRAM MUSIC

Many musical genres have a narrative component: operas, ballads, and song cycles with language; and ballets through gesture and dance. Program music elicits images and events using only the instruments themselves. Numerous composers have used these storytelling possibilities to reenact traditional folk and fairy tales. Opera, with its combination of musical, dramatic, visual, and narrative effects, has proven to be an especially productive fairy-tale medium.

An early example is *Die Zauberflöte* (The Magic Flute, 1791), composed by Wolfgang Amadeus Mozart, with a libretto by Emanuel Schikaneder. The fantasy-filled text does not follow any specific fairy tale, although it is loosely based on the story "Lulu; oder, Die Zauberflöte" (Lulu; or, The Magic Flute), a literary fairy tale inspired by the *1,001 Nights* and written by the now obscure author Jakob August Liebeskind. Complementing the opera's fairy-tale atmosphere is a strong ritualistic element, prompted by Mozart's involvement with Freemasonry, which adds to the work's sense of mystery.

The opera *Undine* (1816), composed by the multigifted E.T.A. Hoffmann, brings together several aspects of fairy lore as it influenced European artistic life in the early nineteenth century. The libretto was written by Friedrich de la Motte Fouqué and patterned after his own successful literary fairy tale with the same name (1811). Fouqué's plot centers around a love relationship between a medieval knight and a mysterious girl who turns out to be a water sprite. The composer was also one of German Romanticism's greatest literary figures, with a special flare for writing surrealistic fairy tales. He is, in fact, the Hoffmann featured in Jacques Offenbach's most enduring work, the opera *Contes d'Hoffmann* (Tales of Hoffmann), first produced in 1881 after the composer's death. Labeled an *opéra-fantastique,* this work incorporates a number of Hoffmann's tales into a frame story.

The first major opera with lasting influence to be patterned after a traditional fairy tale was *La Cenerentola* (Cinderella, 1817) by Gioacchino Rossini, with a libretto by Jacopo Ferretti. The recent success in France of Nicholas Isouard's opera *Cendrillon* (Cinderella), first staged in 1810, may have prompted the Italian composer to turn to Charles Perrault's famous tale for raw material. At Rossini's insistence, his librettist removed all the magic elements from the story, and other alterations were made to Perrault's text as well, such as changing the object used for the bride test from a glass slipper to a bracelet, prompting some contemporary critics to joke that the substitution was made because a prima donna could not be found with appropriately small feet. This criticism notwithstanding, *La Cenerentola* remains a standard offering in opera houses around the world. Rossini's final opera, *Guillaume Tell* (William Tell, 1829), is also based on folkloric material, the story of Switzerland's legendary national hero.

A German contemporary of Rossini's who had no reservations about including magic elements in his operas was Carl Maria von Weber. Steeped in Romanticism, von Weber used folk material throughout his career. Among his earliest operatic attempts was the uncompleted *Rübezahl* (1805), based on a famous forest-spirit trickster from the Riesengebirge Mountains. *Der Freischütz* (1821), his most enduring opera, is based on the widespread European superstition of a marksman who through magic never misses his target. His final opera, *Oberon; or, The Elf King's Oath* (1826), was created for the London stage. Weber was immensely popular both in his native Germany and abroad, and he did much to legitimize the use of folk motifs—including the supernatural—in serious art.

Richard Wagner, the master of nineteenth-century German opera, acknowledged his debt to Weber, both in musical composition and in subject matter. Virtually all of Wagner's operas are based on folkloric, legendary, and mythological themes, and he did not avoid the supernatural in his texts. His first opera, *Die Feen* (The Fairies, 1833), is literally a fairy tale. *Der fliegende Holländer* (The Flying Dutchman, 1843) is based on the legend of the wandering Jew (A-T 777). *Tannhäuser* (1845) recounts the folktale of the knight who, after failing to receive forgiveness from the pope, takes refuge in the forbidden mountain of Venus (A-T 756). *Lohengrin* (1850), based on a medieval legend, is replete with fairy-tale motifs, most famously the boat pulled by a swan. *Tristan und Isolde* (1865), which also retells a medieval legend, centers around a magic love potion, a common folklore motif. While the plot of *Die Meistersinger von Nürnberg* (The Mastersingers of Nürnberg, 1868) is not derived from folklore, it does champion the art of ordinary people, as epitomized by the singing cobbler Hans Sachs. The historical shoemaker Hans Sachs, as Wagner knew, preserved numerous folktales in the texts of his many Shrovetide plays. As is well known, Wagner's great tetralogy *Der Ring des Nibelungen* (The Ring of Nibelung, 1869–1876) is based on Germanic mythology and as such is replete with fairy-tale images and motifs, including dwarfs, sleeping beauties, dragon slayers, magic rings, and supernatural swords. Wagner's final opera, *Parsifal* (1882), returns to the fairy-tale world of medieval legendry. This is a realm with knights, sorcerers, magic healings, transformations, and vanishing castles—all dominated by the search for the Holy Grail.

Nikolay Rimsky-Korsakov wrote a number of operas with plots taken from Russian fairy tales—for example, *The Snow Maiden* (1882). Still better known is his symphonic suite *Scheherazade* (1888). This work's four movements were initially labeled "The Sea and Sinbad's Ship," "The Story of the Kalendar Prince," "The Young Prince and the Young Princess," and "The Festival at Baghdad," indicating a set of four tales. The composer later retracted the idea that his piece was a continuous narration, referring to it instead as a "kaleidoscope of fairy-tale images."

The marksman who never misses his target. Herman Hofberg, *Swedish Fairy Tales* (Chicago: W.B. Conkey, 1893), p. 11.

Following a much lighter vein are the fairy-tale operas of Engelbert Humperdinck (not to be confused with the popular English ballad singer Arnold George Dorsey, who performs under the stage name of the nineteenth-century German opera composer). Humperdinck's opera *Hänsel und*

*Gretel* (1893), a musical dramatization of the Grimms' famous tale, is still performed throughout Germany every Christmas season, in much the same manner that nearly every American ballet company stages Tchaikovsky's *The Nutcracker* during the winter holidays. Humperdinck composed two additional fairy-tale operas, also based on texts by the Grimm brothers: *Die sieben Geißlein* (The Seven Little Kids, 1895) and *Dornröschen* (Brier Rose, 1902).

Jacques Offenbach, mentioned earlier in connection with his opera *Contes d'Hoffmann,* also wrote a number of operettas featuring fairy-tale motifs. Of these the most enduring is *Orphée aux enfers* (Orpheus in the Underworld, 1858). Described as an *opéra-féerique* (a fairylike opera), it features numerous deities from classical mythology in humorous situations, including a riotous, unforgettable cancan dance. For the Viennese stage Offenbach produced the opera-ballet *Die Rheinnixen* (The Rhine Nixies, 1864). The morbid folktale "Bluebeard" (A-T 312), recorded by Charles Perrault and many others, prompted Offenbach's operetta *Barbe-Bleue* (1866). However, Offenbach turns this tale of murder into a hilarious comedy.

Béla Bartók, famous for his work with the folksongs of his native Hungary—both as a collector and arranger—also turned to the Bluebeard folktale for an opera: *A kékszakállú herceg vára* (Duke Bluebeard's Castle, 1911). Unlike Offenbach's comic opera, Bartók's work retains the dark mood of Perrault's tale. Actually, Bartók's librettist Béla Balázs worked primarily from *Ariane et Barbe-bleue,* a dramatic adaptation of Perrault's story by the Belgian symbolist poet Maurice Maeterlinck. Bartók's ballets *The Wooden Prince* (1914–1916) and *The Miraculous Mandarin* (1919) further reflect his interest in fairy-tale motifs.

Another composer who turned to Maeterlinck's Bluebeard drama was Paul Dukas, with his opera *Ariane et Barbe-bleu* (1907). However, Dukas's most famous folktale-based composition is his ingenious orchestral program piece *L'Apprenti sorcier* (The Sorcerer's Apprentice, 1897), based on Johann Wolfgang von Goethe's popular ballad "Der Zauberlehrling," a poetic rendition of Aarne-Thompson type 325*. Dukas's piece featured prominently in Walt Disney's *Fantasia* (1941), with a harried Mickey Mouse playing the role of the sorcerer's apprentice who charmed a broom into carrying water for him but then did not know how to turn off the magic, with nearly catastrophic results.

A similar concert favorite, and one composed at about the same time as Dukas's *L'Apprenti sorcier,* is the tone poem *Till Eulenspiegels lustige Streiche* (Till Eulenspiegel's Merry Pranks, 1894–1895) by Richard Strauss. This descriptive piece, a guaranteed crowd pleaser, effectively uses a full orchestra—with many opportunities for soloists—to depict the shameless exploits of Germany's legendary trickster. Another major work by Strauss based on folklore is his opera *Die Frau ohne Schatten* (The Woman without a Shadow, 1919), which incorporates numerous folktale motifs, including transformations from beast to human and—as indicated by the title—a person without a shadow. The librettist for this piece was the well-known Austrian poet and dramatist Hugo von Hofmannsthal.

Also composed in 1919 was Sergei Prokofiev's opera *The Love for Three Oranges*—sometimes titled *The Love of Three Oranges*—based on a comedy by the eighteenth-century Italian playwright Carlo Gozzi, which in turn was adapted from a widespread traditional fairy tale (A-T 408). Another favorite work by the Russian composer based on a folktale is his *Peter and the Wolf* (1936), a "symphonic fairy tale" for narrator and orchestra. Here, to the delight of children and adults alike, a speaker recites a folktale-like story, accompanied by an orchestra, with selected solo instruments representing the various characters. Additionally, in 1944 Prokofiev composed *Cinderella,* a ballet based on the traditional fairy tale.

Gozzi's plays were used by numerous composers and librettists of the nineteenth and twentieth centuries for opera plots. Giacomo Puccini, for example, based his opera *Turandot* (1926) on a Gozzi play. Turandot is the name of the Persian fairy-tale princess who demands that her suitors solve three riddles or forfeit their lives (A-T 851).

Maurice Ravel composed four major works based on fairy tales, using only two titles. The first, the "fairy overture" *Shéhérazade* (1899), was intended for an opera that never materialized. The same title was used in 1903 for a song cycle for voice and orchestra. Finally, his suite *Ma Mère l'Oye* (My Mother Goose) was first composed as a pianoforte duet (1908–1910), then later orchestrated as a ballet by the composer (1911).

Peter Ilyich Tchaikovsky demonstrated a love of fairy tales throughout his career, but nowhere greater than in his three popular ballets *Swan Lake* (composed 1875–1876), with its obvious relationship to the "Swan Maiden" family of fairy tales (A-T 400*); *The Sleeping Beauty* (composed 1888–1889), based on Perrault's tale; and *The Nutcracker* (composed 1891–1892), based on E.T.A. Hoffmann's literary fairy tale "Nußknacker und Mausekönig" (Nutcracker and Mouse-King).

## MUSICALS

The first half of the twentieth century in America saw the development of a new theater genre: the musical comedy, or simply, the musical. Although this art form inherited many ideas from the European operetta, its typical integration of sentimental comedy, songs, and dance is unique. As was the case with European operas, traditional fairy tales have provided both a general tone as well as specific subject matter for many of the most memorable musical comedies.

The *1,001 Nights* have been especially popular in this regard. One early musical comedy based on this exotic collection was *Sinbad,* composed by Sigmund Romberg and first performed in 1918, with the leading role sung by Al Jolson. The 1950s, arguably the golden age of the musical, saw at least three major plays based on the *1,001 Nights. Kismet* (1953), promoted as a "Musical Arabian Night," featured music originally composed by the nineteenth-century Russian composer Aleksandr Borodin reworked into a popular stage play by George Forrest. Two songs from this play that are still performed are "Stranger in Paradise" and "Baubles, Bangles, and Beads." The following year (1954) saw the opening of a musical play entitled *Arabian Nights* by Carmen Lombardo and John Jacob Loeb. The third musical of that decade inspired by the *1,001 Nights* was Cole Porter's *Aladdin,* which premiered on American television in 1958 and opened on the London stage the following year. This was Porter's second musical based on a folklore theme, the first being *Kiss Me, Kate* (1948), from Shakespeare's dramatization of the tale of the taming of a shrewish wife (A-T 901).

*Once upon a Mattress* (1959) by Mary Rodgers (daughter of Richard Rodgers) and Marshall Barer is a delightfully ironic version of Hans Christian Andersen's "The Princess and the Pea." Carol Burnett starred in the original Broadway cast, helping to launch her career. The play's signature song is titled, appropriately, "Happily Ever After."

"Cinderella," the most popular of all traditional fairy tales, inspired the immensely successful team Richard Rodgers and Oscar Hammerstein to create their own musical *Cinderella,* with the title role written especially for Julie Andrews. This production debuted on American television in 1957. The play was updated in 1997 (also for television) with an all-star cast including Whitney Houston, Bernadette Peters, Jason Alexander, and Whoopi Goldberg.

Indirectly, "Cinderella" is also the theme of *My Fair Lady* (1956), arguably the most successful of all musicals, by composer Frederick Loewe and lyricist Alan Jay Lerner. Their immediate inspiration came from George Bernard Shaw's play *Pygmalion,* a classic reworking of the Cinderella material. Lerner and Loewe created one other musical based on folklore: *Brigadoon* (1947). Here they transport to Scotland the German legend of Germelshausen, a town that appears only once each hundred years.

After "Cinderella," the world's most popular fairy-tale material is "Beauty and the Beast." The Walt Disney stage production of that tale opened in 1994, quickly establishing itself as one of the most successful musicals of the decade. Gaston Leroux's novel *Le fantôme de l'opéra* (The Phantom of the Opera, 1910), although lacking the expected happy ending, is built around the principal motif of "Beauty and the Beast": a beautiful woman who through mysterious circumstances becomes attached to a hideously ugly man. Andrew Lloyd Webber's very successful musical adaptation of this material premiered in London in 1986 and two years later in New York.

Another fairy-tale-like drama lacking a happy ending is *Little Shop of Horrors* (1982) by composer Alan Menken and author Howard Ashman. This offbeat musical, based on the 1960 Roger Corman film with the same name, features a human-eating plant, and by the end of the play, nearly all the characters have been devoured.

Considered only from the perspective of folk and fairy tales, the most important musical of the twentieth century is Stephen Sondheim's *Into the Woods* (1987). Here Sondheim blends four familiar fairy tales ("Cinderella," "Jack and the Beanstalk," "Rapunzel," and "Little Red Riding Hood") into a single original frame story, "The Baker and His Wife." Act one depicts the four traditional tales in a more-or-less expected manner, albeit always with a good portion of irony. Act two reveals the continuing lives of the characters, after the pronouncement of "happily ever after" has been made. For the most part these revelations are not very positive, and some of the characters perish. In the end, however, the survivors recognize that their actions always have consequences, often unforeseeable, both to themselves and to others.

## FILMS

In a very real sense motion pictures, especially television, brought to an end the centuries-old tradition of family storytelling. We still tell—more likely read—bedtime stories to children, but an hour spent with the entire family listening to one of its members reciting traditional tales would now be a rare experience indeed. The demise of such family storytelling began 200 years ago, and more, with the advance of general literacy and the availability of inexpensive reading material; the omnipresence of television sealed its doom.

From the very beginning of filmmaking its writers and producers have recognized the fact that their new art form was an alternative form of storytelling, and they turned immediately to traditional folk and fairy tales for material. The Internet Movie Data Base (http://us.imdb.com/) currently lists 50 films based on fairy tales by Charles Perrault, 89 films based on the Grimm brothers' tales, and 83 films based on Hans Christian Andersen stories. The dates range from the 1890s to the present. Furthermore, a number of popular movies have featured famous storytellers as characters, including *Hans Christian Andersen* (1952), *The Wonderful World of the Brothers Grimm* (1962), and *Ever After* (1998).

Fairy-tale films have served as pioneering pieces in a number of genres. Walt Disney began his cartooning career with a version of *Little Red Riding Hood* (1922), the first of many such short features based on fairy tales. Disney's *Snow White and the Seven Dwarfs* (1937) was the first full-length animated feature, and is still considered a classic. The aforementioned *Wonderful World of the Brothers Grimm* (1962) was the first story film produced using Cinerama, a three-projector, curved-screen presentation process. (John Ford's *How the West Was Won,* released the same year, also claims this distinction.)

Films based on folk and fairy tales cross the entire spectrum of tale types and subgenres. The *1,001 Nights* collection has provided many plots and motifs, including the silent film *The Thief of Bagdad* (1924), starring Douglas Fairbanks; Disney's *Aladdin* (1992); and *Sinbad: Legend of the Seven Seas* (2003). The grim tale of Bluebeard prompted the Charlie Chaplin movie *Monsieur Verdoux* (1947). The tall tales of the so-called "Liar Baron" gave rise to the offbeat *Adventures of Baron Munchausen* (1989). Every little boy's fantasy to be big (realized in traditional folktales of type 650A, "The Young Giant") is given expression in the magical film *Big* (1988), starring Tom Hanks. Numerous fairy-tale motifs are presented in *Toy Story* (1995), *Shrek* (2001), and their sequels.

### Cinderella Films

Fairy-tale films display much the same distribution as do their folklore counterparts. The most frequently told oral tales are the ones most often selected by filmmakers for reenactment. "Cinderella," best known in the version of Charles Perrault, exists in literally hundreds of folklore versions and is probably the world's most popular story. Filmmakers, from the very beginning of their industry, have turned to this story for movie plots. In 1898 the pioneering English filmmaker George Albert Smith produced a silent film based on Perrault's text. His better-known French counterpart Georges Méliès directed no fewer than three Cinderella films (1899, 1909, and 1912). One of Walt Disney's first animation projects was a short film titled *Cinderella* (1922). His full-length animated *Cinderella* of 1950 remains a classic of that genre.

Apart from films that consciously follow Perrault's text, many pieces use the fairy tale's basic outline but rationalize the magic parts by replacing them with chance and good luck. The formula is ageless and crosses cultures easily:

Cinderella. Illustration by Walter Crane. *Household Stories from the Collection of the Brothers Grimm* (London and New York: Macmillan, 1886), p. 125.

Through a lucky break a disadvantaged heroine gains access to a glamorous world, including the promise of romance with a man who by ordinary expectations would not notice her. Elegant clothing usually plays a pivotal role in giving her this entrée into the privileged class. Circumstances, often provoked by a jealous and unworthy female competitor, threaten to expose her as a fraud, but her inner worth reveals itself. The man who at first was attracted only by her external beauty now recognizes her full human value, and she is accepted as his legitimate partner and as a deserving member of the privileged class that he represents. Following are a few of the many films that have used this proven formula:

George Bernard Shaw's masterful comedy *Pygmalion* (first performed in 1913) follows this formula closely, but not without a large portion of irony. It was filmed in 1938 (Shaw received an Academy Award for the screenplay) and turned into an immensely popular musical, *My Fair Lady*, in 1956, which was followed by a motion-picture version in 1964. Here the Cinderella figure is Eliza Doolittle (played by Audrey Hepburn in the film), a Cockney flower peddler. Her magically lucky break comes when a phonetics professor decides to transform her into a lady, starting with her speech and ending with elegant manners and beautiful clothing. In the end she moves into the privileged class inhabited by her instructor, but—given Shaw's penchant for irony—whether they marry and live happily ever after is not entirely settled.

*Educating Rita* (1983), based on a play by Willy Russell, is another *Pygmalion-Cinderella* story. Here the heroine (played by Julie Walters) is an uneducated English hairdresser married to an insensitive husband. Her entrée into a better world comes when she enrolls in an adult-education program. Here the elegant clothing is replaced with intelligent thought, and marriage with a handsome prince replaced with her discovery of herself.

Samuel A. Taylor's play *Sabrina Fair* prompted two films, both titled *Sabrina* (1954, 1995). The Cinderella character (played respectively by Audrey Hepburn and Julia Ormond) is the daughter of a chauffeur who works for a wealthy industrialist family, the Larrabees. Unnoticed by them, she observes the glamour of their life from a perch in a tree in their garden and adjacent to her father's modest apartment. By chance she gets the opportunity to spend two years in Paris and returns a polished, sophisticated, and—of course—elegantly dressed young woman. In the end she marries the Larrabee brother of her choice.

*Working Girl* (1988) fits the Cinderella mold almost perfectly. Heroine Tess McGill (Melanie Griffith), instead of slaving in a kitchen, is stuck in a dead-end secretary's job. Her entrée into the world of decision makers comes when she is mistaken for an executive by Jack Trainer (Harrison Ford), a successful businessman. Clothes play a role here too, but instead of sumptuous ball gowns the heroine wears tailored business suits or smart cocktail dresses, as the occasion dictates. There is even a jealous stepsister type, Tess's boss (played by Sigourney Weaver), who is engaged to marry Jack (a good fairy-tale name) until Tess comes upon the scene. Early in the film Tess makes a wish over her 30th birthday cake. As the film ends, all her wishes have come true. The secretary-Cinderella is now an executive-princess.

*Pretty Woman* (1990) depicts an even greater leap forward and upward for another kind of "working girl." Vivian Ward (Julia Roberts) is a Los Angeles streetwalker, hired by a millionaire businessman (played by Richard Gere) as an escort for social events. Her magical makeover comes during a shopping spree at Beverly Hills clothiers. In the end, her prince recognizes her human qualities, and mounted on a white horse (actually a white limousine) he rescues her from her sordid environment.

Turning back to Perrault's original text, more or less, *Ever After* (1998) features costumes and events from Renaissance Europe (there is even a role for Leonardo da Vinci). Cinderella, here called Danielle (Drew Barrymore), is a strong-willed, athletic feminist who is more than a match for her abusive stepmother and stepsister (she has two stepsisters, but one of them is quite kind).

The title heroine of *The Princess Diaries* (2001) is a San Francisco teenager (played by Anne Hathaway) who discovers that she, through her deceased father, is the successor to the throne of a small country in Europe. Her grandmother (played by Julie Andrews) appears on the scene and turns the awkward adolescent into a beautiful, elegantly dressed, self-confident princess.

Marisa Ventura (Jennifer Lopez), the heroine of *Maid in Manhattan* (2002), is a single mother who works as a maid in a luxury Manhattan hotel. She yields to the temptation of trying on a hotel guest's dress and is seen, beautifully attired, by another guest, Christopher Marshall (Ralph Fiennes), a New York assemblyman and candidate for the United States Senate. Predictable misunderstandings lead to hopes, frustrations, and the also predictable fairy-tale ending.

### Male Cinderellas

From rags to riches is also the path of countless male fairy-tale protagonists. A very common plot in fairy tales is the advancement to wealth and power of a hero initially introduced as a simpleton. A number of popular films follow this formula. *Cinderfella* (1969), starring Jerry Lewis, is a parody of the traditional Cinderella story from the wordplay in the title through the clumsy hero's winning of Princess Charmant.

*Being There* (1979), starring Peter Sellers and Shirley MacLaine, like many fairy tales before it, is a story about chance, both figuratively and literally. Chance is the name of a simple-minded gardener who finds himself wandering aimlessly in the streets following the death of his employer. Dressed in a good suit, essentially his only possession, Chance, through chance, becomes the guest of a wealthy businessman and his wife. A chain of happy coincidences and fortunate misunderstandings transforms Chauncey Gardner (as his hosts have understood his name) into a political insider and a man of prestige and influence.

Another slow-witted fellow who stumbles into good fortune in fairy-tale fashion is the title hero of *Forrest Gump* (1994), starring Tom Hanks. A final example of a male Cinderella story is *Notting Hill* (1999), starring Hugh

Grant and Julia Roberts. Chance rules here as well; unusual circumstances bring together Anna Scott, a Julia Roberts–like world-famous film star, and William Thacker, a very ordinary London bookseller. As in the female rags-to-riches counterparts, misunderstandings lead to hopes and frustrations, but in the end true love triumphs, in spite of initial class differences.

### Beauty and the Beast

Following "Cinderella," the family of tales depicting heroines promised in marriage to animal bridegrooms probably constitutes the next most popular story line in folklore. Extant in hundreds of different versions, the classic form of an animal-bridegroom tale is "La Belle et la Bête" (Beauty and the Beast, 1756) as written by Jeanne-Marie LePrince de Beaumont. Her tale has prompted some 30 film adaptations—mostly titled *Beauty and the Beast*—beginning with a silent movie in 1903, including a popular (among women, at least) CBS television series that ran between 1987 and 1990, and culminating with the animated Disney film (1991) and its associated Broadway musical (1994).

As was the case with the Cinderella plot, the basic formula of a generic "Beauty and the Beast" tale has been adopted by numerous writers and filmmakers, possibly with the traditional magic transformation rationalized into a psychological change on the part of one or more characters. One such example is the classic horror film *King Kong* (1933). At the center of this fantasy thriller is the attraction of a giant gorilla for a petite blonde heroine. The scriptwriters are quite aware of the relationship between their movie and the popular fairy tale. Various characters mention the "Beauty and the Beast" motif repeatedly, but the film departs from the tradition of having the heroine's acceptance of the beast transform him into a human. Instead, his love for her leads to his destruction. In the final words of the film, "It was Beauty killed the Beast."

Another famous adaptation of the "Beauty and the Beast" material is Gaston Leroux's *Le fantôme de l'opéra* (The Phantom of the Opera, 1910), the story of a disfigured musical genius who lives in the catacombs beneath the Paris opera house and his love for a beautiful female singer. This novel has been filmed a number of times, including a memorable silent version starring Lon Chaney as the phantom (1925). A film version of Andrew Lloyd Webber's musical based on this story has been announced for 2004.

*Fairy Legends*

Folklorists define the word *legend* as a believed account. Sincere belief in fairies and other hidden people (elves, dwarfs, trolls, brownies, kobolds, leprechauns, pixies, selkies, and the like) continued well into the twentieth century, especially in Ireland, Cornwall, Wales, Scotland, and the more remote parts of Scandinavia. A number of films depict this belief, and usually in a sympathetic manner. *The Secret of Roan Inish* (1994) investigates a local legend about selkies—seals that can turn into humans—from a remote Irish fishing village. Adding to the mystery is the account of a baby who was carried away by the tide and reputedly is being raised by seals. *FairyTale: A True Story* (1997) reenacts the story of two English children who reportedly took a series of photographs, beginning in 1917, at Cottingley in West Yorkshire that captured the images of fairies. The girls' photographs aroused considerable publicity. Sir Arthur Conan Doyle, himself a true believer in fairies and other psychic phenomena, wrote an account of the affair titled *The Coming of the Fairies,* published in 1922, and is given a role in the movie. *Photographing Fairies* (1997) depicts the same period and culture, but with a professional photographer carefully designing scientific experiments to verify or disprove the existence of the hidden people.

In the end we are given to believe that fairies do indeed exist. This will come as no surprise to the audiences of *Peter Pan* who for more than a century have been clapping their hands to keep Tinker Bell from succumbing to the pirate's poison, for—as observed by Andrew Lang in the preface to his *Yellow Fairy Book* (1894)—"if there are really no fairies, why do people believe in them, all over the world?"

## WORKS CITED

Lang, Andrew. *The Lilac Fairy Book.* London: Longmans, 1910.
———. *The Yellow Fairy Book.* London: Longmans, 1894.

# Glossary

Cross-references are spelled with SMALL CAPITALS.

**Aarne-Thompson (A-T)**. *See* TYPE.

**Active and Passive Folktale Carriers**. An active folktale carrier is a storyteller who remembers a story heard elsewhere, then retells it—with or without alteration—on a new occasion. A passive folktale carrier makes this process possible by being a receptive listener, possibly requesting specific tales from the storyteller, and sometimes prompting or correcting an active storyteller with a temporary memory lapse. This concept was developed by the Swedish folklorist Carl Wilhelm von Sydow.

**Aesopic, Aesopian**. In the manner of Aesop, the legendary Greek composer of FABLES. Although it is possible that there was an ancient storyteller by the name of Aesop, already in antiquity the reputation behind this name expanded to proportions far beyond what a single person could have achieved. Many of the earliest references to didactic tales of the type attributed to Aesop identify them as Aesopic (or Aesopian) fables rather than Aesop's fables. In other words, Aesopic is an adjective that describes a kind of story and a literary tradition but does not claim to identify a specific author.

**Allegory**. A fictional work that, in addition to advancing its own plot, symbolizes a more general set of values. Fables and parables, with their transparent moralizing, typically can be seen as allegories representing such abstractions as justice, good, selflessness, and the like. Fairy tales, too, frequently function as allegories, with individual characters and happenings symbolizing entire classes of people and universal drives or stages of human development. For example, "The Frog King" (Grimm 1) can be read as a simple adventure story about a girl who loses a golden ball down a well; is helped by a frog, under the agreement that later the two will eat and sleep together; is at first repulsed by the frog's advances, especially when he wants to share her bed; then performs an act that turns the frog into a prince; and finally falls in love with and marries the frog. Beneath this simple plot lies the potential for an allegorical reading, not about wells and frogs and beds, but about the loss of childhood, coming of age, and a growing awareness and acceptance of sexuality. *See also* METAPHOR, SIMILE, SYMBOL.

**Analogue**. In folktale research, a narrative that is similar to another one. *See also* VARIANT, VERSION.

**Anecdote**. A short account in prose, usually describing a single event and often constructed with a humorous PUNCH LINE. *See also* JOKE.

**Animal (Beast) Epic**. A long narrative featuring animals as actors and usually comprising many episodes. Popular in medieval and Renaissance Europe, such stories were often allegorical in nature, with various animals symbolizing different human qualities. Thus the fox (frequently named Reynard) stood for a cunning person, while his principal antagonist the wolf (often named Isengrim) represented a greedy and slow-witted cleric. Individual episodes in animal epics were often derived from, or had continuing circulation as, oral folktales.

**Animal (Beast) Fable**. *See* FABLE.

**Animism**. The belief, common among primitive cultures, that inanimate objects as well as living beings have a spirit and thus a conscious life. The prevalence of talking things and animals both in AESOPIC fables and in traditional FAIRY TALES has led to theories that some such tales represent SURVIVALS of very ancient animism beliefs and rituals. *See also* ETHNOLOGY.

**Anthropomorphic**. Having human attributes. The animal and inanimate characters in AESOPIC fables typically display human qualities and can thus be described as being anthropomorphic.

**Anti–Fairy Tale**. A term applied to such works as Kafka's "The Metamorphosis" and the film *Shrek,* where the leading characters, although engaged in typical fairy-tale situations, behave in thoroughly nontraditional, one might say, antiheroic, fashion. *See also* CROSSOVER FAIRY TALE.

**Aphorism**. Composed in the tradition of the PROVERB, an aphorism is a concise formulation of a principle, usually consisting of a single sentence. Aphorisms, sometimes charged with IRONY, are often used in expressing "the MORAL of the story" for a FABLE or in delivering the punch line of an ANECDOTE.

**Application (of a fable)**. *See* MORAL.

**Archetype**. In JUNGIAN psychology, an idea or mode of thought inherited from the past through the COLLECTIVE UNCONSCIOUS. Some interpreters of folklore see such archetypes in many of the repeating images, motifs, and symbols of fairy tales.

**Art Fairy Tale**. A literal translation of the German *Kunstmärchen*. *See* LITERARY FAIRY TALE.

**Ballad**. A narrative, often rhymed, composed in a rhythmic form suitable for singing or chanting. Many traditional folktales in prose have ballad counterparts with essentially the same plots. *See also* CANTE FABLE.

**Belief**. Many fragments of ancient SUPERSTITIONS and beliefs, both religious and secular, have survived in folk and fairy tales. For example, the Aesopic fable "The Swan" speaks of the unbelievably beautiful song sung by a swan (swan song) just before it dies. The Grimms' "Rumpelstiltskin" (55) centers on the widespread ancient belief that a mortal can gain control over an underground person by discovering his or her name. *See also* SURVIVAL.

**Big Rock Candy Mountain**. *See* FOOL'S PARADISE.

**Bogeyman, Bugbear**. An imaginary monster invented by adults to frighten children into good behavior. Many of the threatening creatures in children's CAUTIONARY TALES can be interpreted as bogeymen.

**Bowdlerize**. A synonym for *expurgate*. The term derives from the name of Thomas Bowdler, who created *The Family Shakespeare* (1807), a selection of 20 Shakespeare plays with passages paraphrased or removed that the editor deemed offensive to nineteenth-century British moral standards. Bowdlerization was practiced frequently by COLLECTORS, EDITORS, and publishers of folktales, especially during the nineteenth century. Forewords to these collections often include statements that unspecified changes have been made to the original texts to protect readers from the moral laxness of previous eras and foreign cultures, as well as from the vulgarities of common entertainment.

**Broadside**. A publication consisting of a single printed sheet, usually folded. Soon after the invention of printing in the fifteenth century and well into the nineteenth century, broadsides containing the texts of ballads and other folkloric material were sold at fairs and marketplaces throughout Europe. *See also* CHAPBOOK.

**Calendar Story**. An ANECDOTE, often derived from a folktale, and published in an almanac.

**Cante Fable, Cante Tale**. A story, obviously related to the BALLAD, containing songs or rhymes, typically sung or recited by the characters. In such stories the quoted verse remains remarkably constant across variants from different countries. Examples are the Grimms' "The Juniper Tree" (47) and "Old Hildebrand" (95).

**Catchword**. *See* TAG.

**Cautionary Tale**. A narrative, in prose or verse, that depicts the negative, often tragic consequences of inappropriate conduct. Cautionary tales are found in every culture, from AESOPIC fables to the fairy tales of Hans Christian Andersen, and into the present. A less common term, *exemplary tale,* usually refers to a story emphasizing the positive outcome of good behavior. Many didactic tales combine both the positive and the negative. For example, de Beaumont's classical rendition of "The Beauty and the Beast" describes in dramatic detail the heroine's generous rewards for her piety and selflessness but also the dire punishment meted out to her mean-spirited sisters. *See also* BOGEYMAN.

**Censorship**. *See* BOWDLERIZE.

**Chain Tale**. A formula story consisting of a sequence of EPISODES, each one repeating the previous episode and then adding one new element. Most chain tales are whimsical, virtually to the point of being nonsensical. They are found in the folklore of most countries. The English story "The Old Woman and Her Pig" is typical. A woman, on her way home from market with a pig, comes to a stile, but the pig will not jump over it. She asks a dog to bite the pig, but the dog refuses; so she asks a stick to hit the dog, but the stick refuses; so she asks a fire to burn the stick, and so forth. Each succeeding request is refused, thus lengthening the chain, until

The old woman's pig refuses to jump over a stile. Illustration by John D. Batten. Joseph Jacobs, *English Fairy Tales* (London: David Nutt, 1898), p. 20.

at last a cow gives her some milk. The final sentence, read backward and then forward, summarizes the whole chain: "As soon as the cat had lapped up the milk, the cat began to kill the rat; the rat began to gnaw the rope; the rope began to hang the butcher; the butcher began to kill the ox; the ox began to drink the water; the water began to quench the fire; the fire began to burn the stick; the stick began to beat the dog; the dog began to bite the pig; the little pig in a fright jumped over the stile; and so the old woman got home that night" (Halliwell, *The Nursery Rhymes of England*, pp. 159–60; see bibliography for publication information).

**Chanson de Geste (*pl.,* chansons de geste).** An epic poem from medieval France based on historical people and events but also containing many legendary and folkloric elements.

**Chapbook.** A small, cheaply printed book distributed in Europe (and later North America) between the late fifteenth and early nineteenth centuries. Often illustrated with woodcuts, these books contained popular matter, including legends, folktales, and ballads. The name derives from *chapman,* an old term for *peddler. See also* BROADSIDE.

**Charm.** *See* INCANTATION.

**Child Ballad.** One of the 305 basic types of traditional BALLADS compiled and cataloged by Francis James Child in his *English and Scottish Popular Ballads* (1882–1898).

**Climax.** The turning point or PUNCH LINE in an ANECDOTE.

**Cockaigne, Land of.** *See* FOOL'S PARADISE.

**Collective Composition.** A term applied to a folktale that has undergone revision over several generations of telling and retelling, the end product thus being the result of collective effort. The process can be observed with many of the Grimms' tales, first published in 1812 and 1815. Soon afterward many of these tales found their way from the printed page back into the repertories of oral storytellers, where they continued to evolve.

**Collective Unconscious**. A term defined by Carl Jung to describe that portion of the unconscious mind formed by the brain's structure itself rather than by individual experience, and thus common to all humans. JUNGIAN interpreters of fairy tales see the collective unconscious as contributing heavily to various images, symbols, and patterns common to the myths and folktales of diverse cultures.

**Collector**. With reference to folktales, a person who records orally transmitted stories from live storytellers by means of recording devices, shorthand, or outlining (with details filled in later from memory); or a person who brings together tales from disparate and scattered sources such as chronicles, manuscripts, diaries, letters, broadsides, chapbooks, periodicals, and published books. Folklorists greatly prefer the former method because of its closeness to the people who are themselves part of the tradition being preserved and studied. However, folklorists wanting to preserve and study the oral tales of past generations are dependent upon written or published raw materials. *See also* EDITOR, NARRATIVE SITUATION.

**Contamination**. The addition to a folktale of EPISODES or MOTIFS from another story, or the joining together of two independent stories into one longer and more complex tale. Such mixtures, which usually result from a storyteller's faulty memory, are most often structurally disjointed, although on occasion the new compositions can be artistically satisfying.

**Conte de Fées**. Literally, *tale of fairies,* the French term from which the English word *fairy tale* is derived. Related terms are *conte merveilleux* (magic tale), *conte populaire* (popular tale), and *conte de bonne femme* (old wives' tale).

**Contemporary Legend**. *See* URBAN LEGEND.

**Content and Form**. Students of esthetics have long been interested in the relationship between content and form in a literary work. Fairy tales provide relevant examples. For instance, numerous fairy tales have the following form: childhood—conflict—marriage. This basic form can be filled in with various plot elements (content). For example, in "The Frog King" (Grimm 1) the childhood episode depicts a girl playing with a golden ball; the conflict episode shows her losing the ball, but regaining it by agreeing to eat and sleep with a frog; the final episode describes the frog's transformation into a prince and his subsequent marriage to the heroine. In "Little Brier Rose" (Grimm 50) the childhood episode describes the heroine's birth and christening; the conflict episode shows her pricking her finger and falling into a 100-year sleep; the final episode depicts a prince awakening her, and their subsequent marriage. Thus two quite different tales, in terms of content, can be shown to have essentially the same form.

**Crossover Fairy Tale**. A term suggested by Jack Zipes to designate literary fairy tales using traditional motifs but assigning nontraditional roles to females, ethnic minorities, and other groups. *See also* ANTI–FAIRY TALE, REVISIONIST FAIRY TALE.

**Cumulative Tale**. A story, usually intended for small children, with a simple, repetitive plot and featuring dialogue that builds on itself from episode to episode. An example is "The Gingerbread Boy." *See also* CHAIN TALE.

**Custom**. A traditional practice that serves to define acceptable human behavior, often with the force of a legal code. Many folk and fairy tales allude to ancient customs, such as courtship and marriage practices, gender-related work roles, master-apprentice relations, and the execution of condemned criminals. *See also* FOLKLORE, SURVIVAL.

**Dialect**. Most major languages have regional, social, and ethnic variants called *dialects*. Although dialects often are considered to be substandard to the formal language, a rich variety of orally transmitted folklore has been collected from dialect-speaking informants. COLLECTORS have long agonized about whether stories told in dialect should be rewritten in the standard language. The Grimms solved this problem by writing most of their tales in High German (the standard literary language), but leaving a few sample texts in their original Low German, Swiss German, or Austro-Bavarian dialects. The best-known dialect writer of folklike stories in America is Joel Chandler Harris, whose Uncle Remus tales, based on African American folklore and recorded in African American dialect, are recognized as classics of the genre. *See also* EDITOR, SIGHT DIALECT.

**Didactic Tale**. *See* CAUTIONARY TALE.

**Diffusion**. The process of transmitting an item of folklore from its birthplace by word of mouth to outlying communities, which in turn would serve as starting points for further outward transmission. Diffusion can be continuous, analogous to a circular wave set up by a stone thrown into still water, or it can be intermittent, as when a folklore carrier travels to a distant place before resuming his or her storytelling activities. At every stage a tale might be altered somewhat, reflecting the new audience's values as well as a storyteller's ability to remember and retell a story. *See also* CONTAMINATION, LOCALIZATION, MIGRATORY LEGEND, POLYGENESIS VARIANT.

**Double Entendre**. An expression with two possible meanings, one often risqué. Traditional RIDDLES often depend on double entendres for their solution. The writers of medieval and Renaissance jest books used this device to bring their tales (just barely) into the realm of respectability. Even family tales often contain expressions or entire episodes with dual meanings, thus retaining the interest of older members of the audience without making the stories inappropriate for younger listeners. *See also* LEVELS OF SIGNIFICANCE, SUBTEXT.

**Dream Analysis**. A cornerstone of FREUDIAN psychoanalysis. Freud theorized that dreams reflect unconscious mental activity, although not without distortion and often through symbols. Long before Freud, fairy tales, with their surrealistic imagery and otherworldly logic, were associated with dreams. Psychologists of different persuasions see in both dreams and fairy tales similar expressions of unconscious fears and wishes. *See also* JUNGIAN, OEDIPUS COMPLEX.

**Droll**. A humorous person, or a whimsical story featuring such characters. *See also* JEST.

**Dualism**. The tendency, very common in traditional fairy tales, to divide reality and experience into two mutually exclusive parts—such as good or evil, I or you, yes or no, black or white—resulting in an often simplistic worldview with little delineation between extremes.

**Editor**. With reference to folktale publishing, an editor makes the material provided by the COLLECTOR ready for printing and distribution. Among the many decisions that he or she must make are these: How will such speech imperfections as false starts, unintended repetition, mispronunciations, and grammatical errors be handled? Are sexist or racist remarks, profanity, and obscenities acceptable? If the STORYTELLER has added parenthetical remarks such as apologies or explanations to the story, will these be included in the final text? If dialogue between the storyteller and his or her audience occurs, will this be included? If the storyteller speaks a regional or nonstandard DIALECT, will it be normalized, or spelled out phonetically as spoken? If the storyteller merges two traditional tales into one (CONTAMINATION), will they be treated as separate entities, or published as delivered? There are no easy answers to these and other questions faced by an editor. Each generation has its own standards and expectations. As a rule, scholarly practices of the nineteenth century gave editors great freedom in forming an end product to meet public expectations. In most respects scholarship standards are much tighter today. *See also* BOWDLERIZE, STYLIZATION.

**Enchantment**. *See* TRANSFORMATION.

**Endless Story**. A type of CHAIN TALE that repeats endlessly. Such tales fall into three basic categories. Circular tales, called rounds, turn back on themselves—for example, "Ask your mother for twenty-five cents to see the elephant jump the fence; he jumped so high he skinned his ask your mother for twenty-five cents...." Other endless tales repeat a particular phrase forever, as for example the account of the ogre who granted his victim one last prayer before eating him. The victim prays, "Save me, save me, save me...." A third type describes each step of a monumental task, such as: "There was a barn filled with grain, with a hole in the wall large enough for just one ant. An ant crawled through the hole and took a single grain, then another ant came and took another grain, then another ant came and...."

**Epic**. A long narrative, often in verse, depicting heroic deeds of historic or legendary characters. Most traditional epics evolved as folklore before being formulated and recorded by a specific poet. Many epics, including Homer's *Iliad* and *Odyssey*, contain episodes that have had independent lives as folktales. *See also* ANIMAL EPIC, SAGA.

**Epimythium (*pl.,* epimythia)**. See MORAL.

**Episode**. The account of a brief event, usually one of a sequence of similar incidents. Many folk and fairy tales are constructed by chaining events together. One common technique is the depiction of three very similar events. The first occurrence is described in detail and has a negative outcome. The second one is related with few details and also has a negative outcome. The final one is related with more details than the second, but fewer than the first, and it has a positive outcome. Cinderella's three visits to the ball in the Grimms' version of the tale (no. 21) provide an example of this technique. (Perrault's "Cinderella" describes only two ballroom visits.) Folktales about FOOLS and TRICKSTERS also are typically constructed from numerous episodes, each one comprising a single encounter that can be, and often is, told as an independent story. CHAIN TALES and CUMULATIVE TALES are also episodic in their construction, with each succeeding episode building on the preceding one in a predictable manner.

**Escape Literature**. *See* FANTASY.

**Ethnology**. Essentially a synonym for *cultural* or *social anthropology,* ethnology is the study of the nonbiological aspects of cultures, that is, those parts of culture that are learned, as opposed to those that are inherited. Ethnologists historically have focused more on primitive than on advanced cultures. Because mythmaking and storytelling is common to all known cultures, ethnologists often study myths, legends, and folktales as reflections of cultural beliefs, practices, and values. *See also* ANIMISM.

**Etiologic Tale**. Derived from *etiology,* the study of origins and causes, this term refers to stories that explain why things are as they are. Such stories constitute an important and early branch of the folklore of all cultures. The great popularity of these tales is demonstrated by the large number of folktale titles that begin with *Why* or *How.* The range of explanatory tales, as they have evolved over time, runs from the sublime to the ridiculous. At their most serious, etiologic tales take on the gravity of a creation myth, demanding religious belief from their audience (for example, the Biblical account of the origin of rainbows). At the other end of the spectrum are playful and obviously fictitious fables such as "Why Dogs Dislike Cats" found in the collections of many countries. Etiologic tales are also called *pourquois tales,* from the French word for *why.*

**Exemplary Tale**. *See* CAUTIONARY TALE.

**Exemplum (*pl.,* exempla)**. A short, simple tale that "sets an example," either positively or negatively, and thus illustrates a moral value. Exempla can be built into larger works or can exist as independent stories. *See also* SIMPLE FORMS.

**Explanatory Tale**. *See* ETIOLOGIC TALE.

**Fable**. A short tale illustrating a moral value, which may or may not be expressly stated as a concluding sentence ("The moral of the story is..."). Regardless of their origin, traditional fables are often called AESOPIC, after the legendary Greek storyteller credited with having invented the genre. Fables can have humans, animals, or objects as actors. Those featuring animals are often called animal or beast fables. An author or teller of fables is called a *fabulist. See also* ALLEGORY, MORAL, PARABLE, PROVERB.

**Fabliau (*pl.,* fabliaux)**. A short narrative, usually in verse, popular in medieval France, and often recited by JONGLEURS. Fabliaux often parodied courtly manners and typically were marked by crude humor and antifemale sentiment. *See also* JEST.

**Facetia (*pl.,* facetiae)**. A Latin term often used in English (and other European languages) to designate a witty, frequently ribald anecdote composed in the manner of the Italian humanist Poggio (Gian Francesco Poggio Bracciolini, 1389–1459). *See also* JEST.

**Fairy**. A generic term for any of the hundreds of types of hidden beings formerly believed to share the earth with humans. Each region had one or more species of these creatures. Although the different kinds of fairies differed greatly from each other in size, habitat, and character, they did share some qualities. They lived very close to humans, somehow in a parallel world, but they remained invisible except under special circumstances. When visible, they closely resembled their human counterparts, although they were typically much smaller. Fairies possessed supernatural powers, which they could use either to help or to harm their human neighbors. However malicious the hidden people might be, humans often called them "the good folk" to avoid offending them. With the right charms and rituals (often of a religious nature) humans could gain some control over fairies, and according to some legends, they vacated many Christian areas altogether because of the ringing of church bells. With the advance of secular learning, belief in fairies declined in most areas. Folklore and popular culture have now relegated these little beings to the realm of FANTASY fiction and make-believe. Among the many creatures closely related to fairies are banshees, brownies, dwarfs, elves, genies, gnomes, goblins, hidden people, hobbits, imps, leprechauns, nymphs, pixies, sprites, trolls, and underground people. *See also* FAIRY TALE, FAIRYLAND.

**Fairy Tale, Fairy Story**. Derived from the French *conte de fées,* this is the normal term in English for *magic tale* or *wonder tale,* designating even stories that do not feature fairies per se. Fairy tales, whether told orally or composed on paper, are characterized by FANTASY and MAGIC. Used as an adjective, the term *fairy-tale* carries the connotation of beauty and perfection, as in the expression "fairy-tale wedding." *See also* FOLKTALE, LITERARY FAIRY TALE.

**Fairyland**. According to popular belief, a realm occupied by fairies or similar supernatural beings, traditionally named *Faërie* (also spelled *Faerie* or *Faery*). This land is variously described as being beneath the ground, under water, or above the clouds. Similar to the otherworld of the ancient Celts, fairyland often is depicted as a realm parallel to or overlapping the human world, but invisible and intangible (except under special circumstances) to humans. As the belief in actual fairies diminished, fairyland came to represent a land of make-believe, the setting for FANTASY stories where traditional limitations (physical, social, and psychological) no longer apply, and where WISHES can come true. Alternatively, the fantasy setting of fairy tales also can be seen as a dreamlike reflection of the human psyche, with its overlapping layers of conscious and unconscious memories. Literary fairy tales are often set in otherworldly realms reminiscent of fairyland—for example, L. Frank Baum's Oz, James Barrie's Never Never Land, Lewis Carroll's Wonderland, C.S. Lewis's Narnia, and Charles Kingsley's underwater world.

**Fakelore**. A term coined by Richard M. Dorson to describe stories and other lore artificially created, usually for commercial purposes, in imitation of authentic, orally transmitted material. Fakelore is, in Dorson's words, "a synthetic product claiming to be authentic oral tradition but actually tailored for mass edification" (*Folklore and Fakelore,* p. 5; see bibliography for publication information). His prime example of fakelore is the myriad of Paul Bunyan stories that claim to be lumber camp reminiscences but in truth are the products of commercial writers with little or no knowledge of logging traditions.

The mundane world and its parallel realm fairyland. Illustration by Willy Pogany. W. Jenkyn Thomas, *The Welsh Fairy Book* (London: T. Fisher Unwin, n.d. [1908]), p. 22.

**Fantasy**. Throughout the ages, storytelling (whether by word of mouth, through books, or on a stage) has entertained by providing audiences with an escape from their own existence. This escape may be through the vicarious participation in improbable adventures and romance, albeit in a naturalistic setting, or it may be into a make-believe world governed by totally different physical laws and social customs. Traditional fairy tales excel in both cases and are the foundation of fantasy literature ranging from Shakespeare's *A Midsummer Night's Dream* to the latest Harry Potter novel by J.K. Rowling. *See also* FAIRYLAND, MAGIC.

**Figure of Speech**. *See* FORMULA, TAG.

**Finnish School**. A synonym for the GEOGRAPHIC-HISTORIC METHOD of folktale scholarship, so called because of its development and advocacy by Finnish scholars, preeminently Kaarle Krohn and Antti Aarne.

**First-Person Narrative**. An account where the narrator, identified as "I," is one of the story's participants. This technique is unusual in fairy tales but common in some types of anecdotes, especially FISH STORIES and TALL TALES. *See also* MEMORATE, POINT OF VIEW.

**Fish Story**. A special form of TALL TALE, in which the narrator exaggerates the size of a fish, either one caught or one that got away. By extension, *fish story* can apply to any account involving gross exaggeration, either uncontested or suspected but not proven.

**FOAF**. An acronym, derived from *friend of a friend,* used by students of URBAN LEGENDS, to designate the usual attribution of such tales. For many generations and in many countries people have passed on accounts of ostensibly true occurrences, originally experienced not by the narrator, nor by a firsthand acquaintance, but by the proverbial *friend of a friend.*

**Folk Drama**. Plays that are a part of European FOLKLORE appear in at least two forms, both of which are closely connected to FOLKTALES. One form is the liturgical drama, associated with religious services in the Middle Ages, but with time separating entirely from the church. Liturgical drama performed in vernacular languages can be divided into three main types: miracle plays, morality plays, and mystery plays. Religious themes remained central in all types, but secular (even coarse) episodes were often added for comic relief and audience appeal. A second form of folk drama is the large body of seasonal ceremonies that often included enactments of legendary or historical events. Such plays included SHROVETIDE PLAYS *(Fastnachtspiele)* and mumming or mummers' plays. Folk dramas of all types incorporated existing folktales into their plots; or, conversely, dialogue composed for these plays found its way into the repertories of oral storytellers. For example, a Dutch miracle play, "The Miraculous Apple Tree," features an apple tree that captures anyone who touches it without the owner's permission. This same motif is central to the widespread folktale "The Smith's Three Wishes," with the smith using his magic tree to capture Death, thus gaining additional years of life.

**Folklore**. Coined as a substitute for the awkward phrase *popular antiquities* in the mid-1800s, *folklore* is a collective noun encompassing all information that humans preserve and transmit by personal (as opposed to institutional) demonstration and oral communication. Subcategories of folklore include customs, folk art, folksongs, folktales, proverbs, riddles, games, ceremonies, folk remedies, and superstitions.

**Folktale (*sometimes spelled as two words*, folk tale, *or as a hyphenated word*, folk-tale)**. Strictly speaking, a folktale is any narrative made up within the group that is using it, then preserved and passed on by word of mouth. More generally, the term *folktale* has come to designate a story, regardless of its origin or mode of transmission, that resembles a tale traditionally made up by an unlettered storyteller and then communicated orally to future generations. *See also* GENRE.

**Fool's Paradise**. A place where even a fool can be happy, presumably through self-delusion, but also a fantastic realm, often named Cockaigne and described in numerous folktales from medieval Europe, where rivers flow with wine, roast ducks fly onto one's table, and so forth. American hobo stories and songs about the Big Rock Candy Mountain are derived from these tales.

**Fool's Tale**. A JEST featuring the mistakes of a slow-witted character. These can be authentically stupid blunders, such as losing a fortune by engaging in a series of trades, each time getting something less valuable; or they can be clever tricks, hidden behind a veil of pretended naïveté. Tales of both types use a large number of synonyms for *fool*, including blockhead, booby, dumbbell, dumbhead, dummy, dunce, dunderhead, idiot, knucklehead, moron, natural, nincompoop, noodle, numbskull (numskull), oaf, simpleton, and silly. Fool's tales can also take the form of ANIMAL FABLES, typically with the alligator (in India) and the bear or wolf (in Europe) displaying human foolishness. *See also* GOTHAM, TRICKSTER TALES.

**Form**. *See* CONTENT AND FORM.

**Formula**. A set expression such as "Once upon a time" used as a marker within a story, whether or not the phrase is appropriate within its context. It is even conceivable that a fairy tale could end, "Then the prince and princess died, and they lived happily ever after," with the concluding formula communicating "The story is over," rather than its literal meaning. Set formulas (outlines) are also used in the construction of fairy-tale plots. For example, numerous tales follow this plan: conflict at home—outward quest—magic resolution—marriage. CHAIN TALES offer an extreme example of a prescribed outline determining not only the form but also greatly influencing the content of the story. *See also* CONTENT AND FORM, TAG.

**Fractured Fairy Tale**. A popular term designating an alternate version of a traditional story, possibly a PARODY written for humorous effect or a REVISIONIST tale with altered gender or social roles to make the story compatible with a particular ethical or political philosophy.

**Frame Story**. An external narrative that facilitates the telling of stories within a story. This device has been used by authors and compilers of tales in many cultures and almost from the beginning of published collections. The most famous such collection is probably the *1,001 Nights*, which consists primarily of stories told (but left unfinished until the following night) by Scheherazade to her despotic husband. *The Panchatantra* from India is a prominent example from the Orient.

Two exemplary frame-story collections from Europe are Boccaccio's *Decameron* and Chaucer's *Canterbury Tales*. Less known, but very important as early compilations of fairy tales, are the *Facetious Nights* of Straparola and *The Pentamerone* of Basile.

**Freudian**. Characteristic of Sigmund Freud, the Austrian neurologist and founder of psychoanalysis. The adjective *Freudian,* with reference to fairy tales, usually refers to the connection that such tales have to the unconscious and to the psychosexual development of storytellers and their listeners. Freudian interpreters see in the many traditional myths and folktales that depict incestuous relationships a corroboration of the OEDIPUS COMPLEX, a cornerstone of Freud's teaching.

**Function**. It is legitimate to ask the question *why* a particular tale is told, remembered, then retold in a given culture, or *why* a given book resonates with its audience. The answers to these questions reveal the function that a story or book performs. With folk and fairy tales, entertainment is always an important function. If a story does not entertain, does not satisfy its teller and listener, it will soon be forgotten. Protection of social norms is also a function, but as those norms change, the stories designed to protect them will also fall out of favor. For example, many tales collected in medieval and Renaissance jest books promote wife beating, and it is to be hoped that such tales no longer find a receptive audience. Yet another common function of folk and fairy tales is to provide acceptable outlets for the expression of tabooed subjects. Incest, probably the most universal of all taboos, is a common motif in folktales. *See also* NARRATIVE SITUATION.

**Games**. Many traditional childhood games contain verbal elements and gestures that relate to ancient incantations, ceremonies, and folktales. For example, the words and actions associated with "London Bridge Is Falling Down" are widely interpreted as SURVIVALS of a ritual used to select individuals to be sacrificed in order to protect bridges and other vulnerable structures from storms and floods. Action games, such as "Ghost in the Graveyard" or "Cops and Robbers," often act out, very broadly, the plots of familiar ghost or robber stories. "Kings' X," a call for "time-out" used in children's games well into the twentieth century, derives from a halt in medieval warfare for the exchange of captured kings.

**Genre**. Related to the words *gender* and *kind,* this term refers to a category of art, literature, or music. Basic literary genres such as narrative, drama, and poetry can be (and have been) endlessly subdivided according to style, content, structure, function, and so forth. The most important genres of FOLKTALES include MYTH, LEGEND, FABLE, MAGIC TALE, and ANECDOTE, but these too can be divided into still narrower categories.

**Geographic-Historic Method**. Also called the FINNISH SCHOOL, this method prescribes techniques for tracing the evolution and migration of a given folktale by documenting and analyzing all of its known versions, both oral and literary.

**Gesture**. The importance in storytelling of body language (facial expression, tone of voice, hand gestures, and other motions) can hardly be overstated, but these important modes of communication are largely lost in printed versions of the tales.

Readers of traditional stories should bear in mind that most of the texts were originally acted out by oral STORYTELLERS, whose nonverbal signals could greatly alter the meaning and impact of many passages.

**Ghost Story**. A tale of the supernatural whose primary function is to entertain or instruct by frightening the listener. Such stories fall primarily into two categories: serious accounts about spirits haunting mortals, told as true stories, often with a didactic purpose; and obviously fictitious tales told frivolously and whose only purpose is entertainment.

**Gotham**. A village in Nottinghamshire, England, and the home of the legendary wise fools. These men, hearing that King John (who ruled from 1199 to 1216) was considering a visit to their village, which would bring them additional expense and restrictions, performed numerous ridiculous tasks in the presence of royal messengers, thus dissuading the king from his plans. Many FOOL'S TALES are told about Gothamites, some suggesting method in their madness, others related as simple burlesques about unqualified morons. Other places famous for foolish behavior (sometimes feigned foolishness, sometimes authentic stupidity) include the Mols peninsula in Jutland, Denmark; the legendary town of Schwarzenborn in Germany; and Chelm in Poland.

**Hero Tale**. An adventure story, often presented as truth, whose leading character has extraordinary abilities. The featured hero can be a mythical character such as Hercules, a legendary person such as Robin Hood, a historical person such as Daniel Boone, or an anonymous character identified only as Jack, Hans, Juan, or Ivan. Hero tales can be imbedded into larger works or they can circulate independently as shorter, self-contained tales. For example, dragon-slayer episodes (often with strikingly similar details) commonly appear in MYTHS, FOLK PLAYS, EPICS, and LEGENDS and are also told as individual folk or fairy tales.

**History**. In normal usage, a true account of actual events, but in some older contexts, a synonym for STORY.

**Household Tale**. A story intended for all members of a family, and thus one suitable for different age groups and both genders. Such tales, told by skilled storytellers, will be enjoyable at different levels—easy enough for youngsters to follow but with enough extended meaning to keep the interest of older listeners. The Grimms' so-called "fairy tales" actually appeared in a collection titled *Children's and Household Tales.*

**Image**. In traditional fairy-tale studies, a mental picture induced by the storyteller's words. Such images can be monumental (a beanstalk rising into the clouds); SURREALISTIC (a creature, half boy and half hedgehog, playing bagpipes while riding on a rooster); or fanciful (a glass slipper). Fairy-tale interpreters often compare the images of stories with those of dreams, finding psychological and symbolic meaning behind both. In an oral story the induced images are a product of the listener's own mind, but in an illustrated, printed version, an outside artist provides the visual stimulation, and even more so in a filmed or cartoon enactment. *See also* DREAM ANALYSIS.

The wise men of Gotham attempt to kill an eel by drowning it. Illustration by Arthur Rackham. Flora Annie Steel, *English Fairy Tales* (London and New York: Macmillan, 1918), p. 275.

**Incantation**. A magic phrase recited, sung, or chanted in order to achieve a specific supernatural effect. The belief in incantations plays an important role in fairy tales, and some tales contain the actual magic words *(Open sesame, abracadabra)* used by the practitioners. Some such expressions, still surviving in tales and children's GAMES, sound like total gibberish in today's language (such as "hocus, pocus, dominocus") but can be traced to ancient charms or phrases from the Latin mass.

**Interpretation**. Everyone who reads a text or hears a tale and then forms a judgment about it is practicing the art of interpretation. Fairy tales, especially those transmitted orally, lend themselves to two levels of interpretation: a formal level that presupposes standardized learning and knowledge of certain facts and conventions, and a personal level that asks only, "Why did I like or dislike that story?" At the formal level there are indeed warranted and unwarranted interpretations, but at the personal level a fairy tale is like a Rorschach inkblot, with any interpretation being justifiable. *See also* ALLEGORY, LEVELS OF SIGNIFICANCE, METAPHOR, SYMBOL.

**Irony**. Incongruity between the literal or expected meaning of a statement or situation and the message actually conveyed or the outcome actually experienced. *Socratic irony,* where a character feigns ignorance in order to expose and exploit his or her opponent's weaknesses, is common in folk and fairy tales, especially those featuring TRICKSTERS and so-called FOOLS. Also common in folktales, especially FABLES, is *dramatic irony,* where the characters proceed under their own misguided expectations, with the audience knowing better. An example from Aesop is provided by the wolf who overhears a nurse threaten to throw a noisy child to the wolf, so he waits beneath the window, expecting an easy meal. Seeing the wolf, the nurse sets the dogs on him, and he barely escapes with his life.

**Jack Tale**. A traditional folktale, usually of European origin, from the American South and featuring a hero named Jack. The American folklorist Richard Chase published a collection titled *The Jack Tales* in 1943.

**Jataka**. A tale depicting one of the many births or incarnations of the future Buddha on his route to becoming the Enlightened One. These tales vary greatly in terms of content and length, but each one illustrates a particular virtue important to the future Buddha at that stage of his development.

**Jest**. A short, simple tale, usually told in a humorous manner, either in verse or in prose. A narrative form found in the folklore of all cultures, jests were also among the first folktales collected and published. *See also* ANECDOTE, BROADSIDE, CHAP-BOOK, DROLL, FABLIAU, FACETIA, JEST BOOK, JOKE, SIMPLE FORMS.

**Jest Book**. A collection of JESTS, JOKES, or other similar ANECDOTES. The Renaissance period in Europe saw many such publications, both in Latin and in vernacular languages. As a rule these early collections were marked by earthy humor and a cynical attitude toward clerics and women. Representative titles include Poggio's *Facetiae* (1470) from Italy; the anonymous *Les cent nouvelles nouvelles* (100 New Novellas, 1486) from France; and Pauli's *Schimpf und Ernst* (Frivolity and Seriousness, 1522) from Germany.

**Jocular Tale**. A synonym for JEST.

**Joke**. A brief, tightly constructed humorous tale that elicits laughter through an unexpected turn in the final sentence, the PUNCH LINE. Jokes are among the few folktale forms that are still transmitted orally. Despite joke pages in popular magazines and listings on the Internet, most jokes are still communicated by word of mouth, for centuries the method of all folktale transmission.

**Jongleur**. A professional storyteller in medieval France. In addition to telling stories, both of their own invention and from other sources, jongleurs also performed as musicians and jugglers. *See also* FABLIAU, MINSTREL.

**Jungian**. Characteristic of Carl Gustav Jung, the Swiss psychologist and psychiatrist. The adjective *Jungian,* with reference to fairy tales, usually refers to the connection that such tales have to IMAGES, SYMBOLS, and the COLLECTIVE UNCONSCIOUS, cornerstones of Jung's teaching.

**Just So Story**. Essentially a synonym for an ETIOLOGIC TALE, this term comes from the title of a book of children's stories by Rudyard Kipling, *Just So Stories for Little Children* (1902), a collection of playful, nonsensical explanations of prominent features of selected animals—for example, "How the Camel Got His Hump." These popular stories borrow at least their basic structure from traditional folktales such as "How the Bear Lost His Tail."

**KHM**. The standard abbreviation for *Kinder- und Hausmärchen* (Children's and Household Tales), the title of the Grimms' collection of so-called fairy tales. This collection contains 200 numbered tales plus an appendix of 10 "Children's Legends." KHM numbers are thus a convenient tool for identifying any of the tales in the Grimms' collection.

**Legend**. As folklorists use the term, a legend is an account that claims to be true, in contrast to FAIRY TALES and ordinary FOLKTALES, which are transparently fictitious. However, many traditional legends depict events such as encounters with dragons, fairies, sorcerers, witches, and such—all within the realm of belief for past generations but now normally relegated to the world of SUPERSTITION and FANTASY. The otherworldly nature of many legends and most fairy tales blurs the distinction between the two genres. Thus many tales are classified both as magic folktales and as legends by specialists. For example, "The Sorcerer's Apprentice" (the story of a novice magician who enchants a broom into carrying water but does not know how to stop it, nearly drowning in the ensuing flood) is classified both as a type 325* folktale and as a type 3020 migratory legend. *See also* MIGRATORY LEGEND, SAINT'S LEGEND, SETTING, URBAN LEGEND.

**Leitmotif**. From the German words *leiten* (to lead) and *Motiv* (motive, theme, or subject), this term, in the context of fairy tales, designates a recurring theme that leads the reader through a story. For example, the birds in the Grimms' "Cinderella" (21), which are obviously associated with the heroine's deceased mother, appear repeatedly, first to help Cinderella, then finally to punish her stepsisters.

**Levels of Significance**. Given the fact that many traditional folktales were told in settings where listeners of different ages and backgrounds were present (remember the actual title of the Grimms' so-called fairy tales—*Children's and Household Tales*), it stands to reason that gifted storytellers would speak to all members of the audience, to each on his or her level of understanding. Thus a child might enjoy a story only for its fanciful plot, whereas an adult hearing the same performance may well get caught up in the extended meaning offered by DOUBLE ENTENDRES, IRONY, SYMBOLISM, or external associations.

**Lie**. A special form of anecdote whose primary appeal lies in the outrageous impossibility of its plot. *See also* FISH STORIES, TALL TALES, and NONSENSE TALES are variations of this form.

**Literary Fairy Tale**. A work of fiction created by its author to imitate—in form, style, or function—the traditional oral magic tales of folklore. In Europe the literary fairy tale rose to special prominence during the age of ROMANTICISM (about 1790 to about 1850), and its appeal continues to the present. Literary fairy tales are also called *art fairy tales* (from the German *Kunstmärchen*) or *invented fairy tales*.

**Localization**. The process of altering a migratory story to make it fit in its new environment. For example, in the Aesopic version of the type 1430 tale about "air castles" a milkmaid, daydreaming of future wealth coming from chickens not yet hatched from the eggs she intends to buy from the milk she is carrying, tosses her head and spills the milk. In a version from the Indian *Panchatantra,* the day-dreamer spills rice gruel that he is saving. In a version from the *1,001 Nights,* the fantasizer upsets a table loaded with glassware that he wants to sell. And in a Swedish version, a boy, filled with fantasies about the wealth that will come from a fox he is about to kill, frightens the fox and has nothing. Thus each story, while sharing the main plot with others of the type, incorporates unique details from its local environment. *See also* MIGRATORY LEGEND, OICOTYPE.

**Magic**. Supernatural force, usually interpreted as being separate from the powers ascribed to standard religions. Belief in magic seems to have been universal in preliterate societies and lives on in many cultures and subcultures even today. Magic pervades the world of ancient LEGENDS and traditional FAIRY TALES, often blurring the distinction between those two genres. Fairy tales are so reliant on magic solutions that specialists prefer to call them *magic tales* (a literal translation of the German *Zaubermärchen*). Although the magic world of fairy tales requires a suspension of disbelief in the supernatural by the audience, this world is not without its own logic, order, and restrictions. Thus INCANTATIONS must be recited with precision. Normally invincible werewolves can be killed with a silver bullet, and trolls will turn to stone (or explode) if exposed to sunlight. The plot of many magic tales revolves around the hero's learning and using the rules of magic. *See also* FANTASY, FAIRYLAND, SUPERSTITION, SURVIVAL, WITCHCRAFT.

**Make-Believe, Land of**. A place that exists only in one's fantasy. Fairy tales typically are set in such an imaginary locale. *See also* FAIRYLAND, NEVER NEVER LAND.

**Märchen**. A German term often used in scholarly English publications, sometimes spelled with a lowercase *m, märchen* (in German all nouns are capitalized), and sometimes without the umlaut, *marchen*. Literally, the word *Märchen* means "little tale," but it has come to designate, both in German and as a borrowed word in English, folktales in general. More specific related terms are *Volksmärchen* (folktale), *Zaubermärchen* (magic tale), and *Kunstmärchen* (literary tale).

**Memorate**. A term proposed by Carl Wilhelm von Sydow to designate an oral anecdote based on personal experience. The term has not gained widespread acceptance.

**Merry Tale**. A term used by folklorist Alexander Krappe and others as a synonym for JEST.

**Metaphor**. A figure of speech that combines the qualities of two different concepts into one phrase, thus implying a comparison. Fairy tales, in spite of their expected linguistic simplicity, are rich in metaphors. Cinderella's stepsisters had "dark hearts" (Grimm 21); Little Red Cap saw "sunbeams dancing to and fro through the trees" (Grimm 26); and Bearskin "was always at the very front when it was raining bullets" (Grimm 101). These are standard metaphors, found in all literary forms and even in everyday speech. Still more important in fairy tales are the many unforgettable combinations that linger in one's memory long after the tale is told. Images such as glass slipper, golden ball, Bluebeard, gingerbread house, 100-year sleep, and spinning straw into gold are all more meaningful when interpreted as symbolic metaphors rather than as literal objects and acts. *See also* SIMILE.

**Migratory Legend**. A LEGEND existing in more than one version, each set in its own time and place. Typically the story's plot remains essentially the same across all versions, but place names, dates, and descriptive details change in keeping with each new environment. Good examples are the stories of sleeping heroes, destined to awaken and save their respective countries when the need is greatest. The hero and location of his repose are variously identified as Barbarossa in Mount Kyffhäuser (Germany), Charlemagne in Mount Untersberg (Austria), the three Tells in a cave in the mountains above Waldstätter Lake (Switzerland), King Arthur in Sewing-shields Castle (England), and Holger Danske in Kronborg Castle (Denmark), to name but a few examples of this well-traveled legend. *See also* DIFFUSION, LOCAL-IZATION.

**Mimesis, Mimetic.** From the Greek word for imitation, *mimesis* refers to the re-presentation of reality in a work of art. Thus, a *mimetic* tale is one that faithfully depicts the reality of this world. However, in a culture that accepts the reality of magic, even fairy tales can be called *mimetic*.

**Mimic.** To imitate, often with the intention to ridicule. Many folk and fairy tales in-clude dialogues that mimic sounds of nature, calls of animals, and the language of DIALECT speakers. These features are largely lost in printed versions of the tales, but they can be especially effective when performed by a skilled STORYTELLER.

**Minstrel.** A professional entertainer, often itinerant, common throughout Europe between the twelfth and seventeenth centuries. Although the word often applies primarily to musicians, minstrels were also storytellers, jugglers, acrobats, and so on. They were instrumental in transmitting stories from one location to another. *See also* DIFFUSION, JONGLEUR.

**Monogenesis.** The view that all versions of a given folktale, however widespread, evolved from a single story, first told in only one place. *See also* DIFFUSION, POLY-GENESIS.

**Monomyth.** A term borrowed from James Joyce's *Finnegans Wake* (1939) and used by Joseph Campbell in *The Hero with a Thousand Faces* to designate a structure common to many magic tales and myths, namely the hero's call to adventure, his passing into another realm, a confrontation, then finally his return to "the king-dom of humanity."

**Moral.** The central function of many folktales, especially FABLES and PARABLES, is to deliver a moral teaching. Such tales often end with a PROVERB-like restatement of the tale's moral conclusion. In the case of AESOPIC fables, this summary can come at the beginning of the tale, where it is known to specialists as a *promythium* (plu-ral, *promythia*), or—more commonly—at the end of the tale, where it is called an *epimythium* (plural, *epimythia*). In the *Gesta Romanorum,* a medieval collection of didactic tales, each entry concludes with an "application," a recommendation as to how the moral values of the preceding story might best be applied to everyday life.

**Morphology.** A word borrowed from biology and from linguistics, morphology is the study of form and structure. First used by Vladimir Propp in the context of folktale studies, morphology here is the study of a tale's component parts, their re-lationship to each other, and to the work as a whole.

**Mother Goose.** This name first appeared in print in 1697 in the subtitle of Charles Perrault's pioneering fairy-tale collection *Histoires, ou contes du temps passé, avec des moralités: Contes de ma mère l'Oye* (Stories or Tales from Times Past, with Morals: Tales of Mother Goose). The expression was probably already a familiar one, being akin to terms such as OLD WIVES' TALE found in many languages. Beginning in the mid–eighteenth century a number of FAIRY-TALE and NURSERY-RHYME anthologies featuring Mother Goose's name in their titles were published in England and in America, helping to cement the association between her name and the two genres. In America the name Mother Goose has been especially closely connected to traditional nursery rhymes.

**Motif.** A basic narrative element used in constructing a story. A simple tale may consist of a single motif. Tales typically include a number of motifs, which can be, and often are, used in more than one story. For example, the following motif (no. K1611) is integral to Perrault's version of "Little Thumb": The captive boys exchange their caps for the ogre's sleeping daughters' golden crowns, thus tricking the ogre into killing his own daughters. Essentially the same motif is found in the Grimms' "Sweetheart Roland" (56) and in many other tales. Stith Thompson has described, cataloged, and numbered some 40,000 different motifs found in folk literature in his monumental work *Motif Index of Folk Literature* (1955–1958).

**Mutation.** The development of a folk narrative in two or more directions from one common source. Depending on external influences—for example, stimuli from differing values of storytellers from various ethnic or social backgrounds—two mutant stories can be quite different from their common ancestor.

**Myth, Mythology, Mythos.** One of the SIMPLE FORMS of literature, myths are traditional narratives depicting and explaining universal concerns and fundamental issues, such as the creation of the world, the reasons why humans speak different languages, the origins of social classes, and the like. Typically the leading characters in myths are deities, prophets, and superheroes. Myths have a strong connection with religion, although the stories constituting the myths often outlive the religious beliefs that originally gave them life, as evidenced, for example, by the timeless appeal of Greek and Roman myths, even though the gods they depict no longer are worshipped. The SYMBOLIC nature of myths gives them many LEVELS OF SIGNIFICANCE. They can be interpreted as straightforward stories of adventure, intrigue, and romance; as reflections of the human psyche; or as treatments of interpersonal relationships. The term *mythology* refers both to an entire body of myths within a given tradition as well as to the study of myths. The term *mythos* is used as a synonym both for *myth* and for *mythology*. Given the fantastic or miraculous nature of most myths, the term, in common usage, has also come to mean *falsehood,* although no folklorist or mythologist would use the word in that sense.

**Mythological Method.** The study of fairy tales as remnants of ancient MYTHS and primeval religious rituals. *See also* SURVIVAL.

**Narrative.** The verbal representation of a sequence of events. In most contexts, STORY is a synonym for *narrative.*

**Narrative Situation.** The environment and circumstances in which a STORY is told. Although frequently ignored by folktale editors and publishers, the narrative situation is held to be very important by folklorists, determining—as it does—important aspects of the story, such as mood, tone, and purpose. The following are among the many different narrative situations folklorists have identified and documented: A mother tells a story to children as part of a bedtime ritual; a family member entertains an entire household with stories; a professional minstrel performs stories at a fair or public market; a traveling tailor tells stories in the household where he is making or repairing clothes; women working together in a communal spinning room tell stories (spin yarns) to one another; stonemasons or other craftsmen tell stories to one another at work; athletes in a locker room exchange jokes and anecdotes with each other. Soldiers in an encampment entertain one another with reminiscences and stories; A public speaker inserts a fable or anecdote into his or her speech to emphasize a point. *See also* FUNCTION.

**Narratology**. The study of structure in narrative literature. *See also* MORPHOLOGY.

**Narrator**. The person who is actually speaking the words that make up a story, that is, the STORYTELLER, or a fictitious (and usually unnamed and unseen) person within the story's text who appears to be giving the account its form and its purpose by deciding what to tell and what to omit, how to order the events, what to emphasize, what value judgments to imply or to explicitly state, whose POINT OF VIEW to represent, and the like. *See also* FIRST-PERSON NARRATIVE.

**Never Never Land**. Specifically, the home of the lost boys in J.M. Barrie's *Peter Pan* (1904), but in general a designation for a world that exists only in one's fantasy. East European fairy tales often open with the formula "once and never," drawing attention to the often self-contradictory nature of fairy-tale settings. *See also* FAIRY-LAND, FANTASY.

**Nonsense Tale**. An illogical or self-contradictory story, often told in rhymes, whose appeal lies in the esthetic quality of the words themselves, such as "higgelty, piggelty, my red hen," as well as the brazenness of their contradictions and unexpected juxtapositions. A sampling of this technique is provided by the opening sentences of a traditional English nursery tale: "I saddled my sow with a sieve full of buttermilk, put my foot into the stirrup, and leaped nine miles beyond the moon into the land of Temperance, where there was nothing but hammers and hatchets and candlesticks.... And if that isn't true, you know as well as I" (Briggs, *A Dictionary of British Folk-Tales*, pt. A, vol. 2, p. 537; see bibliography for publication information). *See also* LIE, NURSERY TALE, TALL TALE.

**Noodle**. Popularized by the nineteenth-century folklorist W.A. Clouston with his book *The Book of Noodles: Stories of Simpletons; or, Fools and Their Follies,* this term is one of the many synonyms for FOOL.

**Novella**. From the feminine form of the Italian *novello* (new). In English the plural forms *novelle* (from the Italian) and *novellas* are both used. The novella is a short, concise story, of which the individual tales in Boccaccio's *Decameron* (1348–1353) are exemplary. Although the term usually refers to literary tales, novellas often borrow their subject matter and plot elements from traditional folktales, and conversely, stories that began life as literary novellas sometimes find their way into oral folklore. Like FAIRY TALES, novellas typically depict highly unlikely events, but unlike their supernatural counterparts, novellas rarely rely on magic to achieve their ends.

**Nursery Rhyme, Nursery Tale**. A verse or story intended for small children. *See also* HOUSEHOLD TALE, MOTHER GOOSE.

**Oedipus Complex**. A term coined by Freud reflecting his view that most children (usually between the ages of three and five) go through a stage of hostility toward a parent of the same gender, due to the child's own sexual attraction toward the parent of the opposite sex. For boys this is called an *Oedipus complex,* for girls an *Electra complex.* The names come from Greek mythology, Oedipus unwittingly having killed his father and married his own mother, and Electra having helped to kill her own mother. FREUDIAN interpreters find many details in traditional fairy tales describing or symbolizing rivalry between children and their parents of the same gender, giving—in their view—credibility to this theory. Oedipus is of further interest to students of folklore. His tragic life story gave rise to numerous tales (type 931) about heroes who suffer a similar fate.

**Oicotype**. A term proposed by Carl Wilhelm von Sydow to designate a local or regional form of a migratory tale. *See also* LOCALIZATION.

**Old Wives' Tale**. A foolish story or belief based on superstition rather than reality. The fact that this expression has no masculine counterpart supports the view that certain kinds of folktales (for example, those told primarily to children in a household setting) were invented and passed on primarily by females. Similar constructions are found in other languages—for example, Danish *(ammestuehistorie)*, French *(conte de bonne femme)*, and German *(Altweibermärchen)*. *See also* MOTHER GOOSE.

**Oral Narrative**. An anonymous story passed on by word of mouth.

**Parable**. A short didactic tale similar to a FABLE but featuring humans rather than animals as actors, and usually with a more plausible, true-to-life plot. Most parables can be viewed as ALLEGORIES, with individual characters and events symbolically representing larger abstract values and issues. The parables of Jesus—for example, "The Prodigal Son" and "The Good Samaritan"—are definitive examples of the genre.

**Parody**. A literary, dramatic, or musical work, created in transparent imitation of another work, but exaggerating selected aspects of the original. Parodies can be good-naturedly humorous or scornfully critical. Fairy tales, because they are widely known and exhibit distinctive qualities, are easy to parody, resulting in countless films *(Cinderfella)*, books *(The True Story of the Three Little Pigs,* by A. Wolf), and jokes ("…and the next morning—he was still a frog").

**Passive Folktale Carrier**. *See* ACTIVE AND PASSIVE FOLKTALE CARRIERS.

**Personification**. Representation of human qualities and behavior through non-human agents, especially animals or things, as in Aesopic fables, but also sprites, ogres, dragons, and the like, as in countless myths, legends, and magic tales.

**Perspective**. *See* POINT OF VIEW.

**Plot**. *See* CONTENT AND FORM.

**Point of View**. The position (physical, psychological, or moral) from which a story's NARRATOR, either fictitious or actual, perceives events and then communicates them to a reader or listener. A narrator's point of view, also called perspective, can be that of an omniscient observer who can read all the characters' minds and see into the future or it can be that of a single character, with the result that the listener hears of the events only as the character experiences them. As in other forms of fiction, the narrator's point of view can shift as the story unfolds. For example, the narrator of "Hansel and Gretel" (Grimm 15) tells the listeners that the kindly old woman in the woods is a cannibalistic witch long before the abandoned children learn of her evil intents. However, the children's stepmother dies during their absence, which we do not learn until Hansel and Gretel themselves return home. Point of view also refers to a moral position taken by the story as a whole. In traditional fairy tales the moral point of view is generally simplistic, representing only a single character or group. For example, an impoverished hero is virtually never criticized for taking treasures from (or even killing) a person thought to be an ogre or a witch. *See also* FIRST-PERSON NARRATIVE.

**Polygenesis**. The independent generation of a FOLKTALE or MYTH in two or more different geographic areas. Because all human cultures share certain values (for example, the desire for companionship, offspring, justice, and security) it stands to reason that stories reflecting those values could evolve in separate locations, and that such stories might closely resemble one another, even though their creators had no contact with each other. *See also* DIFFUSION, MONOGENESIS.

**Pourquois Tale**. *See* ETIOLOGIC TALE.

**Primary Form**. According to the FINNISH SCHOOL, the original telling of a folktale prior to its modification through migrations and retellings. The primary form of traditional tales is, of necessity, a theoretical reconstruction based on many variants.

**Promythium**. *See* MORAL.

**Proverb**. A concise saying formulating folk wisdom and beliefs. Commonly used in everyday speech, proverbs also are often quoted in folktales, especially FABLES, where they serve as summaries of moral intent. *See also* APHORISM, MORAL.

**Punch Line**. *See* JOKE.

**Raconteur (*masculine*), Raconteuse (*feminine*)**. A gifted STORYTELLER, especially of anecdotes and personal experiences.

**Realism**. In general, a concern for details of the physical world and a rejection of otherworldly matters; and specifically, a nineteenth-century esthetic movement that favored detailed depictions of ordinary life and reacted against the subjective, sentimental, and fantasy-filled literature and art of the Romantic period. Fairy tales, as a rule, were criticized by realists for their lack of everyday logic. *See also* ROMANTICISM.

**Reception**. As a literary term, *reception* refers to the responses and reactions that a work elicits from the community of book buyers, readers, critics, parodists, imitators, and the like. In this regard, certain folk and fairy-tale collections, most prominently Aesop's fables, the *1,001 Nights,* and the collections by Perrault and the Grimm brothers, are among the most influential books ever produced, prompting countless retellings and imitations for many generations and in all artistic media.

**Religious Tale**. All religions have their stories about faith, devotion, virtue, sacrifice, and divine intervention; and many such tales are found in the repertories of traditional storytellers. (Aarne and Thompson categorize religious tales as types 750–849.) Often the religious components of stories survive even after the people telling them change their religious views. By way of illustration, a number of the Grimms' tales collected in Protestant Germany have Catholic overtones. And even more extreme, remnants of heathen religion can be found in folktales and legends collected in Scandinavia in the nineteenth century, nearly 1,000 years after those beliefs were formally abandoned. *See also* SAINT'S LEGEND, SURVIVAL.

**Revisionist Fairy Tale**. Stories written in a fairy-tale style but in contradiction to expected and traditional values, especially in support of political and social causes that emerged in the 1960s or later. *See also* ANTI–FAIRY TALE, CROSSOVER FAIRY TALE, FRACTURED FAIRY TALE.

**Rhyme**. Many of the oldest folk narratives were composed in rhyme, in part for esthetic purposes but also because rhymed narratives are easier to memorize than those in everyday prose, with each new rhyme word calling to mind the one that will follow. Nursery rhymes offer proof of this claim. Every adult can recite from memory numerous rhymes learned in childhood, but few can remember details of the prose stories heard at the same time.

**Riddle**. One of literature's SIMPLE FORMS, riddles are also among folklore's oldest and most popular genres. Many folktales contain riddles, or are constructed around them. One of the oldest recorded riddles comes from an ancient Greek folktale. The Sphinx, terrorizing the people of Thebes, offered them peace if they could solve her riddle: What goes on all fours, then on two feet, and finally on three? Oedipus solved the puzzle. The answer is man, who crawls on all fours as an infant, walks on two feet as an adult, but requires the aid of a cane in old age. In good fairy-tale fashion Oedipus received as a reward the hand in marriage of the queen of Thebes. But, unbeknown to him, she was his own mother, so this is one fairy tale without a happy ending.

**Ritual, Rite**. A ceremonial event, usually with prescribed words, gestures, and acts and marking a significant point in one's life (name giving) or in the yearly cycle (harvest time), or asking for divine intervention (protection against a flood). There is substantial evidence that fragments of ancient rituals have survived in FOLK DRAMAS, festivals, fairy tales, and even children's GAMES. *See also* CUSTOM, SUPERSTITION, SURVIVAL.

**Romance, Romantic Tale**. The word *romance,* as a literary genre, comes from the medieval French *romanz,* a story marked by love, unexpected turns, and—sometimes—supernatural events. Short versions of these stories are akin to the NOVELLAS of Boccaccio and other Renaissance writers, as well as folktales of types 950–999, which as a rule have little reliance on magic for their unusual outcomes.

**Romanticism**. An esthetic movement of the late eighteenth and early nineteenth centuries that emphasized feeling, the imagination, and otherworldly fantasy, in reaction to the objective logic of the preceding Age of Reason. Romantics, especially in Germany, promoted the FAIRY TALE as natural literature. Most German Romantic authors wrote LITERARY FAIRY TALES, and two sons of the movement,

Jacob and Wilhelm Grimm, became the best-known COLLECTORS and EDITORS of folktales in the world.

**Round**. *See* ENDLESS STORY.

**Saga**. Specifically, a long prose account depicting the first settlers in Iceland. These stories, often including episodes dealing with Norse gods, were passed down by word of mouth for generations, then finally recorded during the twelfth and thirteenth centuries. By extension, the word *saga* refers to any lengthy account. *See also* EPIC.

**Saint's Legend**. Formerly in English the term *legend* applied only to tales about Christian saints. This distinction still applies in German, with *Legende* primarily designating a religious tale, whereas *Sage* (akin to the English *saga*) refers to legends of other types. A vast body of legends about saints and miracles attributed to them evolved in the Middle Ages, many of which have become an important part of the cultural heritage of many lands. For example, the story of Saint George and the dragon is told throughout the Mideast and Europe, with the location of the legendary battle often corresponding with the storyteller's own homeland. Legends about saints nearly always have a didactic function, the exemplary behavior depicted by them serving to enlighten and inspire their readers. *See also* MIGRATORY LEGEND, RELIGIOUS TALE, EXEMPLUM.

**Satire**. A literary work written to expose and ridicule human foibles, especially hypocrisy and folly. Although all genres of folktales lend themselves to satirical use, traditionally FABLES, FOOL'S TALES, and TRICKSTER TALES have most often served this purpose. *See also* IRONY, PARODY.

**Setting**. The time and place of a story's action. Most traditional FAIRY TALES are set in the unspecified distant past and in an imaginary location ("long ago and far away"), although some are connected to actual places. Thus the Grimms' "Bremen Town Musicians" (27) takes place in the woods approaching a real German city, although in truth any other location would have served equally well. By contrast, LEGENDS, which as a rule claim to be true, typically give specific details about the time and place of their action.

**Shape-Shifting**. *See* TRANSFORMATION.

**Shrovetide Play**. A FOLK DRAMA, often burlesque in nature, performed at pre-Lenten carnival (Mardi Gras) celebrations. In many instances such plays were dramatizations of traditional folktales.

**Sight Dialect**. The purposeful misspelling of words (for example, *sez* for *says,* or *wimmin* for *women*) in an attempt to portray the narrator or speaker as uneducated. This device is frequently used (especially in English, with its lack of phonetic spelling) in jests, tall tales, stories about fools, and other folklike anecdotes about simple people. *See also* STYLIZATION.

**Simile**. An explicit comparison, usually including the function words *like* or *as*. Examples can be found in virtually all fairy tales, as in, for instance, the opening paragraph of the Grimms' "Little Snow-White" (53): "Once upon a time in midwinter, when *the snowflakes were falling like feathers from heaven,* a queen sat sewing at her window, which had a frame of black ebony wood. As she sewed she looked up at the snow and pricked her finger with her needle. Three drops of blood fell into the snow. The red on the white looked so beautiful that she thought to herself, 'If only I had *a child as white as snow, as red as blood, and as black as the wood in this frame.'* " (Emphasis added.) *See also* METAPHOR.

**Simple Forms**. A phrase coined by the Dutch scholar André Jolles in his influential study *Einfache Formen* (Simple Forms), first published in 1929. His simple forms are SAINT'S LEGEND, LEGEND, MYTH, RIDDLE, EXEMPLUM, MEMORATE, FOLKTALE (MÄRCHEN), and JEST. They can be defined as preliterary, naïve expressions of human response to external reality. Most specialists agree that the primitive forebears of folk and fairy tales fit in this category but that these tales have developed into a complex and sophisticated literary tradition that can no longer be called "simple."

**Story**. Derived from the Latin *historia,* the term *story* implies a written, factual account, as contrasted with *tale,* which is related to the Old Norse *tala* (talk). The term *story* has evolved in two opposing directions, and the word today can mean *true account,* as in *news story;* or *lie,* as in *That's just a story.* Applied to fictional accounts, *story* and *tale* are synonyms and in most contexts interchangeable.

**Storyteller**. The person who orally performs a story. *See also* GESTURE, NARRATIVE SITUATION, NARRATOR.

**Structuralism**. Any one of several movements—primarily in the fields of psychology, cultural anthropology, linguistics, and literature—that analyze and attempt to integrate patterns of thought, speech, and behavior, linking them to perceived innate structures in the human mind. *See also* CONTENT AND FORM, MORPHOLOGY.

**Structure**. *See* CONTENT AND FORM, FORMULA, MORPHOLOGY.

**Stylization**. Editors and translators often stylize folktale texts to meet personal taste or perceived public expectations. Archaic words may be chosen to give the text an antiquated or exotic sound. Substandard grammar and misspelled words give a text an unlettered look. Simplified language may appeal to (or claim to be from) children. *See also* DIALECT, SIGHT DIALECT.

**Subtext**. The secondary or deeper meaning of a literary text, communicated by implication rather than through explicit statements. One purpose of a subtext is to make a tale interesting to all members of a mixed audience. This is achieved by the use of IRONY, METAPHORS, SYMBOLS, DOUBLE ENTENDRES, and the like. A simple example of a subtext is found in the Grimms' "Thumbthick" (37). A man spent every evening "poking the fire," but still he and his wife had no children. Finally she wished out loud for a child, "even if it were ever so small—no larger than a thumb." Then, we are told, "the wife took ill, and seven months later she gave birth to a child, . . . but he was no larger than a thumb." A child will take no notice of the double entendre "poking the fire," nor of the significance of a seven-month pregnancy, but these details will attract the interest of and provide added meaning for adult listeners. *See also* HOUSEHOLD TALE, LEVELS OF SIGNIFICANCE.

**Superstition**. The superstitions of one era are the cherished beliefs of another. Fairy tales feature many such examples—fairies, omens, shape-shifting, unlucky numbers, thoughtless wishes that come true, magic invulnerability, and witchcraft—

implying that these stories originated at a time when such beliefs were held to be plausible.

**Surrealism**. An art and literary movement that flourished in Europe in the 1920s. The defining characteristic of surrealist art and literature is an unnatural juxtaposition of images and events, designed to reflect the otherworldly logic of the unconscious. Many surrealists felt an affinity for traditional fairy tales, whose anonymous creators arguably were intuitively and naïvely using some of the same techniques.

**Survival**. As used by anthropologists and folklorists, a *survival* is an aspect of ancient culture (for example, a primitive belief or a fragment from a once-common RITUAL) that continues to exist as a motif in a folktale or an element within a traditional game or ceremony. An obvious example is the jealous stepmother's intention to eat Snow-White's liver and lungs in the Grimms' fairy tale (53). According to ancient belief, one could gain the desired qualities (in this case beauty) of other animals or humans by eating their internal organs. *See also* CUSTOM, SUPERSTITION.

**Symbol**. An object or an act that communicates meaning beyond itself. Traditional fairy tales contain many images and events that lend themselves to symbolic interpretation. For example, a glass slipper, through its obvious qualities of transparency (purity) and fragility, might represent virginity. A hero's quest for a magic item might represent anyone's search for fulfillment. *See also* ALLEGORY, INTERPRETATION, LEVELS OF SIGNIFICANCE, METAPHOR, SUBTEXT.

**Taboo**. Also spelled *tabu,* the prohibition of an action, often for religious reasons. Especially well developed in Polynesia (the word *tabu* is Tongan), taboos exist in all cultures and regulate many aspects of life. One of the functions of fairy tales is to provide storytellers and their audiences with a socially acceptable means of addressing "unspeakable" tabooed acts. For example, the most universal of all taboos, incest, is the central topic in many fairy tales, most prominently those of type 510B, of which the Grimms' "All-Kinds-of-Fur" (65) is exemplary.

**Tag**. Sometimes called *catchwords,* tags are FORMULA expressions that mark different points of a story. In English the most famous of these are "Once upon a time" or "Long ago and far away," marking the beginning of a fairy tale, and "They lived happily ever after," marking its ending. Similarly, "Have you heard the one about..." would mark the beginning of a joke, and "When I was in the army..." would mark the beginning of a MEMORATE. Folktales from eastern Europe often begin with a tag that emphasizes the fantasy or nonsense nature of the story to follow. Examples are "Once and never," "There was and there was not," and "This did not happen." Native American storytellers sometimes begin their narratives with "In legend time." Arabic folktales often begin with tags such as "Neither here nor elsewhere" or "Once and never." The Norwegian tale "Katie Woodencloak" ends with the nonsense rhyme "Snipp snapp snute, så er eventyret ute" (Snip snap snout, so this story is out).

**Tale**. *See* STORY.

**Tall Tale**. A special form of NONSENSE TALE that delights in the exaggeration of selected details of an otherwise logical plot. An example would be the account of the grandfather clock that was so old that the pendulum's shadow had worn a hole through the back of the casing. Although especially nurtured in North America, tall tales are told around the world. *See also* LIE, FISH STORY.

**Theme**. The subject matter of a story. Although many different themes present themselves in folk and fairy tales, some have proven to be timeless in their appeal, such as sibling rivalry, coming-of-age conflicts, courtship issues, inheritance problems, and master-servant relationships.

**Traits**. The essential episodes making up a particular tale TYPE.

**Transformation**. From the evidence in myths and legends, the ancients firmly believed in the power of some individuals to transform themselves and others into different creatures and things. Also called *enchantment* or *shape-shifting,* this device can be used to escape from one's enemies, by turning oneself into a bird or a ferocious monster, or to punish an adversary, by turning him or her into a stone or a frog. Sometimes the transformation comes unwittingly because of a reckless curse or thoughtless WISH. Transformations permeate fairy tales, often with the entire tale dedicated to the reversal of a wicked transformation, as, for example, in most animal-bridegroom tales.

**Trickster Tales**. From ancient times (Aesop himself is reported to have been a clever trickster) and in virtually all known cultures, storytellers have delighted their audiences with accounts of individuals (typically underlings) duping their victims. Episodes include confidence games that expose the victim's own dishonesty, sexual exploitation, and slapstick pranks resulting in the victim's physical injury or even death. Tricksters often set up their victims by feigning foolishness, giving these tales a strong kinship with FOOL'S TALES. Famous tricksters (some of whom disguise themselves as jesters or fools) include Aesop (Greece), the god Eshu (Africa), Loki (Scandinavia), Till Eulenspiegel (Germany), Nasreddin Hoca (Turkey), Goha (Egypt), Tenali Rama (South India), Pedro de Urdemalas (Latin America), Coyote or Raven (Native American), Brer Rabbit (African American), the spider Anansi (Africa and the Caribbean), and the fox Kitsune (Japan).

**Turning Point**. The place in a story where the plot reaches a climax (for example, the PUNCH LINE of a JOKE) or where the action shifts toward a previously unexpected outcome. In FAIRY TALES the turning points (there can be more than one) usually come through magic intervention.

**Type**. Folktales within the Indo-European tradition are classified according to a system initiated by the Finnish folklorist Antti Aarne and continued by his American colleague Stith Thompson. This system (usually designated Aarne-Thompson, or simply A-T) identifies some 2,500 basic folktale plots, assigning to each a type number, sometimes further differentiated by letters or asterisks. The Aarne-Thompson system was expanded by Reidar Thoralf Christiansen to include MIGRATORY LEGENDS (type numbers 3000–8025), especially those found in his native Norway. Additional type indexes have been assembled by various scholars to classify folktales outside the Indo-European tradition.

**Unfinished Tale**. A formula tale purposely designed without an ending, thus allowing each listener or reader to arrive at his or her own conclusion. Frank Stockton's

A snake bridegroom, prior to his transformation back into a human being. Illustration by H.J. Ford (1892). Andrew Lang, *The Green Fairy Book* (London: Longmans, Green, and Company, 1892), p. 189.

**The Witch**

Illustration by John D. Batten. Joseph Jacobs, *European Folk and Fairy Tales* (New York: G.P. Putnam's Sons, 1916), p. 180.

"The Lady or the Tiger" offers a famous example, with its final sentence, "And so I leave it with all of you: Which came out of the opened door,—the lady, or the tiger?" Similarly, "The Golden Key" (Grimm 200) tells how a boy finds a chest and a key. The key fits, and the boy begins to unlock the chest. The story ends, "Now we must wait until he has finished unlocking it and has opened the lid. Then we shall find out what kind of wonderful things there were in the little chest." Excluding their appendix of 10 "Children's Legends," this is the last tale in the Grimms' collection. By closing with this enigmatic unfinished tale, the Grimms seem to be saying that folktales, too, are endless. There is no final word.

**Urban Legend.** An account, presented as truth, but rarely verifiable, of some recent horrible, spectacular, or supernatural event. These tales often are attributed to a source two or three times removed from the current storyteller, the proverbial friend of a friend (FOAF). The relationship between urban legends and rumors is very close. In essence, an urban legend is the account of a single event built around a rumor. For example, the rumor that Uncle Joe's Chicken Restaurant also serves deep-fried rat might give rise to the legend that my cousin's boss found a rat tail in his chicken dinner, and was offered a million dollars to not report it. Because so-called urban legends do not necessarily have an urban setting, many specialists prefer the designation *contemporary legend*.

**Variant, Version**. Due to the unreliability of storytellers' memories, or their willful changing of stories heard elsewhere, orally transmitted folktales are rarely recorded from different informants with exactly the same wording. In folktale studies these two terms are often used as synonyms, although strictly speaking, variants of a given story differ only in small details, whereas alternate versions of a story may move in quite different directions. The expression *distant variant* (somewhat of an oxymoron) is used to describe a tale that resembles a standard type in only general terms.

**Wish**. The first tale in the Grimms' collection, "The Frog King," begins "In ancient times, when wishing still did some good..." Wish fulfillment is probably the most common element in FAIRY TALES and helps to explain their enduring popularity. By identifying with the tale's fortunate hero or heroine, the listener can vicariously enjoy rewards brought about by the happy ending. In most traditional fairy tales this occurs through magic intervention, but in NOVELLAS and other naturalistic stories, it is more often brought about by circumstantial good luck.

**Witchcraft**. One of the many SUPERSTITIONS, once actively (and in this instance, perniciously) believed, that have survived in fairy tales. The wicked witch is an even more common feature in fairy tales than is the evil stepmother, although in many stories the two phrases are interchangeable. Belief in witchcraft is exceptionally well documented, largely because of the infamous church-prompted persecution from the Middle Ages well into the eighteenth century. Fairy-tale accounts combined with the historical record suggest that stories of witchcraft reflect a deeply rooted, archetypal fear common to all people. Belief in witches is still a dominant force in the world, although in some instances their ostensible powers are praised as potentially beneficial (as, for example, in the neopagan religion Wicca), rather than feared and condemned as inherently evil. Male witches, called sorcerers or warlocks, also exist, but there are proportionately many fewer of them than females, both in fairy tales and in the annals of witchcraft trials. *See also* MAGIC, SURVIVAL.

**Wonder Tale (sometimes spelled wondertale)**. A synonym for magic tale.

**Yarn**. An unbelievable story—for example, a TALL TALE—often ironically presented as a firsthand true experience.

# Bibliography

## REFERENCE WORKS

Aarne, Antti, and Stith Thompson. *The Types of the Folktale: A Classification and Bibliography.* Helsinki: Suomalainen Tiedeakatemia, 1961. A substantial enlargement of the work first published in 1910 by Aarne under the title *Verzeichnis der Märchentypen.*

Ashliman, D.L. *A Guide to Folktales in the English Language: Based on the Aarne-Thompson Classification System.* Westport, CT: Greenwood, 1987.

Baughman, Ernest. *Type and Motif-Index of the Folktales of England and North America.* The Hague: Mouton, 1966.

Brown, Mary Ellen, and Bruce A. Rosenberg, eds. *Encyclopedia of Folklore and Literature.* Santa Barbara: ABC-CLIO, 1998.

Brunvand, Jan Harold, ed. *American Folklore: An Encyclopedia.* New York: Garland, 1996.

———. *Encyclopedia of Urban Legends.* New York: Norton, 2001.

Carpenter, Humphrey, and Mari Prichard. *The Oxford Companion to Children's Literature.* Oxford: Oxford UP, 1987. First published 1984.

Castro, Rafaela G. *Chicano Folklore: A Guide to the Folktales, Traditions, Rituals, and Religious Practices of Mexican Americans.* New York: Oxford UP, 2001.

Eastman, Mary Huse. *Index to Fairy Tales, Myths, and Legends.* 2 vols. Boston: Faxon, 1937–1952. The forerunner to this index, under the same title, was first published in 1915. It has been continued by Norma Olin Ireland and Joseph W. Sprug.

*Enzyklopädie des Märchens: Handwörterbuch zur historischen und vergleichenden Erzählforschung.* Berlin: de Gruyter, 1975–. Fourteen volumes plus an index volume are planned. Ten volumes are completed.

Green, Thomas A., ed. *Folklore: An Encyclopedia of Beliefs, Customs, Tales, Music, and Art.* Santa Barbara: ABC-CLIO, 1997.

Ireland, Norma. *Index to Fairy Tales, 1949–1972: Including Folklore, Legends, and Myths, in Collections.* Westwood, MA: Faxon, 1973. A continuation of the index begun by Mary Huse Eastman. Additional supplements were published in 1979 (Faxon), 1985 (Metuchen, NJ: Scarecrow), and with Joseph W. Sprug in 1989 (Scarecrow).

Leach, Maria, ed., and Jerome Fried, assoc. ed. *Funk and Wagnalls Standard Dictionary of Folklore, Mythology, and Legend.* San Francisco: Harper, 1984.

MacDonald, Margaret. *The Storyteller's Sourcebook: A Subject, Title, and Motif Index to Folklore Collections for Children.* Detroit: Schuman, 1982.

———, ed. *Traditional Storytelling Today: An International Sourcebook.* Chicago: Fitzroy Dearborn, 1999.

*MLA International Bibliography.* New York: Modern Language Association. Published annually in print form. Also available by subscription in electronic form (both CD and Internet versions). The folklore section includes the history and study of folklore, folk literature, folk music, folk art, folk belief systems, and folk rituals.

Sprug, Joseph W. *Index to Fairy Tales, 1987–1992: Including 310 Collections of Fairy Tales, Folktales, Myths, and Legends, with Significant Pre-1987 Titles Not Previously Indexed.* Metuchen, NJ: Scarecrow, 1994. A continuation of the index begun by Mary Huse Eastman and Norma Ireland.

Thompson, Stith. *Motif-Index of Folk-Literature: A Classification of Narrative Elements in Folktales, Ballads, Myths, Fables, Mediaeval Romances, Exempla, Fabliaux, Jest-Books, and Local Legends.* Rev. and enl. ed. 6 vols. Bloomington: Indiana UP, 1955.

Zipes, Jack, ed. *The Oxford Companion to Fairy Tales.* Oxford: Oxford UP, 2000.

## TOOLS FOR TEACHERS

Arbuthnot, May Hill, ed. *The Arbuthnot Anthology of Children's Literature.* Chicago: Scott, 1961.

Haviland, Virginia, et al. *Children's Literature: A Guide to Reference Sources.* Washington: Library of Congress, 1966.

Joy, Flora. *Treasures from Europe: Stories and Classroom Activities.* Englewood, CO: Libraries Unlimited, 2003.

Livo, Norma J. *Bringing Out Their Best: Values Education and Character Development through Traditional Tales.* Englewood, CO: Libraries Unlimited, 2003.

Schmidt, Gary D., and Donald R. Hettinga. *Sitting at the Feet of the Past: Retelling the North American Folktale for Children.* Westport, CT: Greenwood, 1992.

Shannon, George W.B. *Folk Literature and Children: An Annotated Bibliography of Secondary Materials.* Westport, CT: Greenwood, 1981.

Sierra, Judy. *Multicultural Folktales for the Feltboard and Readers' Theater.* Phoenix: Oryx, 1996.

## REGIONAL AND NATIONAL COLLECTIONS

### Africa (Excluding North Africa)

Abrahams, Roger D. *African Folktales: Traditional Stories of the Black World.* New York: Pantheon, 1983.

Arnott, Kathleen. *African Myths and Legends.* London: Oxford UP, 1962.

Bascom, William R. *African Dilemma Tales.* The Hague: Mouton, 1975.

Bennett, Martin. *West African Trickster Tales.* Oxford: Oxford UP, 1994.

Dadié, Bernard Binlin. *The Black Cloth: A Collection of African Folktales.* Amherst: U of Massachusetts P, 1987.

Dayrell, Elphinstone. *Folk Stories from Southern Nigeria, West Africa.* London: Longmans, 1910.

Feldmann, Susan. *African Myths and Tales.* New York: Dell, 1963.

Frobenius, Leo, and Douglas C. Fox. *African Genesis.* New York: Stackpole, 1937.

Glew, Robert S., and Chaibou Babalé. *Hausa Folktales from Niger.* Athens: Ohio U Center for International Studies, 1993.

Lewis, I. Murphy, and Izak Barnard. *Why Ostriches Don't Fly and Other Tales from the African Bush.* Englewood, CO: Libraries Unlimited, 1997.

Matateyou, Emmanuel. *An Anthology of Myths, Legends, and Folktales from Cameroon: Storytelling in Africa.* Lewiston, NY: Mellen, 1997.

McNeil, Heather. *Hyena and the Moon: Stories to Tell from Kenya.* Englewood, CO: Libraries Unlimited, 1994.

Radin, Paul. *African Folktales.* New York: Schocken, 1983.

Smith, Alexander McCall. *Children of Wax: African Folk Tales.* New York: Interlink, 1991.

Theal, George McCall. *Kaffir Folk-Lore: A Selection from the Traditional Tales Current among the People Living on the Eastern Border of the Cape Colony.* London: Sonnenschein, 1886.

Walker, Barbara K., and Warren S. Walker. *Nigerian Folk Tales, as Told by Olawale Idewu and Omotayo Adu.* Hamden, CT: Archon, 1980.

### Asia

#### ARABIC COUNTRIES, IRAN

Abdallah, Ali Lutfi. *The Clever Sheikh of the Butana and Other Stories: Sudanese Folk Tales.* New York: Interlink, 1999.

Al-Shahi, Ahmed, and F.C.T. Moore. *Wisdom from the Nile: A Collection of Folk-Stories from Northern and Central Sudan.* Oxford: Clarendon, 1978.

Bushnaq, Inea. *Arab Folktales.* New York: Pantheon, 1986.

Clouston, William Alexander. *Flowers from a Persian Garden.* London: Nutt, 1890.

El-Shamy, Hasan M. *Folktales of Egypt.* Chicago: U of Chicago P, 1980.

Hanauer, J.E. *Folk-Lore of the Holy Land: Moslem, Christian, and Jewish.* London: Sheldon, 1935.

Mitchnik, Helen. *Egyptian and Sudanese Folk-Tales.* Oxford: Oxford UP, 1978.

Muhawi, Ibrahim, and Sharif Kanaana. *Speak, Bird, Speak Again: Palestinian Arab Folktales.* Berkeley: U of California P, 1989.

Petrie, W.M. Flinders. *Egyptian Tales.* Mineola, NY: Dover, 1999. A republication of *Egyptian Tales: Translated from the Papyri.* 2 vols. London: Methuen, 1895–1913.

Picard, Barbara Leonie. *Tales of Ancient Persia: Retold from the Shah-Nama of Firdausi.* Oxford: Oxford UP, 1993.


## Thousand and One Nights

Burton, Richard F., trans. *The Book of the Thousand Nights and a Night: A Plain and Literal Translation of the Arabian Nights Entertainments.* 10 vols. plus 6 supplemental vols. Privately printed by the Burton Club, 1885–1888.

Lane, Edward William, trans. *The Arabian Nights' Entertainments; or, the Thousand and One Nights.* New York: Tudor, 1939.

Mathers, Powys, trans. *The Book of the Thousand Nights and One Night.* Trans. from the literal and complete French translation of Dr. J.C. Mardrus. 4 vols. London: Routledge, 1964.


## Australia, Pacific Islands

Cole, Mabel Cook. *Philippine Folk Tales.* Chicago: McClurg, 1916.

Eugenio, Damiana L. *Philippine Folk Literature: An Anthology.* Quezon City: Folklore Studies Program, U of the Philippines, 1982.

Faurot, Jeannette. *Asian Pacific Folktales and Legends.* New York: Simon, 1995.

Kalakaua, King David. *The Legends and Myths of Hawaii: The Fables and Folk-Lore of a Strange People.* Honolulu: Mutual, 1990. First printed 1888.

McKay, Helen F., et al. *Gadi Mirrabooka: Australian Aboriginal Tales from the Dreaming.* Englewood, CO: Libraries Unlimited, 2001.

Miller, John Maurice. *Philippine Folklore Stories.* Boston: Ginn, 1904.

Parker, Mrs. K. Langloh. *Australian Legendary Tales: Folklore of the Noongahburrahs as Told to the Picaninnies.* London: Nutt, 1896.

Stewart, Pamela J., and Andrew Strathern. *Gender, Song, and Sensibility: Folktales and Folksongs in the Highlands of New Guinea.* Westport, CT: Praeger, 2002.


## China, Indochina, Japan, Korea, Vietnam

Birch, Cyril, *Chinese Myths and Fantasies.* Oxford: Oxford UP, 1961.

Bunanta, Murti, and Margaret Read MacDonald. *Indonesian Folktales.* Englewood, CO: Libraries Unlimited, 2003.

Illustration by an unnamed native of Australia. Mrs. K. Langloh Parker, *Australian Legendary Tales* (London: David Nutt, 1896), p. 119.

Chin, Yin-lien C., Yetta S. Center, and Mildred Ross. *Traditional Chinese Folktales.* Armonk, NY: Sharpe, 1989.

Curry, Lindy Soon, and Chan-eung Park. *A Tiger by the Tail and Other Stories from the Heart of Korea.* Englewood, CO: Libraries Unlimited, 1999.

Davis, F. Hadland. *Myths and Legends of Japan.* London: Harrap, 1913.

Dracott, Alice Elizabeth. *Folk Tales from Simla [Himalayas].* New York: Hippocrene, 1998.

Eberhard, Wolfram. *Folktales of China.* Chicago: U of Chicago P, 1965.

*Folk Tales from China.* Series 1–5. Peking: Foreign Languages P, 1957–1960.

*Korean Lore.* Seoul: Office of Public Information, Republic of Korea, 1953.

Livo, Norma J., and Dia Cha. *Folk Stories of the Hmong: Peoples of Laos, Thailand, and Vietnam.* Englewood, CO: Libraries Unlimited, 1991.

Mayer, Fanny Hagin. *Ancient Tales in Modern Japan: An Anthology of Japanese Folk Tales.* Bloomington: Indiana UP, 1984.

McAlpine, Helen. *Japanese Tales and Legends.* Oxford: Oxford UP, 1958.

Metternich, Hilary Roe. *Mongolian Folktales.* Boulder, CO: Avery P, in association with the U of Washington P, 1996.

Minford, John. *Favourite Folktales of China.* Peking: New World, 1983.

Mitford, A.B. *Tales of Old Japan.* London: Macmillan, 1871.

O'Conner, W.F. *Folk Tales from Tibet.* London: Hurst, 1906.

Riordan, James. *Korean Folk-Tales.* Oxford: Oxford UP, 1994.

Roberts, Moss. *Chinese Fairy Tales and Fantasies.* New York: Pantheon, 1979.

Schiefner, F. Anton von. *Tibetan Tales: Derived from Indian Sources.* London: Routledge, 1926.

Seki, Keigo. *Folktales of Japan.* Chicago: U of Chicago P, 1963.

*Seven Sisters, The: Selected Chinese Folk Stories.* Peking: Foreign Languages P, 1965.

Shelton, A.L. *Tibetan Folk Tales.* New York: Doran, 1925.

Shrestha, Kavita Ram, and Sarah Lamstein. *From the Mango Tree and Other Folktales from Nepal.* Englewood, CO: Libraries Unlimited, 1997.

Smith, Richard Gordon. *Ancient Tales and Folklore of Japan.* London: Black, 1908.

Song Ngu. *Truyên Dân Gian Viêt Nam: Vietnamese Folktales.* Retold by Vo Van Thang and Jim Lawson. Danang: Danang Publishing, 1993. Vietnamese and English on facing pages.

Skeat, Walter. *Fables and Folk-Tales from an Eastern Forest [Malay Peninsula].* Cambridge: Cambridge UP, 1901.

Terada, Alice M. *Under the Starfruit Tree: Folktales from Vietnam.* Honolulu: U of Hawaii P, 1989.

Tyler, Royall. *Japanese Tales.* New York: Pantheon, 1987.

Vathanaprida, Supaporn, and Margaret Read MacDonald. *Thai Tales: Folktales of Thailand.* Englewood, CO: Libraries Unlimited, 1994.

Zŏng, In-Sŏb. *Folk Tales from Korea.* London: Routledge, 1952.


INDIA, PAKISTAN, TIBET, SRI LANKA

Beck, Brenda E.F., et al. *Folktales of India.* Chicago: U of Chicago P, 1987.

Bidpai. *The Tortoise and the Geese and Other Fables of Bidpai.* Retold by Maude Barrows Dutton. Boston: Houghton, 1908.

Blackburn, Stuart. *Moral Fictions: Tamil Folktales from Oral Tradition.* Helsinki: Academia Scientiarum Fennica, 2001.

Bompas, Cecil Henry. *Folklore of the Santal Parganas.* London: Nutt, 1909.

Frere, Mary. *Old Deccan Days; or, Hindoo Fairy Legends Current in Southern India.* London: Murray, 1868.

Ghose, Sudhin N. *Folk Tales and Fairy Stories from India.* London: Golden Cockerel, 1961.

Gordon, E.M. *Indian Folk Tales, Being Side-Lights on Village Life in Bilaspore, Central Provinces.* London: Stock, 1908.

Gray, John E.B. *Indian Tales and Legends.* London: Oxford UP, 1961.

Jacobs, Joseph. *Indian Fairy Tales.* London: Nutt, 1892.

*Jataka, The; or, Stories of the Buddha's Former Births.* 6 vols. Ed. E.B. Cowell. Cambridge: Cambridge UP, 1895–1913. Rpt. 1999 by Motilal Banarsidass, Delhi.

Kingscote, Georgiana Wolff, and Natêsá Sástrî. *Tales of the Sun; or, Folklore of Southern India.* London: Allen, 1890.

Knowles, J. Hinton. *Folk-Tales of Kashmir.* 2nd ed. London: Kegan Paul, 1893.

McNair, J.F.A., and Thomas Lambert Barlow. *Oral Tradition from the Indus, Comprised in Tales, to Which Are Added Explanatory Notes.* Brighton: Gosden, 1908.

*Ocean of Story, The [Katha-saritsagara].* Trans. Charles H. Tawney. 10 vols. London: privately printed, 1924–1928. Compiled about 1050 in Kashmir.

O'Flaherty, Wendy Doniger. *Tales of Sex and Violence: Folklore, Sacrifice, and Danger in the Jaiminiya Brahmana.* Chicago: U of Chicago P, 1985.

Illustration by David Gentleman. Flora Annie Steel, *Tales of the Punjab* (London and New York: Macmillan and Company, 1894), p. 183.

*Pañcatantra: The Book of India's Folk Wisdom.* Trans. Patrick Olivelle. Oxford: Oxford UP, 1997.

*Panchatantra, The.* Trans. Arthur W. Ryder. Chicago: U of Chicago P, 1964.

Parker, Henry. *Village Folk-Tales of Ceylon.* 3 vols. London: Luzac, 1910–1914.

Siddiqui, Ashraf, and Marilyn Lerch. *Pakistani Folk Tales.* New York: Hippocrene, 1998.

Spagnoli, Cathy, and Paramasivam Samanna. *Jasmine and Coconuts: South Indian Tales*. Englewood, CO: Libraries Unlimited, 1999.

Steel, Flora Annie. *Wide-Awake Stories: A Collection of Tales Told by Little Children between Sunset and Sunrise in the Panjab and Kashmir*. Bombay: Education Society's P, 1884. Reissued as *Tales of the Punjab*. London: Macmillan, 1894.

Swynnerton, Charles. *Indian Nights' Entertainment; or, Folk-Tales from the Upper Indus*. London: Stock, 1892.

*Twenty-two Goblins*. Trans. from the Sanskrit by Arthur W. Ryder. London: Dent, [1917].


ISRAEL, INCLUDING JEWISH FOLKTALES FROM OTHER AREAS

Ausubel, Nathan. *A Treasury of Jewish Folklore*. New York: Crown, 1948.

Berdichevsky, Micah Joseph. *Mimekor Yisrael: Selected Classical Jewish Folktales*. Collected by Micha Joseph bin Gorion. Ed. Emanuel bin Gorion. Trans. I.M. Lask. Bloomington: Indiana UP, 1990.

Buber, Martin. *Tales of the Hasidim: The Early Masters*. New York: Schocken, 1975.

Hanauer, J.E. *Folk-Lore of the Holy Land: Moslem, Christian, and Jewish*. London: Sheldon, 1935.

Noy, Dov. *Folktales of Israel*. Chicago: U of Chicago P, 1963.

Rappoport, Angelo S. *The Folklore of the Jews*. London: Soncino, 1937.

Sabar, Yona. *The Folk Literature of the Kurdistani Jews: An Anthology*. New Haven: Yale UP, 1982.

Sadeh, Pinhas. *Jewish Folktales*. Trans. from the Hebrew by Hillel Halkin. New York: Anchor, 1989.

Schwartz, Howard. *Elijah's Violin and Other Jewish Fairy Tales*. New York: Harper, 1985.

———. *Miriam's Tambourine: Jewish Folktales from around the World*. Oxford: Oxford UP, 1988.

Weinreich, Beatrice Silverman. *Yiddish Folktales*. New York: Pantheon, 1988.


*Europe*

ENGLAND, WALES, SCOTLAND, IRELAND

Addy, Sidney Oldall. *Household Tales with Other Traditional Remains*. London: Nutt, 1895.

Aitken, Hannah. *A Forgotten Heritage: Original Folk Tales of Lowland Scotland*. Totowa, NJ: Rowman, 1973.

Briggs, Katherine M. *British Folktales*. New York: Pantheon, 1977.

———. *A Dictionary of British Folk-Tales in the English Language*. Pt. A, 2 vols. Pt. B, 2 vols. London: Routledge, 1970–1971.

Briggs, Katharine M., and Ruth L. Tongue. *Folktales of England*. Chicago: U of Chicago P, 1965.

Campbell, J.F. *Popular Tales of the West Highlands: Orally Collected*. 4 vols. London: Gardner, 1890–1893.

Campbell, Lord Archibald. *Waifs and Strays of Celtic Tradition: Argyllshire Series [Craignish Tales and Others]*. London: Nutt, 1889.

Chambers, Robert. *Popular Rhymes of Scotland*. New ed. London and Edinburgh: Chambers, 1870. Preface to 3rd ed. dated 1841.

Chaucer, Geoffrey. *The Canterbury Tales*. Trans. Nevill Coghill. Harmondsworth, Middlesex, Eng.: Penguin, 1977.

———. *The Complete Works of Geoffrey Chaucer*. Ed. F.N. Robinson. 2nd ed. London: Oxford UP, 1957. A standard edition in Middle English.

Child, Francis James. *The English and Scottish Popular Ballads*. 5 vols. Boston: Houghton, 1882–1898.

Crossley-Holland, Kevin. *Folk-Tales of the British Isles*. New York: Pantheon, 1985.

Curtin, Jeremiah. *Myths and Folk-Lore of Ireland*. Boston: Little, 1890.

———. *Tales of the Fairies and the Ghost-World, Collected from Oral Tradition in South-West Munster*. London: Nutt, 1895.

Douglas, George. *Scottish Fairy and Folk Tales*. London: Scott, [1901].

*Gesta Romanorum: or, Entertaining Moral Stories; Invented by the Monks as a Fireside Recreation, and Commonly Applied in Their Discourses from the Pulpit*. London: Bell, 1877.

Glassie, Henry. *Irish Folktales*. New York: Pantheon, 1985.

Gregor, Walter. *Notes on the Folk-Lore of the North-East of Scotland*. London: Folk-Lore Society, 1881.

Gutch, Mrs. [Eliza], and Mabel Peacock. *County Folk-Lore: Lincolnshire*. London: Nutt, 1908.

Halliwell[-Phillips], James Orchard. *The Nursery Rhymes of England: Collected Principally from Oral Tradition*. London: printed for the Percy Society by T. Richards, 1842.

Halliwell-Phillips, James Orchard. *Popular Rhymes and Nursery Tales: A Sequel to the Nursery Rhymes of England*. London: Smith, 1849.

Hartland, Edwin Sidney. *English Fairy and Other Folk Tales*. London: Scott, [1890].

Hazlitt, William Carew. *Tales and Legends of National Origin or Widely Current in England from Early Times*. London: Sonnenschein, 1899.

Henderson, William. *Notes on the Folk-Lore of the Northern Counties of England and the Borders: With an Appendix on Household Stories by S. Baring-Gould*. London: Longmans, 1866.

Hewett, Sarah. *Nummits and Crummits: Devonshire Customs, Characteristics, and Folk-Lore*. London: Burleigh, 1900.

Hunt, Robert. *Popular Romances of the West of England; or, The Drolls, Traditions, and Superstitions of Old Cornwall*. 2nd ed. London: Hotten, 1871.

Hyde, Douglas. *Beside the Fire: A Collection of Irish Gaelic Folk Stories*. London: Nutt [1910].

Jacobs, Joseph. *Celtic Fairy Tales*. New York: Putnam's, [1899].

———. *English Fairy Tales*. 3rd ed. New York: Putnam's, [1898].

————. *More Celtic Fairy Tales.* London: Nutt, 1894.

————. *More English Fairy Tales.* New York: Putnam's, 1894.

Jones, Gwyn. *Welsh Legends and Folk-Tales.* London: Oxford UP, 1955.

Kennedy, Patrick. *Legendary Fictions of the Irish Celts.* London: Macmillan, 1866.

Leather, Ella Mary. *The Folk-Lore of Herefordshire.* London: Sidgwick, 1912.

MacDougall, James. *Folk and Hero Tales.* London: Nutt, 1891. Trans. of Gaelic tales collected in Argyllshire, Scotland.

————. *Folk Tales and Fairy Lore in Gaelic and English, Collected from Oral Tradition.* Edinburgh: Grant, 1910.

Mackenzie, Donald A. *Wonder Tales from Scottish Myth and Legend.* New York: Stokes, 1917.

MacManus, Seumas. *Donegal Fairy Stories.* New York: McClure, 1900.

McGarry, Mary. *Great Folktales of Old Ireland.* New York: Bell, 1972.

McNeil, Heather, and Nancy Chien-Eriksen. *The Celtic Breeze: Stories of the Otherworld from Scotland, Ireland, and Wales.* Englewood, CO: Libraries Unlimited, 2001.

Moore, A.W. *The Folk-Lore of the Isle of Man, Being an Account of Its Myths, Legends, Superstitions, Customs, and Proverbs.* London: Nutt, 1891.

Morrison, Sophia. *Manx Fairy Tales.* London: Nutt, 1911.

Nicolson, John. *Some Folk-Tales and Legends of Shetland.* Edinburgh: Allan, 1920.

O'Faolain, Eileen. *Irish Sagas and Folk-Tales.* London: Oxford UP, [1957].

O'Sullivan, Sean. *Folktales of Ireland.* Chicago: U of Chicago P, 1966.

Owen, Elias. *Welsh Folk-Lore: A Collection of the Folk-Tales and Legends of North Wales.* Oswestry: Wrexham, [1896].

Philip, Neil. *The Penguin Book of English Folktales.* London: Penguin, 1992.

————. *The Penguin Book of Scottish Folktales.* London: Penguin, 1995.

Reeves, James. *English Fables and Fairy Stories.* London: Oxford UP, 1954.

Rhys, John. *Celtic Folklore: Welsh and Manx.* 2 vols. Oxford: Oxford UP, 1901.

Simpson, Eve Blantyre. *Folk Lore in Lowland Scotland.* London: Dent, 1908.

Steel, Flora Annie. *English Fairy Tales.* New York: Macmillan, 1918.

Stephens, James. *Irish Fairy Tales.* New York: Macmillan, 1920.

Swinson, Cyril. *Twenty Scottish Tales and Legends.* New York: Hippocrene, 1998.

Thomas, W. Jenkyn. *The Welsh Fairy Book.* London: Unwin, [1908].

Wilde, Lady. *Ancient Legends, Mystic Charms, and Superstitions of Ireland: With Sketches of the Irish Past.* London: Ward, 1888.

Williamson, Duncan, and Linda Williamson. *A Thorn in the King's Foot: Stories of the Scottish Travelling People.* Harmondsworth, Middlesex, Eng.: Penguin, 1987.

Wilson, Barbara Ker. *Scottish Folk-Tales and Legends.* London: Oxford UP, 1954.

Yeats, William Butler. *Fairy and Folk Tales of Ireland.* New York: Macmillan, 1983. Contains *Fairy and Folk Tales of the Irish Peasantry,* first published 1888, and *Irish Fairy Tales,* first published 1892.

Young, Ella. *Celtic Wonder-Tales.* Dublin: Maunsel, 1910.

Zipes, Jack. *Victorian Fairy Tales: The Revolt of the Fairies and Elves.* New York and London: Methuen, 1987.

FRANCE

Brun, Samuel Jacques. *Tales of Languedoc: From the South of France.* New York: Hippocrene, 1998.

Delarue, Paul. *The Borzoi Book of French Folk Tales.* Trans. Austin E. Fife. New York: Knopf, 1956.

*Hundred Tales, The: Les Cent Nouvelles Nouvelles.* Trans. Rossell Hope Robbins. New York: Crown, 1960. Written anonymously in about 1460, and first published in Paris in 1486, this collection of *100 New Novellas* is a conscious imitation of *The Decameron.*

Johnson, W. Branch. *Folktales of Provence.* London: Chapman, 1927.

La Fontaine, Jean de. *The Fables of La Fontaine.* Trans. Walter Thornbury. New York: Cassell, [1868].

Margaret of Navarre. *The Heptameron of the Tales of Margaret, Queen of Navarre.* Trans. George Saintsbury. London: privately printed for the Navarre Society, 1922. First published 1558 under the title *Histoire des amans fortunez.* Published 1559 as *Heptameréron des nouvelles.*

Marie de France. *Fables.* Ed. and trans. Harriet Spiegel. Toronto: U of Toronto P, 1987.

Massignon, Geneviève. *Folktales of France.* Trans. Jacqueline Hyland. Chicago: U of Chicago P, 1968.

Perrault, Charles. *The Complete Fairy Tales of Charles Perrault.* Trans. Neil Philip and Nicoletta Simborowski. New York: Clarion, 1993.

———. *The Fairy Tales of Charles Perrault.* Trans. Angela Carter. New York: Avon, 1979.

———. *Histoires, ou contes du temps passé, avec des moralitez.* Paris: Barbin, 1697.

———. *Old-Time Stories Told by Master Charles Perrault.* Trans. A.E. Johnson. New York: Mead, 1921.

———. *Perrault's Fairy Tales.* Trans. S.R. Littlewood. London: Herbert, 1912.

Picard, Barbara Leonie. *French Legends, Tales, and Fairy Stories.* London: Oxford UP, 1955.

Pourrat, Henri. *French Folktales from the Collection of Henri Pourrat.* Trans. Royall Tyler. New York: Pantheon, 1989.

———. *A Treasury of French Tales.* Trans. Mary Mian. Boston: Houghton, 1954.


GERMANY, AUSTRIA, SWITZERLAND, NETHERLANDS

Arndt, E.M. *Fairy Tales from the Isle of Rügen.* Trans. Anna Dabis. London: Nutt, 1896.

Grimm, Jacob, and Wilhelm Grimm. *The Complete Fairy Tales of the Brothers Grimm.* Trans. Jack Zipes. 2 vols. New York: Bantam, 1987.

———. *Kinder- und Hausmärchen.* Ed. Heinz Rölleke. 3 vols. Stuttgart: Reclam, 1980. Based on the 7th edition of 1857.

Leeuw, Adèle de. *Legends and Folk Tales of Holland.* New York: Hippocrene, 1999. First published 1963.

Muller-Guggenbuhl, Fritz. *Swiss-Alpine Folk-Tales.* London: Oxford UP, 1958.

Picard, Barbara Leonie. *German Hero-Sagas and Folk-Tales.* London: Oxford UP, 1958.

Ranke, Kurt. *Folktales of Germany.* Trans. Lotte Baumann. Chicago: U of Chicago P, 1966.


### Greece

Abbott, G.F. *Macedonian Folklore.* Cambridge: Cambridge UP, 1903.

Dawkins, R.M. *Forty-Five Stories from the Dodecanese.* Cambridge: Cambridge UP, 1950.

————. *Modern Greek Folktales.* Oxford: Clarendon, 1953.

————. *More Greek Folktales.* London: Clarendon, 1955.

Garnett, Lucy M.J. *Greek Wonder Tales.* London: Black, 1927.

Mitakidou, Soula, et al. *Folktales from Greece: A Treasury of Delights.* Englewood, CO: Libraries Unlimited, 2002.

Megas, Georgios A. *Folktales of Greece.* Chicago: U of Chicago P, 1970.


### Aesopic Fables

*Aesop without Morals: The Famous Fables, and a Life of Aesop.* Trans. and ed. Lloyd W. Daly. New York: Yoseloff, 1961.

*Aesop's Fables.* Trans. and ed. Laura Gibbs. Oxford: Oxford UP, 2002.

*Aesop's Fables.* Trans. V.S. Vernon Jones. Ed. D.L. Ashliman. New York: Barnes and Noble, 2003.

*Fables of Aesop.* Trans. and ed. S.A. Handford. Harmondsworth, Middlesex, Eng.: Penguin, 1964.

Perry, Ben Edwin. *Babrius and Phaedrus: Newly Edited and Translated into English, together with an Historical Introduction and a Comprehensive Survey of Greek and Latin Fables in the Aesopic Tradition.* Cambridge: Harvard UP, 1984.


### Gypsy (Romany)

Groome, Francis Hindes. *Gypsy Folk-Tales.* London: Hurst, 1899.

Sampson, John. *Gypsy Folk Tales.* Salem, NH: Salem, 1984.

Tong, Diane. *Gypsy Folktales.* New York: Harcourt, 1989.


### Hungary

Dégh, Linda. *Folktales of Hungary.* Chicago: U of Chicago P, 1965.

Rédei, Károly. *Zyrian Folklore Texts.* Budapest: Akadémiai Kiadó, 1978.

ITALY

Basile, Giambattista. *The Pentamerone*. Trans. from the Italian of Benedetto Croce. Ed. N.M. Penzer. 2 vols. New York: Dutton, 1932. First published 1634–1636 as *Lo cunto de li cunti.*

Boccaccio, Giovanni. *The Decameron*. Trans. G.H. McWilliam. Harmondsworth, Middlesex, Eng.: Penguin, 1972.

Calvino, Italo. *Italian Folktales*. Trans. George Martin. New York: Pantheon, 1980.

Crane, Thomas Frederick. *Italian Popular Tales*. Boston and New York: Houghton, 1885.

Falassi, Alessandro. *Folklore by the Fireside: Text and Context of the Tuscan Veglia.* Austin: U of Texas P, 1980.

Hundred Old Tales, The. *Il Novellino: The Hundred Old Tales*. Ed. and trans. Edward Storer. London: Routledge, [1926]. First ed. printed in Bologna in 1525 by Carlo Gualteruzzi under the title *Le Ciento Novelle antike*. The usual Italian title of this work is *Cento novelle antiche.*

Poggio Bracciolini, Gian Francesco. *The Facetiae of Poggio*. Paris: Liseux, 1879. A standard edition in Latin.

———. *The Facetiae of Poggio and Other Medieval Story-Tellers*. Ed. and trans. Edward Storer. London: Routledge, [1928]. Selections from the Italian humanist's *Liber facetiarum,* or simply *Facetiae,* first published in 1470.

Romano, Lilia E. *Italian Fairy Tales*. New York: Hippocrene, 1999.

Sacchetti, Franco. *Tales from Sacchetti*. Trans. Mary G. Steegmann. London: Dent, 1908.

Straparola, Giovanni Francesco. *The Facetious Nights of Straparola*. Trans. W.G. Waters. 4 vols. London: privately printed for members of the Society of Bibliophiles, 1898.


ROMANIA

Creanga, Ion. *Folk Tales from Roumania*. London: Routledge, 1952.

Gaster, M. *Rumanian Bird and Beast Stories*. London: Folk-Lore Society, 1915.


SCANDINAVIA AND FINLAND

Andersen, Hans Christian. *The Complete Fairy Tales and Stories*. Trans. Erik Christian Haugaard. Garden City, NY: Doubleday, 1983.

———. *The Stories of Hans Christian Andersen*. Trans. Diana Crone Frank and Jeffrey Frank. Boston: Houghton Mifflin, 2003.

Asbjørnsen, Peter Christen. *Fairy Tales from the Far North*. Trans. H.L. Brækstad. New York: Burt, 1897.

———. *Round the Yule Log: Norwegian Folk and Fairy Tales*. Trans. H.L. Brækstad. Philadelphia: Lippincott, [1930].

Asbjørnsen, Peter Christen, and Jørgen Moe. *Norwegian Folk Tales.* Trans. Pat Shaw and Carl Norman. New York: Pantheon, 1960.

――――. *East o' the Sun and West o' the Moon: Fifty-nine Norwegian Folk Tales.* Trans. George Webbe Dasent. New York: Dover, 1970.

――――. *Popular Tales from the Norse, with an Introductory Essay on the Origin and Diffusion of Popular Tales.* Trans. Sir George Webbe Dasent. London: Routledge, n.d.

Bay, J. Christian. *Danish Folk Tales, from the Danish of Svend Grundtvig, E.T. Kristensen, Ingvor Bondesen, and L. Budde.* New York: Harper, 1899.

Blecher, Lone Thygesen, and George Blecher. *Swedish Folktales and Legends.* New York: Pantheon, 1993.

Bødker, Laurits, et al. *European Folk Tales.* Copenhagen: Rosenkilde, 1963.

Booss, Claire. *Scandinavian Folk and Fairy Tales: Tales from Norway, Sweden, Denmark, Finland, Iceland.* New York: Avenel, 1984.

Boucher, Alan. *Icelandic Folktales.* 3 vols. Reykjavik: Icelandic Review Library, 1977.

Braekstad [Brækstad], H.L. *Swedish Fairy Tales.* New York: Hippocrene, 1998.

Christiansen, Reidar. *Folktales of Norway.* Trans. Pat Shaw Iversen. Chicago: U of Chicago P, 1964.

Djurklou, Gabriel. *Fairy Tales from the Swedish of G. Djurklo [Djurklou].* Trans. H.L. Brækstad. Philadelphia: Lippincott, 1901.

Grundtvig, Svendt. *Danish Fairy Tales.* Boston: Badger, 1912.

Hofberg, Herman. *Swedish Fairy Tales.* Trans. W.H. Myers. Chicago: Conkey, 1893.

Jones, Gwyn. *Scandinavian Legends and Folk-Tales.* London: Oxford UP, 1956.

Lindow, John. *Swedish Legends and Folktales.* Berkeley: U of California P, 1978.

Livo, Norma J., and George O. Livo. *The Enchanted Wood and Other Tales from Finland.* Englewood, CO: Libraries Unlimited, 1999.

Lönnrot, Elias. *The Kalevala; or, Poems of the Kaleva District.* Trans. Francis Peabody Magoun Jr. Cambridge: Harvard UP, 1963.

Saxo Grammaticus. *The First Nine Books of the Danish History of Saxo Grammaticus [Gesta Danorum].* Trans. Oliver Elton. London: Nutt, 1894.

Simpson, Jacqueline. *Icelandic Folktales and Legends.* Berkeley: U of California P, 1972.

――――. *Scandinavian Folktales.* London: Penguin, 1988.

Thorpe, Benjamin. *Yule-Tide Stories: A Collection of Scandinavian and North German Popular Tales and Traditions from the Swedish, Danish, and German.* London: Bohn, 1853.

SLAVIC

Afanas'ev [Afanasyev], Aleksandr. *Russian Fairy Tales.* Trans. Norbert Guterman. New York: Pantheon, 1945.

Afanasyev, Aleksandr. *Erotic Tales of Old Russia.* Trans. Yury Perkov. Oakland: Scythian, 1980. English and Russian on facing pages.

———. *Russian Secret Tales: Bawdy Folktales of Old Russia.* New York: Brussel, 1966.

Bloch, Marie Halun. *Ukrainian Folk Tales.* New York: Hippocrene, 1999.

Chodsko, Alex. *Fairy Tales of the Slav Peasants and Herdsmen.* Trans. Emily J. Harding. New York: Dodd, 1896.

Curcija-Prodanovic, Nada. *Yugoslav Folk-Tales.* London: Oxford UP, 1957.

Curtin, Jeremiah. *Myth and Folk-Tales of the Russians, Western Slavs, and Magyars.* Boston: Little, 1890.

Downing, Charles. *Armenian Folk-Tales and Fables.* Oxford: Oxford UP, 1993.

———. *Russian Tales and Legends.* London: Oxford UP, 1956.

Fillmore, Parker. *Czech, Moravian, and Slovak Fairy Tales.* New York: Hippocrene, 1998.

Hodgetts, Edith M.S. *Tales and Legends from the Land of the Tzar: A Collection of Russian Stories.* New York: Merrill, 1892.

Mackenzie, Donald A. *Folk Tales from Russia.* New York: Hippocrene, 1998.

Marshall, Bonnie C., and Vasa D. Mihailovich. *Tales from the Heart of the Balkans.* Englewood, CO: Libraries Unlimited, 2001.

Mijatovies, Csedomille. *Serbian Folk-Lore: Popular Tales.* London: Isbister, 1874.

Oparenko, Christina. *Ukrainian Folk-Tales.* Oxford: Oxford UP, 1996.

Ralston, W.R.S. *Russian Folk-Tales.* London: Smith, 1873.

Riordan, James. *The Sun Maiden and the Crescent Moon: Siberian Folk Tales.* New York: Interlink, 1991.

Steele, Robert. *The Russian Garland of Fairy Tales: Being Russian Folk Legends, Translated from a Collection of Chapbooks Made in Moscow.* New York: McBrude, 1916.

Suwyn, Barbara J., and Natalie O. Kononenko. *The Magic Egg and Other Tales from Ukraine.* Englewood, CO: Libraries Unlimited, 1997.

Wardrop, Marjory. *Georgian Folk Tales.* London: Nutt, 1894.

Wenig, Adolf. *Folk Tales from Bohemia.* New York: Hippocrene, 1998.

Wratislaw, A.H. *Sixty Folk-Tales from Exclusively Slavonic Sources.* London: Stock, 1889.

## TURKEY

Kent, Margery. *Fairy Tales from Turkey.* London: Routledge, 1946.

Nesin, Aziz. *The Tales of Nasrettin Hoca.* Retold in English by Talat Halman. Istanbul: Dost Yayinlari, 1988.

Ramsay, Allan, and Francis McCullagh. *Tales from Turkey.* London: Simpkin, 1914.

Sheykh-Zada. *The History of the Forty Vezirs; or, The Story of the Forty Morns and Eves.* Trans. E.J.W. Gibb. London: Redway, 1886.

## North America

### AFRICAN AMERICAN

Abrahams, Roger D. *African American Folktales: Stories from Black Traditions in the New World.* New York: Pantheon, 1999.

Bascom, William R. *African Folktales in the New World*. Bloomington: Indiana UP, 1992.

Courlander, Harold. *A Treasury of Afro-American Folklore: The Oral Literature, Traditions, Recollections, Legends, Tales, Songs, Religious Beliefs, Customs, Sayings, and Humor of Peoples of African Descent in the Americas*. New York: Smithmark, 1996.

Crowley, Daniel J. *African Folklore in the New World*. Austin: U of Texas P, 1977.

Dance, Daryl Cumber. *From My People: 400 Years of African American Folklore*. New York: Norton, 2002.

Dorson, Richard M. *American Negro Folktales*. Greenwich, CT: Fawcett, 1967.

———. *Negro Folktales in Michigan*. Cambridge: Harvard UP, 1956.

Harris, Joel Chandler. *The Complete Tales of Uncle Remus*. Comp. Richard Chase. Boston: Houghton, 1955. Contents: *Uncle Remus: His Songs and His Sayings,* new and rev. ed. (1896); *Nights with Uncle Remus: Myths and Legends of the Old Plantation* (1883); *Daddy Jake, the Runaway: And Short Stories Told after Dark* (1889); *Uncle Remus and His Friends: Old Plantation Stories, Songs, and Ballads with Sketches of Negro Character* (1892); *Told by Uncle Remus: New Stories of the Old Plantation* (1905); *Uncle Remus and Brer Rabbit* (1907); *Uncle Remus and the Little Boy* (1910); *Uncle Remus Returns* (1918); *Seven Tales of Uncle Remus* (1948).

Hurston, Zora Neale. *Every Tongue Got to Confess: Negro Folk-Tales from the Gulf States*. New York: Harper, 2001.

Jones, Charles Colcock. *Gullah Folktales from the Georgia Coast*. Athens: U of Georgia P, 2000.

Lester, Julius. *Black Folktales*. New York: Grove, 1970.

Levine, Lawrence W. *Black Culture and Black Consciousness: Afro-American Folk Thought from Slavery to Freedom*. Oxford: Oxford UP, 1977.

Lindahl, Carl, et al. *Swapping Stories: Folktales from Louisiana*. Jackson: U of Mississippi P, 1997.

Peck, Catherine. *A Treasury of North American Folktales*. New York: Norton, 1998.


EUROPEAN AMERICAN (EXCEPT SPANISH AMERICAN)

Baker, Ronald L. *Jokelore: Humorous Folktales from Indiana*. Bloomington: Indiana UP, 1986.

Barrick, Mac E. *German-American Folklore*. Little Rock: August, 1987.

Blair, Walter. *Tall Tale America: A Legendary History of Our Humorous Heroes*. Chicago: U of Chicago P, 1987. First published 1944.

Brunvand, Jan Harold. *The Vanishing Hitchhiker: American Urban Legends and Their Meanings*. New York: Norton, 1981. The first of Brunvand's numerous carefully researched collections of urban legends.

Burrison, John A. *Storytellers: Folktales and Legends from the South*. Athens: U of Georgia P, 1991.

Campbell, Marie. *Tales from the Cloud Walking Country [Kentucky]*. Bloomington: Indiana UP, 1958.

Chase, Richard. *American Folk Tales and Songs, and Other Examples of English-American Tradition as Preserved in the Appalachian Mountains and Elsewhere in the United States.* New York: Dover, 1971.

———. *Grandfather Tales: American-English Folk Tales.* Boston: Houghton, 1976.

———. *The Jack Tales: Told by R.M. Ward and His Kindred in the Beech Mountain Section of Western North Carolina and by Other Descendents of Council Harmon (1803–1896) Elsewhere in the Southern Mountains; with Three Tales from Wise County, Virginia.* Boston: Houghton, 1971.

Coffin, Tristram P., and Hennig Cohen. *Folklore in America: Tales, Songs, Superstitions, Proverbs, Riddles, Games, Folk Drama, and Folk Festivals.* Garden City, NY: Doubleday, 1966.

Dorson, Richard M. *America in Legend: Folklore from the Colonial Period to the Present.* New York: Pantheon, 1973.

———. *Bloodstoppers and Bearwalkers: Folk Traditions of the Upper Peninsula.* Cambridge: Harvard UP, 1952.

———. *Buying the Wind: Regional Folklore in the United States.* Chicago: U of Chicago P, 1964.

Emrich, Duncan. *Folklore on the American Land.* Boston: Little, 1972.

Erdoes, Richard. *Legends and Tales of the American West.* New York: Pantheon, 1998.

Fowke, Edith. *Folklore of Canada.* Toronto: McClelland, 1976.

Georges, Robert A. *Greek-American Folk Beliefs and Narratives.* New York: Arno, 1980.

Glimm, James York. *Flatlanders and Ridgerunners: Folktales from the Mountains of Northern Pennsylvania.* Pittsburgh: U of Pittsburgh P, 1983.

Klymasz, Robert B. *Ukrainian Folklore in Canada: An Immigrant Complex in Transition.* New York: Arno, 1980.

Lindahl, Carl, et al. *Swapping Stories: Folktales from Louisiana.* Jackson: U of Mississippi P, 1997.

Malpezzi, Frances M., and William M. Clements. *Italian-American Folklore.* Little Rock: August, 1992.

Mathias, Elizabeth, and Richard Raspa. *Italian Folktales in America.* Detroit: Wayne State UP, 1985.

McCormick, Dell J. *Paul Bunyan Swings His Axe.* Caldwell, ID: Caxton, 1936.

———. *Tall Timber Tales: More Paul Bunyan Stories.* Caldwell, ID: Caxton, 1939.

Musick, Ruth Ann. *Green Hills of Magic: West Virginia Folktales from Europe.* Lexington: UP of Kentucky, 1970.

———. *The Telltale Lilac Bush and Other West Virginia Ghost Tales.* Lexington: U of Kentucky P, 1965.

Peck, Catherine. *A Treasury of North American Folktales.* New York: Norton, 1998.

Randolph, Vance. *The Devil's Pretty Daughter and Other Ozark Folk Tales.* New York: Columbia UP, 1955.

———. *Hot Springs and Hell and Other Folk Jests and Anecdotes from the Ozarks.* Hatboro, PA: Folklore Associates, 1965.

———. *Ozark Superstitions.* New York: Columbia UP, 1947.

————. *Pissing in the Snow and Other Ozark Folktales*. New York: Avon, 1977.

————. *Sticks in the Knapsack and Other Ozark Folk Tales*. New York: Columbia UP, 1958.

————. *The Talking Turtle and Other Ozark Folk Tales*. New York: Columbia UP, 1957.

————. *Who Blowed Up the Church House? and Other Ozark Folk Tales*. New York: Columbia UP, 1952.

Reaver, J. Russell. *Florida Folktales*. Gainesville: U of Florida P, 1987.

Roberts, Leonard W. *South from Hell-fer-Sartin: Kentucky Mountain Folk Tales*. Berea, KY: Council of Southern Mountains, 1964.

Sackett, S.J., and William E. Koch. *Kansas Folklore*. Lincoln: U of Nebraska P, 1961.

Saucier, Corinne L. *Folk Tales from French Louisiana*. New York: Exposition, 1962.

Stevens, James. *The Saginaw Paul Bunyan*. Detroit: Wayne State UP, 1987. First published 1932.

Thomas, Rosemary Hyde. *It's Good to Tell You: French Folktales from Missouri*. Columbia: U of Missouri P, 1981.

Thompson, Harold W. *Body, Boots, and Britches: Folktales, Ballads, and Speech from Country New York*. Lippincott, 1939.

Welsch, Roger L. *Mister, You Got Yourself a Horse: Tales of Old-Time Horse Trading*. Lincoln: U of Nebraska P, 1987.

————. *Shingling the Fog and Other Plains Lies*. Lincoln: U of Nebraska P, 1980.

————. *A Treasury of Nebraska Pioneer Folklore*. Lincoln: U of Nebraska P, 1984. First published 1939.

Welsch, Roger L., and Linda K. Welsch. *Catfish at the Pump: Humor and the Frontier*. Lincoln: U of Nebraska P, 1986.

Young, Richard, and Judy Dockrey. *Ozark Tall Tales: Collected from the Oral Tradition*. Little Rock: August, 1989.


NATIVE AMERICAN

Brown, Dee. *Dee Brown's Folktales of the Native American, Retold for Our Times*. New York: Holt, 1993.

Coffin, Tristram Potter. *Indian Tales of North America: An Anthology for the Adult Reader*. Philadelphia: American Folklore Society, 1961.

Erdoes, Richard, and Alfonso Ortiz. *American Indian Myths and Legends*. New York: Pantheon, 1984.

Leland, Charles G. *The Algonquin Legends of New England; or, Myths and Folk Lore of the Micmac, Passamaquoddy, and Penobscot Tribes*. Boston: Houghton, 1884.

Linderman, Frank B. *Kootenai Why Stories*. New York: Scribner's, 1926.

Millman, Lawrence. *A Kayak Full of Ghosts: Eskimo Tales*. Santa Barbara: Capra, 1987.

Norman, Howard. *Northern Tales: Traditional Stories of Eskimo and Indian Peoples*. New York: Pantheon, 1990.

GLOOSKAP TURNING A MAN INTO A CEDAR-TREE.

Illustration by an unnamed Native American artist.
Charles G. Leland, *The Algonquin Legends of New England* (Boston: Houghton, Mifflin and Company, 1884), facing p. 98.

Parker, Arthur C. *Seneca Myths and Folk Tales.* Buffalo: Buffalo Historical Society, 1923.

Peck, Catherine. *A Treasury of North American Folktales.* New York: Norton, 1998.

Pelton, Mary Helen, et al. *Images of a People: Tlingit Myths and Legends.* Englewood, CO: Libraries Unlimited, 1992.

Thompson, Stith. *European Tales among the North American Indians: A Study in the Migration of Folk-Tales.* Colorado Springs: Colorado College, 1919.

————. *Tales of the North American Indians.* Cambridge: Harvard UP, 1929.

### Latin America

Aiken, Riley. *Mexican Folktales from the Borderland.* Dallas: Southern Methodist UP, 1980.

Bierhorst, John. *Latin American Folktales: Stories from Hispanic and Indian Traditions.* New York: Pantheon, 2002.

Dance, Daryl C. *Folklore from Contemporary Jamaicans.* Knoxville: U of Tennessee P, 1985.

Espinosa, Aurelio M. *The Folklore of Spain in the American Southwest: Traditional Spanish Folk Literature in Northern New Mexico and Southern Colorado.* Norman: U of Oklahoma P, 1985.

Hughes, Brenda. *Folk Tales from Chile.* New York: Hippocrene, 1998.

Louis, Liliane Nerette, and Fred J. Hay. *When Night Falls, Kric! Krac! Haitian Folktales.* Englewood, CO: Libraries Unlimited, 1999.

McCartney, Norma. *Tales of the Immortelles: A Collection of Caribbean Folk Tales.* London: Macmillan, 1989.

Miller, Elaine K. *Mexican Folk Narrative from the Los Angeles Area.* Austin: U of Texas P, 1973.

Paredes, Américo. *Folktales of Mexico.* Chicago: U of Chicago P, 1970.

Pino-Saavedra, Yolando. *Folktales of Chile.* Chicago: U of Chicago P, 1967.

Sherlock, Philip Manderson. *West Indian Folk-Tales.* London: Oxford UP, 1966.

Vigil, Angel. *The Corn Woman: Stories and Legends of the Hispanic Southwest.* Englewood, CO: Libraries Unlimited, 1994.

———. *The Eagle on the Cactus: Traditional Stories from Mexico.* Englewood, CO: Libraries Unlimited, 2000.

West, John O. *Mexican-American Folklore: Legends, Songs, Festivals, Proverbs, Crafts, Tales of Saints, of Revolutionaries, and More.* Little Rock: August, 1988.

Wolkstein, Diane. *The Magic Orange Tree and Other Haitian Folktales.* New York: Knopf, 1978.

## MULTINATIONAL COLLECTIONS

Ashliman, D.L. *Voices from the Past: The Cycle of Life in Indo-European Folktales.* 2nd ed. Dubuque: Kendall/Hunt, 1995.

Barchers, Suzanne I. *Wise Women: Folk and Fairy Tales from around the World.* Englewood, CO: Libraries Unlimited, 1990.

Carter, Angela. *The Old Wives' Fairy Tale Book.* New York: Pantheon, 1990. The British ed. has the title *The Virago Book of Fairy Tales.*

———. *Sleeping Beauty and Other Favourite Fairy Tales.* Boston: Otter, 1991.

———. *Strange Things Sometimes Still Happen: Fairy Tales from around the World.* Boston: Faber, 1994.

Clarkson, Atelia, and Gilbert B. *World Folktales: A Scribner Resource Collection.* New York: Scribner's, 1980.

Cole, Joanna. *Best-Loved Folktales of the World.* Garden City, NY: Anchor-Doubleday, 1982.

Dorson, Richard M. *Folktales Told around the World.* Chicago: U of Chicago P, 1975.

Haviland, Virginia. In 1959 Haviland began publishing illustrated fairy-tale anthologies, with the stories retold for younger readers. Each book comprises about 90 pages, and the titles follow the pattern *Favorite Fairy Tales Told in England.* All were published in Boston by Little, Brown. Following are the countries included, with the year of first publication: England (1959), France (1959), Germany (1959), Ireland (1961), Norway (1961), Russia (1961), Poland (1963), Scotland (1963), Spain (1963), Italy (1965), Czechoslovakia (1966), Sweden (1966), Japan (1967), Greece (1970), Denmark (1971), India (1973).

Jacobs, Joseph. *European Folk and Fairy Tales: Restored and Retold*. New York: Putnam's, 1916.

Lang, Andrew. In 1889 Lang published the first of his colored fairy books. An eminent folklorist, he drew on collections in many languages and from around the world, then cautiously rewrote the tales to meet Victorian standards. The books are handsomely illustrated, for the most part by H.J. Ford. The entire series has been reprinted by Dover, and most of the volumes are available in electronic form on the Internet. The original publisher was Longmans, Green of London. Each title follows the pattern *The Blue Fairy Book*. The 12 colors, with the year of first publication, are as follows: Blue (1889), Red (1890), Green (1892), Yellow (1894), Pink (1897), Grey (1900), Violet (1901), Crimson (1903), Brown (1904), Orange (1906), Olive (1907), and Lilac (1910).

Opie, Iona, and Peter Opie, eds. *The Classic Fairy Tales*. New York: Oxford UP, 1980.

Shah, Idries. *World Tales: The Extraordinary Coincidence of Stories Told in All Times, in All Places*. New York: Harcourt, 1979.

Tatar, Maria. *The Annotated Classic Fairy Tales*. New York: Norton, 2002.

———. *The Classic Fairy Tales*. New York: Norton, 1999.

Thompson, Stith. *One Hundred Favorite Folktales*. Bloomington: Indiana UP, 1974.

Vos, Gail de, and Anna E. Altmann. *New Tales for Old: Folktales as Literary Fictions for Young Adults*. Englewood, CO: Libraries Unlimited, 1999.

———. *Tales, Then and Now: More Folktales as Literary Fictions for Young Adults*. Englewood, CO: Libraries Unlimited, 2001.

Yolen, Jane. *Favorite Folktales from around the World*. New York: Pantheon, 1986.

Zipes, Jack. *The Great Fairy Tale Tradition: From Straparola and Basile to the Brothers Grimm*. New York: Norton, 2000.

———. *Spells of Enchantment: The Wondrous Fairy Tales of Western Culture*. New York: Viking, 1991.

## NONTRADITIONAL COLLECTIONS

Lurie, Alison. *The Oxford Book of Modern Fairy Tales*. Oxford: Oxford UP, 1993.

Mieder, Wolfgang. *Disenchantments: An Anthology of Modern Fairy Tale Poetry*. Hanover, NH: UP of New England, 1985.

Phelps, Ethel Johnston. *The Maid of the North: Feminist Folk Tales from around the World*. New York: Holt, 1981.

———. *Tatterhood and Other Tales*. New York: Feminist P at the City U of New York, 1978.

Zipes, Jack. *Don't Bet on the Prince: Contemporary Feminist Fairy Tales in North America and England*. Aldershot: Gower, 1986.

Illustration by H.J. Ford from "Beauty and the Beast." Andrew Lang, *The Blue Fairy Book* (London: Longmans, Green, and Company, 1889), p. 117.

## PARODIES

Garner, James Finn. *Politically Correct Bedtime Stories.* New York: Macmillan, 1994.

Scieszka, Jon. *The Frog Prince Continued.* New York: Viking, 1991.

Scieszka, Jon, and Lane Smith. *The Stinky Cheese Man and Other Fairly Stupid Tales.* New York: Viking, 1992.

————. *The True Story of the 3 Little Pigs, by A. Wolf.* New York: Viking, 1989.

Thurber, James. *Fables for Our Time, and Famous Poems Illustrated.* New York: Harper, 1983. First published 1939.

## BOOKS ABOUT FOLK AND FAIRY TALES

Bottigheimer, Ruth B., ed. *Fairy Tales and Society: Illusion, Allusion, and Paradigm.* Philadelphia: U of Pennsylvania P, 1986.

Brunvand, Jan Harold. *The Study of American Folklore: An Introduction.* New York: Norton, 1978.

Campbell, Joseph. *The Hero with a Thousand Faces.* 2nd ed. Princeton: Princeton UP, 1968. First published 1949.

Clouston, W.A. *Popular Tales and Fictions: Their Migrations and Transformations.* 2 vols. Edinburgh: Blackwood, 1887.

Dorson, Richard M. *Folklore.* Bloomington: Indiana UP, 1972.

———. *Folklore and Fakelore: Essays toward a Discipline of Folk Studies.* Cambridge: Harvard UP, 1976.

———, ed. *Folklore and Folklife: An Introduction.* Chicago: U of Chicago P, 1972.

———, ed. *Peasant Customs and Savage Myths: Selections from the British Folklorists.* 2 vols. Chicago: U of Chicago P, 1968.

Dundes, Alan, ed. *The Study of Folklore.* Englewood Cliffs, NJ: Prentice, 1965.

Fine, Elizabeth. *The Folkloric Text: From Performance to Print.* Bloomington: Indiana UP, 1984.

Frazer, James George. *The Golden Bough: A Study in Magic and Religion.* 3rd ed. 12 vols. London: Macmillan, 1911–1916. The first ed. appeared in 1890 under the title *The Golden Bough: A Study in Comparative Religion.* 2 vols.

Hartland, Edwin Sidney. *The Science of Fairy Tales: An Inquiry into Fairy Mythology.* London: Scott, 1891.

Jones, Steven Swann. *The Fairy Tale: The Magic Mirror of Imagination.* New York: Twayne, 1995.

King, James Roy. *Old Tales and New Truths: Charting the Bright-Shadow World.* Albany: State U of New York P, 1992.

Legman, G. *The Horn Book: Studies in Erotic Folklore and Bibliography.* New Hyde Park, NY: University Books, 1964.

Lüthi, Max. *The European Folktale: Form and Nature.* Trans. John D. Niles. Philadelphia: Institute for the Study of Human Issues, 1982.

———. *The Fairy Tale as Art Form and Portrait of Man.* Trans. Jon Erickson. Bloomington: Indiana UP, 1985.

———. *Once upon a Time: On the Nature of Fairy Tales.* Trans. Lee Chadeayne and Paul Gottwald. New York: Ungar, 1970.

Mieder, Wolfgang. *Tradition and Innovation in Folk Literature.* Hanover, NH: UP of New England, 1987.

Propp, Vladimir. *The Morphology of the Folktale.* Trans. Laurence Scott. 2nd ed. Austin: U of Texas P, 1968. First published 1928 in Russian.

———. *Theory and History of Folklore.* Trans. Ariadna Y. Martin, Richard P. Martin, et al. Ed. Anatoly Liberman. Minneapolis: U of Minnesota P, 1984.

Röhrich, Lutz. *Folktales and Reality.* Trans. Peter Tokofsky. Bloomington: Indiana UP, 1991.

Sale, Roger. *Fairy Tales and After: From Snow White to E.B. White.* Cambridge: Harvard UP, 1978.

Stone, Kay F. *Burning Brightly: New Light on Old Tales Today.* Peterborough, Ontario: Broadview, 1998.

Tatar, Maria. *The Annotated Classic Fairy Tales.* New York: Norton, 2002.

———. *Off with Their Heads! Fairy Tales and the Culture of Childhood.* Princeton: Princeton UP, 1992.

Thompson, Stith. *The Folktale.* Berkeley: U of California P, 1977. First published 1946.

Tolkien, J.R.R. *Tree and Leaf.* Boston: Houghton, 1989. Includes the essay "On Fairy-Stories" and the tale "Leaf by Niggle."

Warner, Marina. *From the Beast to the Blonde: On Fairy Tales and Their Tellers.* New York: Farrar, 1994.

Yolen, Jane. *Touch Magic: Fantasy, Faerie, and Folklore in the Literature of Childhood.* New York: Philomel, 1981.

Zipes, Jack. *Breaking the Magic Spell: Radical Theories of Folk and Fairy Tales.* Austin: U of Texas P, 1979.

———. *Fairy Tale as Myth/Myth as Fairy Tale.* Lexington: UP of Kentucky, 1994.

———. *Fairy Tales and the Art of Subversion: The Classical Genre for Children and the Process of Civilization.* New York: Wildman, 1983.

———. *Happily Ever After: Fairy Tales, Children, and the Culture Industry.* New York: Routledge, 1997.

## REGIONAL STUDIES

Brown, Carolyn S. *The Tall Tale in American Folklore and Literature.* Knoxville: U of Tennessee P, 1987.

Canepa, Nancy, ed. *Out of the Woods: The Origins of the Literary Fairy Tale in Italy and France.* Detroit: Wayne State UP, 1997.

Dégh, Linda. *Folktales and Society: Storytelling in a Hungarian Peasant Community.* Trans. Emily M. Schossberger. Bloomington: Indiana UP, 1969.

Gose, Elliott B., Jr. *The World of the Irish Wonder Tale: An Introduction to the Study of Fairy Tales.* Toronto: U of Toronto P, 1985.

Hoffman, Daniel. *Paul Bunyan: Last of the Frontier Demigods.* Lincoln: U of Nebraska P, 1983. First published 1952.

Lindfors, Bernth, ed. *Forms of Folklore in Africa: Narrative, Poetic, Gnomic, Dramatic.* Austin: U of Texas P, 1977.

Yassif, Eli. *The Hebrew Folktale: History, Genre, Meaning.* Trans. from Hebrew by Jacqueline S. Teitelbaum. Bloomington: Indiana UP, 1999.

## PSYCHOLOGICAL APPROACHES

Bettelheim, Bruno. *The Uses of Enchantment: The Meaning and Importance of Fairy Tales.* New York: Knopf, 1976.

Edmunds, Lowell, and Alan Dundes, eds. *Oedipus: A Folklore Casebook.* New York: Garland, 1983.

Franz, Marie-Louise von. *The Interpretation of Fairy Tales.* Rev. ed. Boston: Shambhala, 1996.

———. *An Introduction to the Psychology of Fairy Tales.* New York: Spring, 1970.

———. *Problems of the Feminine in Fairytales.* Dallas: Spring, 1972.

————. *Shadow and Evil in Fairy Tales.* Boston: Shambhala, 1995.

Fromm, Erich. *The Forgotten Language: An Introduction to the Understanding of Dreams, Fairy Tales, and Myths.* New York: Rinehart, 1951.

Heuscher, Julius. *A Psychiatric Study of Myths and Fairy Tales.* Springfield: Thomas, 1974.

Mallet, Carl-Heinz. *Fairy Tales and Children: The Psychology of Children Revealed through Four of the Grimms' Fairy Tales.* Trans. Joachim Neugroschel. New York: Schocken, 1980.

Róheim, Géza. *Fire in the Dragon and Other Psychoanalytic Essays on Folklore.* Ed. Alan Dundes. Princeton: Princeton UP, 1992.

## GENDER ISSUES

Auerbach, Nina, and U.C. Knoepflmacher, eds. *Forbidden Journeys: Fairy Tales and Fantasies by Victorian Women Writers.* Chicago: U of Chicago P, 1992.

Bacchilega, Cristina. *Postmodern Fairy Tales: Gender and Narrative Strategies.* Philadelphia: U of Pennsylvania P, 1997.

Bernheimer, Kate, ed. *Mirror, Mirror on the Wall: Women Writers Explore Their Favorite Fairy Tales.* New York: Anchor, 1998.

Bly, Robert. *Iron John: A Book about Men.* New York: Addison, 1990.

Estés, Clarissa Pinkola. *Women Who Run with the Wolves: Myths and Stories of the Wild Woman Archetype.* New York: Ballantine, 1997.

Farrer, Claire, ed. *Women and Folklore.* Austin: U of Texas P, 1975.

Jurich, Marilyn. *Scheherazade's Sisters: Trickster Heroines and Their Stories in World Literature.* Westport, CT: Greenwood, 1998.

Knoepflmacher, U.C. *Ventures into Childland: Victorians, Fairy tales, and Femininity.* Chicago: U of Chicago P, 1998.

Kolbenschlag, Madonna. *Kiss Sleeping Beauty Good-bye: Breaking the Spell of Feminine Myths and Models.* New York: Doubleday, 1979.

Leavy, Barbara Fass. *In Search of the Swan Maiden: A Narrative on Folklore and Gender.* New York: New York UP, 1994.

Seifert, Lewis C. *Fairy Tales, Sexuality, and Gender in France, 1690–1715: Nostalgic Utopias.* Cambridge: Cambridge UP, 1996.

Taggart, James M. *Enchanted Maidens: Gender Relations in Spanish Folktales of Courtship and Marriage.* Princeton: Princeton UP, 1990. Includes English trans. of tales collected in various villages in Spain in the 1980s.

## STUDIES OF INDIVIDUAL AUTHORS AND COLLECTORS

### Aesop

Holzberg, Niklas. *The Ancient Fable: An Introduction.* Trans. Christine Jackson-Holzberg. Bloomington: Indiana UP, 2002.

Jacobs, Joseph. *History of the Aesopic Fable.* New York: Franklin, 1970. First published in 1889.

Patterson, Annabel M. *Fables of Power: Aesopian Writing and Political History.* Durham: Duke UP, 1991.

### Andersen, Hans Christian

Bredsdorff, Elias. *Hans Christian Andersen: The Story of His Life and Work, 1805–1875.* New York: Scribner's, 1975.

Grønbech, Bo. *Hans Christian Andersen.* Boston: Twayne, 1980.

### Basile, Giambattista

Canepa, Nancy. *From Court to Forest: Giambattista Basile's Lo Cunto de li Cunti and the Birth of the Literary Fairy Tale.* Detroit: Wayne State UP, 1999.

### Disney, Walt

Holliss, Richard, and Brian Sibley. *Walt Disney's "Snow White and the Seven Dwarfs" and the Making of the Classic Film.* New York: Simon, 1987.

Schickel, Richard. *The Disney Version: The Life, Times, Art, and Commerce of Walt Disney.* New York: Simon, 1968.

### Grimm, Jacob and Wilhelm

Bolte, Johannes, and Georg Polívka. *Anmerkungen zu den Kinder- und Hausmärchen der Brüder Grimm.* 5 vols. Leipzig: Dieterich, 1913–1932. Reprint Hildesheim: Olms, 1963.

Bottigheimer, Ruth B. *Grimms' Bad Girls and Bold Boys: The Moral and Social Vision of the "Tales."* New Haven: Yale UP, 1987.

Ellis, John M. *One Fairy Story Too Many: The Brothers Grimm and Their Tales.* Chicago: U of Chicago P, 1983.

Haase, Donald, ed. *The Reception of Grimms' Fairy Tales: Responses, Reactions, Revisions.* Detroit: Wayne State UP, 1993.

Kamenetsky, Christa. *The Brothers Grimm and Their Critics: Folktales and the Quest for Meaning.* Athens: Ohio UP, 1992.

McGlathery, James M., ed. *The Brothers Grimm and Folktale.* Urbana: U of Illinois P, 1988.

———. *Fairy Tale Romance: The Grimms, Basile, and Perrault.* Urbana: U of Illinois P, 1991.

———. *Grimm's Fairy Tales: A History of Criticism on a Popular Classic.* Columbia, SC: Camden, 1993.

Sutton, Martin. *The Sin-Complex: A Critical Study of English Versions of the Grimms' Kinder- und Hausmärchen in the Nineteenth Century.* Kassel: Brüder Grimm-Gesellschaft, 1996.

Tatar, Maria. *The Hard Facts of the Grimms' Fairy Tales.* Princeton: Princeton UP, 1987.

Zipes, Jack. *The Brothers Grimm: From Enchanted Forests to the Modern World.* New York and London: Routledge, 1988.


### Harris, Joel Chandler

Bickley, R. Bruce, Jr., and Hugh T. Keenan. *Joel Chandler Harris: An Annotated Bibliography of Criticism, 1977–1996; with Supplement, 1892–1976.* Westport, CT: Greenwood, 1997.

Brookes, Stella Brewer. *Joel Chandler Harris: Folklorist.* Athens: U of Georgia P, 1950.


### Perrault, Charles

Barchilon, Jacques, and Peter Flinders. *Charles Perrault.* Boston: Twayne, 1981.

Lewis, Philip. *Seeing through the Mother Goose Tales: Visual Turns in the Writings of Charles Perrault.* Stanford: Stanford UP, 1996.

Perrault, Charles. *Charles Perrault: Memoirs of My Life.* Ed. and trans. Jeanne Morgan Zarucchi. Columbia: U of Missouri P, 1989.


### Straparola, Giovanni Francesco

Bottigheimer, Ruth B. *Fairy Godfather: Straparola, Venice, and the Fairy Tale Tradition.* Philadelphia: U of Pennsylvania P, 2002.


## INDIVIDUAL TALE TYPES

### Beauty and the Beast

Hearne, Betsy. *Beauties and Beasts.* Phoenix: Oryx, 1993.

———. *Beauty and the Beast: Visions and Revisions of an Old Tale.* Chicago: U of Chicago P, 1989.


### Cinderella

Cox, Marian Roalfe. *Cinderella: Three Hundred and Forty-five Variants of Cinderella, Catskin, and Cap o' Rushes.* Ed. Andrew Lang. London: Nutt, 1893.

Dundes, Alan, ed. *Cinderella: A Folklore Casebook.* New York: Garland, 1982.

Philip, Neil. *The Cinderella Story: The Origins and Variations of the Story Known as "Cinderella."* London: Penguin, 1989.

Rooth, Anna Brigitta. *The Cinderella Cycle.* Lund, Sweden: Gleerup, 1951.

## Little Red Riding Hood

Dundes, Alan, ed. *Little Red Riding Hood: A Folklore Casebook*. Madison: U of Wisconsin P, 1989.

Orenstein, Catherine. *Little Red Riding Hood Uncloaked: Sex, Morality, and the Evolution of a Fairy Tale*. New York: Basic, 2002.

Zipes, Jack. *The Trials and Tribulations of Little Red Riding Hood*. 2nd ed. New York: Routledge, 1993.

## Miscellaneous

Anderson, Rachel. *Renard the Fox*. Oxford: Oxford UP, 1986.

Clouston, W.A. *The Book of Noodles: Stories of Simpletons; or, Fools and Their Follies*. London: Stock, 1888.

Dundes, Alan, ed. *The Walled-Up Wife: A Casebook*. Madison: U of Wisconsin P, 1996.

Gerould, Gordon Hall. *The Grateful Dead: The History of a Folk Story*. London: Nutt, 1908.

Goldman, Shalom. *The Wiles of Women/The Wiles of Men: Joseph and Potiphar's Wife in Ancient Near Eastern, Jewish, and Islamic Folklore*. Albany: State U of New York P, 1995.

Roberts, Warren E. *The Tale of the Kind and the Unkind Girls: Aa-Th 480 and Related Titles*. Detroit: Wayne State UP, 1994.

Travers, P.L. *About the Sleeping Beauty*. London: Collins, 1977.

## JOURNALS

*Fabula: Zeitschrift für Erzählforschung/Journal of Folktale Studies/Revue d'Etudes sur le Conte Populaire*.

*Folk-Lore: A Quarterly Review of Myth, Tradition, Institution, and Custom*.

*Journal of American Folklore*.

*Marvels and Tales: Journal of Fairy-Tale Studies*.

# Web Resources

## INTRODUCTION

In the following presentation book titles are given in *italic type* and Web site names in **bold type.**

A vast amount of valuable folk and fairy-tale information resides on the Internet, although—as is the case with most fields—some information is of questionable credibility or even legality (due to copyright infringements). Furthermore, new material is added daily, with old sites often changing their addresses or disappearing altogether, making the maintenance of an up-to-date list of working sites a daunting if not impossible task. In an attempt to keep this chapter as current as possible, and to make it more computer friendly, the sites listed herein will be included as links on my Web site **Folklinks** (http://www.pitt.edu/~dash/folklinks.html).

## SEARCH ENGINES

The best tool for Internet research is not a comprehensive list of favorite sites but rather a repertory of a few efficient search engines and reliable indexes, together with a basic understanding of how to use them. The starting place for almost any Internet search is **Google** (http://www.google.com). This site's use of keywords is simple and efficient. Word groups set off by quotation marks are treated as single units. Thus the search term *"fairy tales"* will find only Web sites containing that phrase, and not the same words appearing separately. The keywords *"little mermaid" copenhagen* will find sites containing *Copenhagen* and *Little Mermaid* in any order, but *Little Mermaid* must appear as an unbroken phrase. **Google,** like most search engines, is not case sensitive; lowercase letters can substitute for uppercase ones, and vice versa.

Although **Google** is very thorough, one can usually locate further sites by conducting the same search with additional engines. The following are proven performers:

- **All the Web** (http://www.alltheweb.com).
- **Alta Vista** (http://www.altavista.com).
- **DMOZ** (http://dmoz.org).
- **Excite** (http://www.excite.com).
- **Lycos** (http://www.lycos.com).
- **Teoma** (http://www.teoma.com).
- **Webcrawler** (http://www.webcrawler.com).
- **WiseNut** (http://www.wisenut.com).
- **Yahoo!** (http://www.yahoo.com).

## ENCYCLOPEDIAS AND GENERAL REFERENCE WORKS

Folktale and fairy-tale researchers should not overlook general encyclopedias as sources for basic information about authors, collectors, movements, genres, and the like. The following are reliable, easy to use, and gratis, except as noted.

*The Columbia Encyclopedia* has long served as the standard for one-volume reference works, and it is now available online at the following sites, each with its own search engine:

- **Bartleby.com** (http://www.bartleby.com/65/).
- **Encyclopedia.com** (http://www.encyclopedia.com/).
- **Infoplease.com** (http://www.infoplease.com/).

The **MSN Learning and Research** site is an easy-to-use interface that combines results from Microsoft's *Encarta Encyclopedia* with those from external Web pages. Enter a word or phrase (for example, *folktale* or *fairy tale*) in the "Search Learning" field for a list of articles and sites. Some articles from the *Encarta Encyclopedia* can be accessed without charge, while others require a paid subscription. The articles "Folktales" and "Fairy and Fairy Tale" (both gratis) are particularly useful (http://encarta.msn.com/).

The justly famous *Encyclopaedia Britannica* of 1911 is available online, identified only as "the 1911 encyclopedia." The Web version is flawed by innumerable typographical errors introduced in scanning the original text, as well as by irritating pop-up advertisements, but it still provides much information available nowhere else on the Internet (http://75.1911encyclopedia. org/).

The *Dictionary of the History of Ideas* (1973–1974), long out of print but now available online, is a compendium of essays about pivotal ideas in all fields. It contains much information that integrates folklore studies with other disciplines. Its online search feature enables a user to find articles anywhere in the work containing desired terms, such as *folk* or *fairy tale* (http://etext.lib.virginia.edu/DicHist/dict.html).

## RESEARCH LIBRARIES

Online catalogs of large libraries are excellent sources of bibliographic information about published folktale books. However, please note that these catalogs do not provide access to the books themselves. The following electronic catalogs are well designed and provide information about immense collections:

- **COPAC**. A union catalog combining the resources of the largest university libraries in the United Kingdom and Ireland plus the British Library (http://copac.ac.uk/copac/).

- **Gabriel**. The World Wide Web service of Europe's national libraries (http://www.kb.nl/gabriel/).

- **Library of Congress** (http://www.loc.gov/). Of special interest at the Library of Congress is the **Folklife Sourcebook** (http://www.loc.gov/folklife/source/sourcebk.html).

- **Libweb**. Internet resources from libraries in more than 115 countries (http://sunsite.berkeley.edu/Libweb/).

- **Melvyl**. The online catalog of the University of California Libraries (http://melvyl.cdlib.org/).

## ELECTRONIC TEXT INDEXES

Thousands of books and shorter pieces, many of them relevant to folk and fairy-tale studies, are available gratis on the Internet as electronic texts. The most comprehensive index of such texts in English is the University of Pennsylvania's **Online Books**, which currently lists more than 20,000 titles. It also includes links to numerous foreign-language electronic libraries (http://digital.library.upenn.edu/books/).

To assist in finding a desired text among its thousands of listed titles, **Online Books** includes a number of search tools. Two hints for browsing:

- Search for the word *fairy, folk, folktale, folktales, tale,* or *tales* in the title field. Note that the search function uses only whole words, so a search for *tale* will not find a title with the plural form *tales* (http://onlinebooks.library.upenn.edu/titles.html).

- Browse in the subject-matter section under the Library of Congress classification GR, *folklore* (http://onlinebooks.library.upenn.edu/webbin/book/subjectstart?GR).

The **Online Books** database is also available through the **World eBook Library**, which includes links to a large number of reference works (dictionaries, multilingual dictionaries, thesauri, encyclopedias), academic libraries worldwide, and other research tools (http://www.netlibrary.net/).

**Digital Book Index** combines and integrates the free books listed through **Online Books** with commercial titles available for a fee. The subject-matter search tool is very useful. A search under the category "folklore, myths, legends, fables" yielded more than 100 titles. This site requires a sign-on procedure, but its use is without charge (http://www.digitalbookindex.com/).

## DIRECTORIES OF ELECTRONIC TEXT SITES (ALL SUBJECTS)

- **DMOZ** directory of electronic text archives (http://dmoz.org/Arts/Literature/Electronic_Text_Archives/).
- **Google** directory of electronic text archives (http://directory.google.com/Top/Arts/Literature/Electronic_Text_Archives/).
- **Yahoo!** directory of electronic literature (http://dir.yahoo.com/Arts/Humanities/Literature/Electronic_Literature/).

## DIRECTORIES OF FAIRY-TALE AND FOLKTALE SITES

- **Google** directory for fairy tales (http://directory.google.com/Top/Society/Folklore/Literature/Tales/Fairy_Tales/).
- **Yahoo!** directory for folk and fairy tales (http://dir.yahoo.com/Society_and_Culture/Mythology_and_Folklore/Folklore/Folk_and_Fairy_Tales/).
- **DMOZ** directory for myths and folktales (http://dmoz.org/Arts/Literature/Myths_and_Folktales/).

- **DMOZ** directory for fairy tales (http://dmoz.org/Society/Folklore/Literature/Tales/Fairy_Tales/).
- **Folklinks**. Links to folktale and fairy-tale sites, maintained by D.L. Ashliman, University of Pittsburgh (http://www.pitt.edu/~dash/folklinks.html).
- **Snow White Links**. Compiled by Kay E. Vandergrift, Rutgers University, these links are to sites dealing with folklore, mythology, and fairy tales in general, with special emphasis on "Snow White," "Cinderella," and "Little Red Riding Hood" (http://scils.rutgers.edu/~kvander/swlinks.html).

## LIBRARIES OF ELECTRONIC TEXTS

Each of the following electronic text libraries contains a substantial collection of works relating to folk and fairy tales:

- **Arthur's Classic Novels** includes numerous traditional and literary fairy tales, mostly borrowed from other Internet sites, then attractively reformatted (http://arthursclassicnovels.com/arthurs/).
- **Baldwin Project**, according to its mission statement, brings yesterday's classics to today's children. It currently lists nearly 2,000 stories, many of them folk and fairy tales. The site is indexed by grade level, genre (including fables, fairy tales, and legends), book title, and other categories. The texts are handsomely formatted and easy to read (http://www.mainlesson.com/).
- **Bartleby.com** is one of the pioneering electronic text sites. Its strong points include a very useful search mechanism, a large collection of integrated reference works, plus a good assortment of carefully edited classics (http://www.bartleby.com/).
- **Bibliomania** lists more than 2,000 classic texts (http://www.bibliomania.com/).
- **Children's Books Online** (the Rosetta Project) is a large collection of illustrated children's books, mostly from the nineteenth and early twentieth centuries. The books are reproduced as single-page, full-color image files, resulting in accurate and appealing replicas of the originals. An added attraction is the text-file translations of many of the stories into various languages (http://www.childrensbooksonline.org/index.htm).
- **ClassicReader.com** contains books and short stories by more than 200 authors. The children's section includes numerous collections of traditional fairy tales, and the short-story section contains many literary fairy tales (http://www.classicreader.com/).

- **eBooks@Adelaide**, sponsored by the University of Adelaide, Australia, contains more than 500 carefully formatted classic works (http://etext.library.adelaide.edu.au/).

- **Electronic Text Center** at the University of Virginia is a pioneer in the editing and distribution of electronic texts in various formats. Included in the section for young readers are many folk and fairy-tale related items (http://etext.lib.virginia.edu/ebooks/subjects/subjects-young.html).

- **Fables and Fairy Tales** contains a selection of traditional fairy tales, scanned and edited by C.E. Vance from unidentified collections (http://fairytales4u.com/).

- **Fairy Tales**, from the University of Maryland Electronic Reading Room, includes texts of numerous traditional tales, plus links to outside sites (http://www.inform.umd.edu/EdRes/ReadingRoom/Fiction/FairyTales/).

- **Folktexts**, compiled by D.L. Ashliman, University of Pittsburgh, offers a variety of folklore and mythology texts, arranged in groups of closely related stories (http://www.pitt.edu/~dash/folktexts.html).

- **Hockliffe Project** is centered around the Hockliffe Collection of early British children's books held by De Montfort University in Leicester and Bedford, England. The books are scanned into image files, rather than text files, yielding exact replicas of each page (http://www.cta.dmu.ac.uk/projects/Hockliffe/).

- **Internet Public Library**. University of Michigan (http://www.ipl.org/).

- **Kellscraft Studio** specializes in illustrated books from the period 1890–1920, including many fairy-tale collections. Take special notice of two books beautifully illustrated by Blanche McManus: *The True Mother Goose* and *Told in the Twilight* (http://www.kellscraft.com/textcontents.html).

- **The Literature Network** presents biographies of and texts by nearly 100 authors (http://www.online-literature.com/).

- **Literature.org** offers books by a number of authors with folk or fairy-tale connections (http://www.literature.org).

- **Page by Page Books** is a collection of classics, formatted one page per file, which allows for fast loading but limits utility in other ways. An anthology of unattributed fairy tales is included under the author identified as "Unknown" (http://www.pagebypagebooks.com/authorlist.html).

- **Peace Corps Folktales** contains some 20 tales from around the world collected by U.S. Peace Corps volunteers (http://www.peacecorps.gov/wws/students/folktales/).

- **Perseus Digital Library**, sponsored by Tufts University, is an extensive and well-engineered site combining images, texts, and scholarship. The principal fields represented are Greek and Roman civilization and the English Renaissance. Of special interest to students of folktales are the fables of Phaedrus (http://www.perseus.tufts.edu/).

- **Project Gutenberg**, begun in 1971, is the Internet's oldest producer of free electronic books, and with more than 6,000 online books, it is among the largest. With the help of many volunteers the library is expanding at the rate of about one new book per day. **Project Gutenberg**'s text-only and easily downloadable files are among the most carefully scanned and proofread digital texts available (http://www.gutenberg.net/).

- **Rick Walton's Online Library** contains about 1,000 classic tales and fables, compiled by a successful author of children's books (http://www.rickwalton. com/navlib.htm).

- **Sacred Text Archive**. This remarkable site's name does not say it all. In addition to housing the scriptures of many religions, it contains mythology and folklore texts from around the world. Each of the following topics, selected from a list at the lower left side of the site's index page, yields a number of folklore texts: African, Americana, Australia, Buddhism, Celtic, Egyptian, England, Greek/Roman, Hinduism, Judaism, Legends/Sagas (includes the *1,001 Nights*), Native American, Pacific, and Tolkien (http://www.sacred-texts.com/).

## GENERAL FAIRY-TALE SITES

- **Endicott Studio Forum**. Essays, stories, and musings on folklore, modern magical fiction, and related topics. Most of the fairy-tale essays are by Terri Windling. Other authors include Heinz Insu Fenkl, Midori Snyder, Gregory Frost, and Helen Pilinovsky (http://www.endicott-studio.com/forum.html).

- **Fairy Tales**. Directed by William Barker, Memorial University of Newfoundland (http://www.ucs.mun.ca/~wbarker/fairies/).

- **Fairy Tales, Folk Tales, and Mythology WebRing**. A collection of sites linked into a ring (http://b.webring.com/hub?sid = &ring = fairytale&id = &index).

- **Myths and Legends**. Christopher B. Siren's large site emphasizes (as its title states) myths and legends, but with some folk and fairy-tale material (http://members.bellatlantic.net/~vze33gpz/myth.html).

- **Once upon a Time**. A site dedicated to novels (mostly of the romance variety) based on fairy tales (http://www.skyehidesigns.com/mainbook.html).

- **SurLaLune Fairy Tale Pages** is an attractive, extensive, and well-organized site maintained by Heidi Anne Heiner. Included are essays, illustrations, annotated texts, links to outside sites, and a discussion bulletin board (http://www.surlalunefairytales.com/).

- **Types of the Folktale**. A descriptive essay by Virginia Wolf and Michael Levy, University of Wisconsin–Stout (http://www.uwstout.edu/lib/irs/folktale.htm).

## BIBLIOGRAPHY OF FOLKTALE AND FAIRY-TALE ELECTRONIC TEXTS

A search in **Online Books** (http://digital.library.upenn.edu/books/) will yield most of the following items, many of which are housed at more than one electronic library, often in alternate formats—typically HTML and text-only. If **Online Books** does not list the item, then repeat the search with **Google**.

Aesop. The most important of the many Aesop sites on the Internet is **Aesopica.net**. This ambitious project, sponsored by Laura Gibbs, publishes electronic versions of the Greek and Latin texts of Aesop's fables, together with indexes and different English translations. No other site dedicated to Aesop's fables approaches this project in scope, thoroughness, and authority (http://www.mythfolklore.net/aesopica/).

Alden, Raymond Macdonald. *Why the Chimes Rang and Other Stories.*

Andersen, Hans Christian. This famous Danish author has prompted numerous Internet sites. These two are among the best:

- **Hans Christian Andersen: Fairy Tales and Stories**. Included here are a chronological listing of Andersen's tales, electronic texts of most stories, and links to additional information (http://hca.gilead.org.il/).
- **Hans Christian Andersen**. A course offered by the University of Wisconsin (http://scandinavian.wisc.edu/hca/).

Apuleius, Lucius. *The Golden Asse;* plus separate listings for the story "Cupid and Psyche."

Asbjørnsen, Peter Christen, and Jørgen Moe. *Popular Tales from the Norse.*

Babbitt, Ellen C. *Jataka Tales; More Jataka Tales.*

Baldwin, James. *Fairy Stories and Fables.*

Baring-Gould, Sabine. *A Book of Folklore; A Book of Nursery Songs and Rhymes; The Book of Were-Wolves;* and other titles.

Barrie, J.M. *Peter Pan* (the novel, also known as *Peter and Wendy*); *Peter Pan in Kensington Gardens.*

Basile, Giovanni Battista. *Stories from the Pentamerone.*

Baum, L. Frank. *American Fairy Tales; The Wonderful Wizard of Oz;* and many other Oz titles.

Bleek, W.H.I., and L.C. Lloyd. *Specimens of Bushman Folklore.*

Boccaccio, Giovanni. The best starting point for Internet study of *The Decameron* is Brown University's **Decameron Web** (http://www.brown.edu/Departments/ Italian_Studies/dweb/dweb.shtml).

Bray, Anna Eliza. *A Peep at the Pixies; or, Legends of the West.*

Browne, Frances. *Granny's Wonderful Chair.*

Bryant, Sara Cone. *How to Tell Stories to Children, and Some Stories to Tell.*

Bulfinch, Thomas. *The Age of Fable, or Beauties of Mythology.* An especially useful site is **Bulfinch's Mythology**, maintained by Bob Fisher (http://www.bulfinch.org/ welcome.html).

Burgess, Thornton W. *Old Mother West Wind;* and other titles.

Carroll, Lewis. *Alice's Adventures in Wonderland; Through the Looking-Glass and What Alice Found There.* See also the home page of the **Lewis Carroll Society** (http://www.lewiscarroll.org/).

Chamisso, Adelbert von. *Peter Schlemihl.*

Chaucer, Geoffrey. *The Canterbury Tales.* Harvard University's **Chaucer Home Page** is especially useful (http://icg.fas.harvard.edu/~chaucer/).

Clodd, Edward. *Tom Tit Tot: An Essay on Savage Philosophy in Folk-Tale.*

Collodi, Carlo. *The Adventures of Pinocchio.*

Colum, Padraic. *The Boy Who Knew What the Birds Said;* and other titles.

Craik, Dinah Maria Mulock. *The Adventures of a Brownie; The Little Lame Prince;* and other titles.

Croker, Thomas Crofton. *Fairy Legends and Traditions.*

Crossing, William. *Tales of the Dartmoor Pixies.*

Curtin, Jeremiah. *Myths and Folklore of Ireland; Tales of Fairies and of the Ghost World.*

Dasent, George Webbe, trans. *Popular Tales from the Norse.*

Dickens, Charles. *A Christmas Carol in Prose; The Chimes: A Goblin Story; The Cricket on the Hearth: A Fairy Tale of Home;* and other titles.

Douglas, George. *Scottish Fairy and Folk Tales.*

Dutton, Maude Barrows. *The Tortoise and the Geese, and Other Fables of Bidpai.*

Evans-Wentz, W.Y. *The Fairy-Faith in Celtic Countries.*

Ewing, Juliana Horatia. *The Brownies and Other Tales;* and additional titles.

Farjeon, Eleanor. *Martin Pippin in the Apple Orchard.*

Faulding, Gertrude M. *Fairies.*

Fillmore, Parker. *Czechoslovak Fairy Tales.*

Fiske, John. *Myths and Myth-Makers: Old Tales and Superstitions Interpreted by Comparative Mythology.*

Fouqué, Friedrich de la Motte. *Undine.*

Frere, Mary. *Old Deccan Days: or, Hindoo Fairy Legends Current in Southern India.*

Ginzberg, Louis. *Legends of the Jews.*

Grahame, Kenneth. *The Wind in the Willows;* and other titles.

Grimm, Jacob, and Wilhelm Grimm. An immense amount of material about the Grimms (in English, German, and other languages) exists on the Internet. A good starting place is the **Grimm Brothers' Home Page** (http://www.pitt.edu/~dash/grimm.html).

Harrison, Elizabeth. *In Story-Land.*

Hartland, Edwin Sidney. *English Fairy and Other Folk Tales; The Science of Fairy Tales.*

Hawthorne, Nathaniel. *A Wonder-Book for Girls and Boys; Tanglewood Tales for Girls and Boys; Twice-Told Tales;* and other titles.

Hearn, Lafcadio. *Kwaidan: Stories and Studies of Strange Things* (traditional tales from Japan).

Hoffmann, Heinrich. *Struwwelpeter* (in German, English, and French), trans. Mark Twain.

Homer. *The Iliad* and *The Odyssey.*

Honey, James A. *South African Folk-Tales.*

Hunt, Robert. *Popular Romances of the West of England.*

Hyde, Douglas. *Beside the Fire* (Irish folk stories).

Ingelow, Jean. *Mopsa the Fairy;* and other titles.

Irving, Washington. "The Legend of Sleepy Hollow"; "Rip Van Winkle"; and "The Spectre Bridegroom"—all from *The Sketchbook of Geoffrey Crayon.*

Jacobs, Joseph. *Aesop's Fables; Celtic Fairy Tales; English Fairy Tales; Indian Fairy Tales; More Celtic Fairy Tales; More English Fairy Tales.*

Jacobs, W.W. "The Monkey's Paw."

*Jataka Tales of the Buddha,* retold by Ken and Visakha Kawasaki, are found in three files:

Part 1 (http://www.accesstoinsight.org/lib/bps/leaves/bl135.html)
Part 2 (http://www.accesstoinsight.org/lib/bps/leaves/bl138.html)
Part 3 (http://www.accesstoinsight.org/lib/bps/leaves/bl142.html).

Johnson, Clifton. *The Oak-Tree Fairy Book.*

Kafka, Franz. "The Metamorphosis" (called by some critics an "anti–fairy tale").

Keightley, Thomas. *The Fairy Mythology.*

Kennedy, Patrick. *Legendary Fictions of the Irish Celts.*

Kingsley, Charles. *The Water-Babies: A Fairy Tale for a Land-Baby;* and other titles.

Kipling, Rudyard. *Just So Stories.*

Kirk, Robert. *The Secret Common-Wealth* (a classic study of Scottish fairy lore).

La Fontaine, Jean de. *Fables.*

Lamb, Charles. "Beauty and the Beast."

Lang, Andrew. *The Arabian Nights Entertainment; The Blue Fairy Book;* additional colored fairy books; and other titles.

Leroux, Gaston. *The Phantom of the Opera;* and other texts.

Linderman, Frank B. *Indian Why Stories.*

Lindsay, Maud. *Mother Stories.*

Lofting, Hugh. *The Story of Doctor Dolittle; The Voyages of Doctor Dolittle.*

*The Mabinogion* (Welsh myths and folktales).

Macdonald, George. *At the Back of the North Wind* (1871); *The Princess and the Goblin* (1872); *The Princess and Curdie* (1873).

Mackenzie, Donald A. *Egyptian Myth and Legend; Indian Myth and Legend; Myths of Crete and Pre-Hellenic Europe.*

MacManus, Seumas. *Donegal Fairy Stories; In Chimney Corners: Merry Tales of Irish Folk Lore.*

Macpherson, James. *The Poems of Ossian.*

Mawr, E.B. *Roumanian Fairy Tales and Legends.*

Moore, A.W. *The Folk-Lore of the Isle of Man, Being an Account of Its Myths, Legends, Superstitions, Customs, and Proverbs.*

Morrison, Sophia. *Manx Fairy Tales.*

Muhawi, Ibrahim, and Sharif Kanaana. *Speak, Bird, Speak Again: Palestinian Arab Folktales.*

Mulock [Craik], Dinah Maria. *The Fairy Book.*

Olcott, Frances Jenkins. *Good Stories for Great Holidays.*

Orczy, Emmuska. *Old Hungarian Fairy Tales.*

Ovid. *Metamorphoses.*

Ozaki, Yei Theodora. *Japanese Fairy Tales.*

Perrault, Charles. For texts of his stories, both in English and French, see **Charles Perrault's Mother Goose Tales** (http://www.pitt.edu/~dash/perrault.html).

Poe, Edgar Allan. "The Thousand-and-Second Tale of Scheherazade."

Potter, Beatrix. *The Tale of Peter Rabbit;* and other titles.

Pyle, Howard, and Katharine Pyle. *The Wonder Clock.*

Quiller-Couch, Arthur. *The Sleeping Beauty and Other Fairy Tales.*

Ramaswami Raju, P.V. *Indian Fables.*

Rapaport, Samuel. *Tales and Maxims from the Midrash.*

Rhys, John. *Celtic Folklore: Welsh and Manx.*

Ripperton, Lisa M. *The Rainbow Book of Fairy Tales for Five-Year-Olds.*

Rolleston, Thomas. *Myths and Legends of the Celtic Race.*

Ruskin, John. *The King of the Golden River.*

Ryder, Arthur W., trans. *Twenty-Two Goblins.*

Shaw, George Bernard. *Androcles and the Lion.*

Shedlock, Marie L. *The Art of the Story-Teller; Eastern Stories and Legends.*

Shelley, Mary. *Frankenstein;* and other titles.

Sikes, Wirt. *British Goblins* (Welsh fairy lore).

Steel, Flora Annie. *English Fairy Tales; Tales of the Punjab.*

Stephens, James. *Irish Fairy Tales.*

Stevenson, Robert Louis. *The Bottle Imp;* and other titles.

Stockton, Frank R. *The Lady, or the Tiger?* and other titles.

Stoker, Bram. *Dracula;* and other titles.

Swift, Jonathan. *Gulliver's Travels.*

Taylor, Bayard. *Beauty and the Beast.*

Thompson, Stith. *Tales of the North American Indians.*

Theal, George McCall. *Kaffir Folk-Lore,* also listed as *Kaffir (Xhosa) Folk Tales* by Georg McCall Theal.

Thomas, W. Jenkyn. *The Welsh Fairy Book.*

*Thousand and One Nights* (Arabian Nights' Entertainment). There is an insurmountable amount of material on the Internet dealing with the *1,001 Nights.* A good starting point is the **Arabian Nights' Resource Centre** compiled by John Crocker (http://www.crock11.freeserve.co.uk/arabian.htm).

Wells, H.G. Fantasy short stories, including "A Moonlight Fable," "The Magic Shop," "The Story of the Inexperienced Ghost," and "Mr. Skelmersdale in Fairyland."

Wiggin, Kate Douglas. *Fairy Stories Every Child Should Know;* and other titles.

Wilde, Oscar. *The Happy Prince and Other Tales;* plus additional titles.

Young, Ella. *Celtic Wonder Tales.*

Zola, Emile. "The Fairy Amoureuse."

## SITES DEDICATED TO INDIVIDUAL STORIES AND TYPES

- **Beauty and the Beast**. A wide-ranging site bringing together information about the written story plus film, television, and stage versions, compiled by Rebecca Smallwood (http://beauty.rivkashome.com/).

- **Cinderella: A Bibliography**. A thorough and scholarly annotated bibliography of texts, analogues, criticism, modern versions, parodies—ranging from ancient folklore through recent popular culture, modern scholarship, and pornographic films. Organized by Russell A. Peck, University of Rochester (http://www.lib.rochester.edu/camelot/cinder/cinintr.htm).

- **Noodleheads**. The wisdom of fools in folktales (http://www.eldrbarry.net/roos/books/nood.htm).

- **Snow White**. A comprehensive academic site maintained by Kate E. Vandergrift, Rutgers University. Included are variant texts, essays, and teaching aids (http://scils.rutgers.edu/~kvander/snowwhite.html).

## FILM AND FAIRY TALES

A good place to begin research on the use of fairy-tale topics in film and television is the **Internet Movie Database** (http://us.imdb.com/search). Tom Davenport is an American filmmaker who has created a successful series of short films placing familiar Grimm fairy tales in settings from the American South (http://www.davenportfilms.com./).

## STORYTELLING

- **Storyteller.net**. A center for news, essays, texts, and contacts for storytellers (http://www.storyteller.net/).

- **Storytelling Resources**. A bibliography of printed materials by Brian W. Sturm (http://www.ils.unc.edu/~sturm/storytelling/resources.html).

## FOR CHILDREN, PARENTS, AND TEACHERS

- **Andersen Fairy Tales**. In English or French (http://www.andersenfairytales.com/).

- **Animated Tall Tales**. Features the exploits of Paul Bunyan (http://www.ani-matedtalltales.com/).

- **Grimm Fairy Tales**. In English or French (http://www.grimmfairytales.com/).

- **Internet Public Library: Story Hour**. Sponsored by the University of Michi-gan (http://www.ipl.org/div/kidspace/storyhour/).

- **Myths, Folktales, and Fairy Tales**. Resources for teachers of grades 1–8, spon-sored by Scholastic, Inc. (http://teacher.scholastic.com/writewit/mff/).

- **Wired for Books: The Kids' Corner**. From Ohio University, the site features texts, pictures, audio files, and videos of a number of folk and literary tales ap-propriate for children (http://wiredforbooks.org/kids.htm).

## ORGANIZATIONS AND JOURNALS

- **American Folklife Center** at the Library of Congress (http://www.loc.gov/folklife/).

- **American Folklore Society** (http://afsnet.org/).

- **Children's Literature Association** (http://ebbs.english.vt.edu/chla/).

- **Cultural Analysis.** An interdisciplinary forum on folklore and popular culture (http://ist-socrates.berkeley.edu/~caforum/about.html).

- **Folklore Fellows** at the Kalevala Institute of the University of Turku, Finland. An important contribution of this organization is its ongoing monograph se-ries *Folklore Fellows' Communications,* established in 1910 (http://www.folk-lorefellows.fi).

- **Folklore Society** (UK). Founded in 1878, this is one of the first organizations in the world devoted to the study of traditional culture (http://www.folklore-society.com/).

- **Marvels & Tales**. A journal of fairy-tale studies edited by Donald Haase, Wayne State University (http://www.langlab.wayne.edu/MarvelsHome/Mar-vels_Tales.html).

- **Modern Language Association of America**. Founded in 1883, this organiza-tion promotes the study of languages and literature. Of special relevance to fairy tales at this site are the following radio discussions (links from the main page are easy to follow): "Fairy Tales" (1997), "Walt Disney: Modern Mythmaker" (1998), "The Big Bad Wolf: Scary Characters in Children's Literature" ( 2000), and "Children's Literature That Appeals to Adults" (2000) (http://www.mla.org/).

- **Trickster's Way**. An online journal dedicated to trickster research (http://www.trinity.edu/org/tricksters/TrixWay/).

# FOREIGN-LANGUAGE SITES

## Danish/Norwegian

- **Eventyr—et prosjekt i Norsk nettskole**. A study project, based on the collection of Asbjørnsen and Moe (http://www.av-senteret.no/nettskolen/kurs/eventyr/).
- **H.C. Andersen**. Links to Andersen's works in Danish. This site is sponsored by the Royal Library (det Kongelige Bibliotek) of Denmark (http://www.kb.dk/elib/lit/dan/andersen/).
- **H.C. Andersen-Centret**. A treasure trove of information from the H.C. Andersen Center in Odense, Denmark. Click the British flag for an English-language version of this site (http://www.andersen.sdu.dk/).
- **Mytologi og folklore > Eventyr**. A Yahoo! directory for Norway (http://no.dir.yahoo.com/Samfunnsliv/Mytologi_og_folklore/Eventyr/).
- **Mytologi, eventyr og folkesagn**. A Yahoo! directory for Denmark (http://dk.dir.yahoo.com/Samfund/Mytologi__eventyr_og_folkesagn/).
- **Norske Folkeeventyr**. The Norwegian texts of 152 tales, sponsored by Project Runeberg (http://www.lysator.liu.se/runeberg/folkeven/).
- **Svend Grundtvigs Eventyr og den mundtlige Tradition**. A study project based on Denmark's pioneering folktale collector Svend Grundtvig (http://www.dafo.dk/grundtvig/index.htm).

## Dutch

- **Er war eens...De geschiedenis van de sprookjes**. A history of fairy tales (http://web.planet.nl/specials/sprookjes/).

## French

- **A la découverte de Jean de La Fontaine**. Annotated texts of La Fontaine's fables, plus much supplementary information (http://www.lafontaine.net/).
- **Contes**. A Yahoo! directory for France (http://fr.dir.yahoo.com/Art_et_culture/Litterature/Genres/Contes/).
- **Contes de Perrault**. Texts of 10 fairy tales by Charles Perrault (http://www.alyon.org/litterature/livres/XVIII/esprit_salon/perrault/).
- **Il était une fois...les contes de fées**. A very attractive, well-engineered, and authoritative fairy-tale study, sponsored by the Bibliothèque nationale de France (http://expositions.bnf.fr/contes/).

- **Les contes de Madame d'Aulnoy**. A biography of Marie-Cathérine le Jumel de Barneville de la Motte, Comtesse d' Aulnoy, plus the texts of 12 of her tales (http://www.chez.com/feeclochette/aulnoy.html).

## German

- **Europäische Märchengesellschaft**. The European Fairy-Tale Society (http://www.maerchen-emg.de/).
- **Märchen und Sagen**. A Yahoo! directory for Germany (http://de .dir.yahoo.com/unterhaltung_und_kunst/literatur/genres/kinder__und_ju-gendliteratur/maerchen_und_sagen/).
- **Märchenlexikon**. Edited by Kurt Derungs (http://www.maerchenlexikon. de/).
- **Projekt Gutenberg-DE**. A massive German-language site containing some 50,000 electronic texts (http://www.gutenberg2000.de/). Folk and fairy-tale collections within the Projekt Gutenberg-DE include the following:

  Fairy tales (http://www.gutenberg2000.de/maerchen/index.htm)
  Legends (http://www.gutenberg2000.de/info/genres/34.htm)
  The Grimm brothers (http://www.gutenberg2000.de/autoren/grimm.htm).
- **Sagen.at**. A large collection of legends and folktales, mostly from Austria, edited by Wolfgang Morscher, University of Innsbruck (http://www.sagen.at/).

## Italian

- **Favole e racconti**. A Yahoo! directory for Italy (http://it.dir.yahoo.com/ arte_e_cultura/lettere_e_filosofia/letteratura/generi/favole_e_racconti/).

## Portuguese

- **Mitologia e Folclore**. A Yahoo! directory for Brazil (http://br.yahoo.com/so-ciedade/Mitologia_e_Folclore/).

## Russian

- **Russian Folklore** (http://www.folklore.ru/).

## Spanish

- **Mitología y folclor**. A Yahoo! directory for Argentina (http://ar.dir.yahoo .com/sociedad/Mitologia_y_folclor/).

- **Mitología y folclor**. A Yahoo! directory for Mexico (http://mx.dir.yahoo.com/ sociedad/Mitologia_y_folclor/).

- **Mitología y folclor**. A Yahoo! directory for Spain (http://es.dir.yahoo.com/so-ciedad/mitologia_y_folclor/).

## Swedish

- **Mytologi och folklore**. A Yahoo! directory for Sweden (http://se.dir.yahoo. com/samhaelle_och_kulturer/mytologi_och_folklore/).

- **Svenska Sagor**. Attractive .pdf files from the fairy-tale collection of Gunnar Olof Hyltén-Cavallius and George Stephens (http://www.omnibus.se/sven-skasagor/).

## Turkish

- **Uysal-Walker Archive of Turkish Oral Narrative**. Texas Tech University's immense collection of Turkish folklore, including many tales translated into English (http://aton.ttu.edu/).

## DMOZ Foreign-Language Sites

A well-chosen selection of foreign-language sites is available through the **DMOZ** directory for myths and folktales (http://dmoz.org/Arts/Litera-ture/Myths_and_Folktales/). From that page follow the links to related sites in Danish, French, German, Japanese, Russian, Swedish, and Taiwanese.

# Index

## About the Author

D.L. ASHLIMAN is Professor Emeritus of German at the University of Pittsburgh. His previous publications include *Voices from the Past: The Cycle of Life in Indo-European Folktales* (1993, 1995), *Once upon a Time: The Story of European Folktales* (1994), and *A Guide to Folktales in the English Language* (Greenwood, 1987).